Sept. 23, 2022

Sandi,
Hope you enjoy this book as
much as I am.
It's fun getting to know you
and I am appreciating your insights
and your generosity of time!
Warmly, Suzanne Dames

Praise for *Live No Lies*

"This is the book I've been waiting for and one of the most important books a follower of Jesus will ever read. It will become a classic."

—Christine Caine, founder of A21 and Propel Women

"John Mark Comer is a gift to the church. He writes with adept cultural nuance, theological savvy, and refreshing spiritual depth. In *Live No Lies,* he's taken on a multilayered, ancient topic and brilliantly rearticulated it for our generation. I found myself swiftly turning pages and underlining far too many sentences. This is a gem."

—Rich Villodas, lead pastor of New Life Fellowship and author of *The Deeply Formed Life*

"If your soul feels depleted and beat up, *Live No Lies* is the book you need to pick up and read. Right now. It is brilliant, deep, scriptural, and will equip you to face the enemy and fight."

—Jennie Allen, *New York Times* bestselling author of *Get Out of Your Head* and founder and visionary of IF:Gathering

"John Mark Comer has a rare and remarkable ability to apply ancient wisdom to contemporary questions, taking complex ideas and making them transformational in our everyday lives. They say that the longest journey is from the head to the heart, but this book breaks the rule. Again and again your heart will be stirred by the clarity of insight herein."

—Pete Greig, founder of 24-7 Prayer International, senior pastor of Emmaus Rd, and author of *How to Pray: A Simple Guide for Normal People*

"In a time that feels full of contradictions and confusion, John Mark does a masterful job of laying out what is true, what true is, and why it matters deeply that we know the truth. This is the book for our day."

—Annie F. Downs, *New York Times* bestselling author of *That Sounds Fun*

"John Mark Comer is an inspired communicator who speaks with honesty, wisdom, and insight into the challenges of our time."

—Nicky Gumbel, vicar of Holy Trinity Brompton and pioneer of Alpha

"I devoured every word of this book and found myself deeply stirred and nourished. John Mark speaks to the mind and soul, as he uncovers in his usual thoughtful way the three great enemies to our peace—the world, the flesh, and the devil. You will emerge better after reading these pages."

—Bryan Loritts, author of *Insider Outsider*

"Every day we are dealing with temptations in multiple forms that draw us away from faithfulness to the Way of Jesus. In this compelling work, John Mark gives a vision of the beauty of Jesus in a culture of lies."

—Jon Tyson, pastor of Church of the City New York and author of *The Intentional Father*

"In *Live No Lies,* John Mark Comer gives us an incredibly important and timely book for every Christ-follower walking out discipleship in a society rippling and raging with new echoes of Pilate's old question 'What is truth?' This is a robust psychological, philosophical, and theological framework for engaging in spiritual formation and recognizing deformation in the modern era. And perhaps most excitingly, it makes a compelling and, dare I say, irrefutable case for biblical freedom."

—Brooke Ligertwood, Grammy Award–winning songwriter, co-founder of Creatr, and head of Hillsong Worship

"Like few in our time can do, Comer takes the unknown and misunderstood and simplifies the story so we see the active role we must play to not only survive but also thrive."

—Gabe Lyons, president of Q Ideas and co-author of *Good Faith*

"This book is a godsend. It exposes our spiritual enemy of untruth—a foe impacting our societies on a global scale. In a world where everyone tries to live their own 'truth,' this book reveals and challenges the many lies that have become common, normal, and accepted in our everyday conversations and decisions. This is a must-read."

—Albert Tate, lead pastor of Fellowship Church

"What I love about John Mark is that he continues to keep Jesus and his words fastened closely together. Our culture tends to like Jesus (or their ideas of him) but not his words. Authors like John Mark give me hope for the future church."

—Nathan Finochio, founder of TheosU

"Comer has personally helped me on my faith journey and I believe he is one of the greatest teachers of our generation. As you read *Live No Lies,* your heart will be strengthened and your eyes opened to the daily war waged against our personal peace."

—Rich Wilkerson Jr., pastor of VOUS Church

"In a time where deception seems to have settled upon the land like a dense fog, *Live No Lies* offers us a clearing to see how we have been deceived, to learn how we deceive ourselves, and to flee from the one who deceives. As the fog clears, the radiant light of Christ cuts through, offering us a narrow but truthful path. An essential guide for discernment in our contested age."

—Mark Sayers, senior leader of Red Church in Melbourne, Australia, and author of a number of books including *Strange Days* and *Reappearing Church*

Also by John Mark Comer

Loveology

Garden City

God Has a Name

The Ruthless Elimination of Hurry

LIVE
NO
LIES

LIVE
NO
LIES

Recognize and Resist
the Three Enemies
That Sabotage Your Peace

JOHN
MARK
COMER

WATERBROOK

Live No Lies

All Scripture quotations, unless otherwise indicated, are taken from the Holy Bible,
New International Version®, NIV®. Copyright © 1973, 1978, 1984, 2011
by Biblica Inc.™ Used by permission of Zondervan. All rights reserved worldwide.
(www.zondervan.com). The "NIV" and "New International Version" are trademarks
registered in the United States Patent and Trademark Office by Biblica Inc.™
Scripture quotations marked (KJV) are taken from the King James Version.
Scripture quotations marked (NKJV) are taken from the New King James Version®.
Copyright © 1982 by Thomas Nelson. Used by permission. All rights reserved.

Italics in Scripture quotations reflect the author's added emphasis.

Published in association with the literary agency of Yates & Yates.

Author photo by Ryan Garber

Grateful acknowledgment is made for the use of some content taken from
Renovation of the Heart by Dallas Willard. Copyright © 2002. Used by permission of
NavPress, represented by Tyndale House Publishers. All rights reserved.

Library of Congress Cataloging-in-Publication Data
Names: Comer, John Mark, 1980– author.
Title: Live no lies : recognize and resist the three enemies that sabotage your peace / by John Mark Comer.
Description: First edition. | [Colorado Springs] : WaterBrook, an imprint of Random House,
a division of Penguin Random House LLC, [2021] | Includes bibliographical references.
Identifiers: LCCN 2020056881 | ISBN 9780525653127 (hardcover) | ISBN 9780525653134 (ebook)
Subjects: LCSH: Spiritual warfare. | Temptation. | Truthfulness and falsehood—Religious aspects—
Christianity. | Christianity and culture.
Classification: LCC BV4509.5 .C655 2021 | DDC 235/.4—dc23
LC record available at https://lccn.loc.gov/2020056881

Printed in Canada on acid-free paper

waterbrookmultnomah.com

9 8 7 6 5 4 3 2 1

First Edition

Interior book design by Ryan Wesley Peterson

SPECIAL SALES Most WaterBrook books are available at special quantity discounts when purchased in bulk
by corporations, organizations, and special-interest groups. Custom imprinting or excerpting can also be
done to fit special needs. For information, please email specialmarketscms@penguinrandomhouse.com.

Contents

During this earthly pilgrimage our life cannot be free from temptation, for none of us comes to know ourselves except through the experience of temptation, nor can we be crowned until we have come through victorious, nor be victorious until we have been in battle, nor fight our battles unless we have an enemy and temptations to overcome.

—Saint Augustine, AD 418

From all the deceytes of the worlde, the fleshe, and the deuill: God lorde deliuer us.

—*The Book of Common Prayer,* AD 1549

As an experiment in psychology, basic instincts, and the effect of propaganda, it couldn't be surpassed—!

—Emmet Riordan to Orson Welles, October 30, 1938

The war on lies

You may not know this story, but it really did happen.

All of it.

Just after sundown on October 30, 1938, aliens invaded America; the harbingers of an advanced Martian civilization, come to enslave the land of the free.

The first wave landed in an unsuspecting farming town called Grovers Mill, not far from Princeton University in New Jersey and just a short trek from Manhattan. Professor Richard Pierson was standing watch at Princeton's observatory; he had scoped eruptions of blue flames on Mars's surface just an hour before, assumed it was a rare meteor shower, and rushed to the scene to investigate. But upon arrival, instead of the detritus of space rock, he found a large metal cylinder in the open field, still steaming from entry and broadcasting odd scraping noises from inside its shell. As the reporters, first responders, and onlookers examined the crash site, the cylinder began to open, and a terrifying monstrosity of alien violence unfolded.

On-site reporter Carl Phillips broadcast this chilling report live across CBS's airwaves:

> Ladies and gentlemen, this is the most terrifying thing I have ever witnessed. . . . I can see peering out of that black hole two luminous disks. . . . Are they eyes? It might be a face. . . .
>
> But that face, it . . . Ladies and gentlemen, it's indescribable. I can hardly force myself to keep looking at it. The eyes are black and gleam like a serpent. The mouth is V-shaped with saliva dripping from its rimless lips that seem to quiver and pulsate. . . .
>
> What's that? There's a jet of flame springing from [the alien], and it leaps right at the advancing men. It strikes them head on! Good Lord, they're turning into flame!
>
> Now the whole field's caught fire. The woods . . . The barns . . . The gas tanks of automobiles . . . It's spreading everywhere. It's coming this way.[1]

At this point, Phillips's voice abruptly cut out, followed by the eerie hiss of radio static.

Five long seconds later, the report resumed and announced Americans' worst fear: aliens had landed on the Eastern Seaboard. The National Guard had been called in, and bells rang to warn people to evacuate Manhattan. The Secretary of the Interior urged all Americans to join the fight and stand for "the preservation of human supremacy."[2]

Then came word of more alien landfalls—Chicago, then St. Louis.

It was pandemonium in the streets. Urbanites fled in terror. People took refuge in churches. Pregnant women went into labor early. People committed suicide. Looting broke out in the streets. It being America, men got out their guns and made ready to make a final stand.

One woman ran into a church prayer meeting in Indianapolis and screamed, "New York has been destroyed. I believe the end of the world has come. . . . You might as well go home to die."[3]

Life, as we know it, was over.

Now, as much as my conspiracy-theory friends would love this story to be true ("The moon landing was really in Iceland! The royal family are lizard people! The earth is flat!"),[4] the entire story was a lie.

I know; I know—shocking.

There was no alien invasion. But everything else really did happen.

It wasn't a full-on lie; it was more like fiction gone awry.

Here's the backstory . . .

The late 1930s were a tumultuous time in America. Not only did many scientists speculate there was alien life on Mars,[5] but closer to home, people were living with a fever pitch of anxiety. America was on the verge of war with Germany. The economy was still recovering from the Great Depression, and food scarcity was a growing threat. Just weeks before, those living in the Northeast had endured the Great New England Hurricane of 1938, the most devastating storm to ever strike New England, leaving over seven hundred dead and about sixty-three thousand homeless.[6] Add to the mix that it was after dark on the night before Halloween, and you've got an emotional tinderbox just waiting for a spark.

Enter Orson Welles, the twenty-three-year-old actor and director of *The Mercury Theatre on the Air,* a new radio program on CBS. Radio was still a new art form, in its golden era, ripe for creative exploration, and exploitation. It was the first medium to blur the lines between fact and fiction, news and entertainment. And Welles was a prodigy. His *Mercury Theatre* was only seventeen weeks in and was already the darling child of critics. But as is the case with much indie art, it failed to garner a large audience. Welles still had no commercial sponsor, and his time slot was up against the most popular show of the day, *The Chase and Sanborn Hour.*

Welles knew he had to do something drastic or *Mercury Theatre* would fail, so he bought the rights to H. G. Wells's novel *The War of the Worlds* and had his screenwriter simplify it from a literary critique of Western colonialism down to an hour-long sci-fi story designed to entertain.[7] He then updated the setting from Victorian England to current-day New Jersey.

As far as we can tell, Welles had zero malevolent intent.[8] Here's the most plausible theory for how it all went sideways: Most Americans weren't listening to Welles's show when it started; they were listening to the more popular *The Chase and Sanborn Hour.* That week's episode of *Chase and Sanborn* started with a short comedy sketch that ended at 8:15 p.m. So, around 8:16, legions of people turned the dial and were shocked by very realistic-sounding news alerts of mayhem up and down the Eastern Seaboard, including an emergency broadcast from an actor whose voice mimicked President Franklin D. Roosevelt's with near-perfect accuracy.[9] Due to the unrest in Europe, people were used to having their radio shows interrupted with breaking news stories, all bad. Many latecomers interpreted it to be a German invasion with some kind of advanced weaponry. The horror of Germany's use of poisonous gas in WWI was still fresh in people's memory.

As you would imagine, people freaked out.

There's no way to know for sure the extent of the hysteria. The next morning, the *New York Times* ran a front-page story describing it as a "wave of mass hysteria."[10] The *New York Daily News* headline read, "Fake Radio 'War' Stirs Terror Through U.S." in the same font usually reserved for the announcement of a real war.[11] Adolf Hitler even weighed in on the drama, citing the supposed panic as "evidence of the decadence and corrupt condition of democracy."[12]

Welles feared his career was over. Instead, all the publicity landed him a dream contract in Hollywood. As the saying goes, "All publicity is good publicity." Three years later, Welles wrote, directed, and starred in *Citizen Kane,* a movie some critics argue is the best film ever made.

Now, why do I tell you this bizarre story?

Because: I find it an apt metaphor to capture the thesis of this short book. I know your time is precious, so let me get to the point.

We are at war.

Not with aliens from Mars, but with an enemy far more dangerous: *lies.* But unlike *The War of the Worlds,* our enemy isn't the figment of an overactive imagination. In this case, there's no hoax. Our enemy is real.

A manifesto for exile

Okay, hold up. After a lead-in rife with military metaphors, you're expecting an angry tirade about the decline of Western civilization and the looming secular apocalypse, an us-versus-them call to arms, my foray into the culture wars . . .

Take a deep breath.

This isn't that.

Our nation is more divided than it's been since the Civil War, and the last thing we need is more gas on the fire. All I want to do is name the felt experience of following Jesus in our cultural moment, and I just can't find a better metaphor: *it feels like a war for the soul.*

We feel this constant conflict not just "out there" in culture or in our digital newsfeeds but inside the fabric of our own minds and bodies. A kind of inner tug-of-war that is emotionally exhausting and spiritually depleting, a tearing at the fabric of our souls' peace.

On paper, everything is fine: I live in a beautiful home in a great city with the best coffee in the world. I have a job as a pastor. I'm free to teach the Way of Jesus, at least for now. Heck, my kids and I even get to walk the dog to the park and stop along the way for ice cream.

Why do I feel so tired? Worn down? Not in body, but in mind?

Why do I feel so battered and bruised?

Why does every day feel like a battle just to stay faithful, to keep following Jesus?

Here's an idea: maybe because it *is*.

Our generation has a low comfort level with military metaphors and faith. We prefer to think of following Jesus as a journey or lifestyle rather than a war. But our spiritual ancestors didn't share our reticence with war imagery. They were far more adroit at naming the reality of spiritual conflict than we are today. For centuries, teachers of the Way of Jesus used a paradigm that's been lost in the modern era, that of "the three enemies of the soul."

The world.

The flesh.

And the devil.[1]

They saw the three enemies of the soul as alien invaders from hell and a kind of counter-trinity to God himself.

While the exact phrase *the world, the flesh, and the devil* isn't used by Jesus or the writers of the New Testament, the language and categories are.[2] If you've read the apostle Paul, you know he regularly likened following Jesus to a war.[3] One of Paul's most famous sayings is "Fight the good fight of the faith."[4] He told the Ephesians to "put on the full armor of God, so that you can take your stand against the devil's schemes"[5] and prayed that their pastor Timothy would "fight the battle well."[6] Careful to note that "our struggle is not against flesh and blood, but . . . against the spiritual forces of evil"[7] and that "the weapons we fight with are not the weapons of the world," he nonetheless claimed we have "divine power to demolish strongholds."[8]

This was very counterintuitive language for a church that grew up around the life and teachings of a rabbi who was fiercely nonviolent. Who chose to die for his enemies in love, not kill them in battle.

Still, the writers of the New Testament and the early church fathers and mothers—who until the fourth century were almost all pacifists[9]—regularly used this imagery of war to describe the inner dynamics of the soul. As thoroughly unmodern as it sounds to us now, my proposal is that they were naming the challenge of the human experience in a way that we often struggle to articulate in a secular age.

Honestly, many of us, even in the church, have left these ideas behind as relics of the premodern world.

We laugh at the devil as a premodern myth, akin to Thor's hammer or Santa Claus.

We scratch our heads at the New Testament's language of *the flesh* in a sensual culture where people equate feeling good with being good.

And when we hear *the world,* we envision a spittle-spewing street preacher with a bullhorn in a public park, railing about the dangers of AC/DC and the impending rapture.

Whether consciously or subconsciously, we're quick to dismiss these categories all together. But then we wonder why we feel an incessant tug-of-war in our chests that sabotages our peace. And we're mystified by the chaos in our newsfeeds. Why is the world such a mess? Why am *I*?

My intent with this book is to reinterpret the ancient paradigm of the three enemies of the soul for the modern age. While it's easy to scoff at the ancient categories, I believe the world, the flesh, and the devil are alive and well; and aided by our skepticism, they are wreaking havoc in our souls and society.

But hear me loud and clear: Our war against the three enemies of the soul is not a war of guns and bombs. It's not against other people at all. It's a war on lies. And the problem is less that we *tell* lies and more that we *live* them; we let false narratives about reality into our bodies, and they wreak havoc in our souls.

Here's my working theory: as followers of Jesus, we are at war with the world, the flesh, and the devil, and the three enemies' stratagem is as follows:

Deceptive ideas...	▶	that play to disordered desires...	▶	that are normalized in a sinful society.
(the DEVIL)		(the FLESH)		(the WORLD) [10]

Two and a half millennia ago, in *The Art of War,* the Chinese military savant Sun Tzu gave this sagacious advice: "Know your enemy."[11] That's the goal of this book: to unmask the face of our enemies and develop a strategy to fight back. *Vive la résistance.*

For those of you who are already hunting for the receipt to return this book, I simply invite you to suspend judgment. Give me a few more pages to win you over.

Surely, we can agree that our world is not thriving. The last few years in my country have been marked by social unrest, online outrage, and widespread disillusionment over the status quo. The pain of 2020 gave birth to one of the largest protest movements in American history. And as much as we'd love to blame "them"—be they liberals or conservatives, Antifa or the Proud Boys, or whomever it is we fear or hate—we all know that something is off deep within *us,* inside our own souls.

The war is raging on, yet many of us feel like a shell-shocked soldier, lost and confused in the chaos of the battlefield. Our generation is living through three tectonic shifts in Western culture.[12]

The first is *from the majority to the minority.*

While 49 percent of millennials and 65 percent of American adults as a whole still identify as "Christian" in national surveys (though we're hemorrhaging millions of young people each year),[13] a recent in-depth analysis by the Barna Group, a Christian think tank, put the number of young adults who are "resilient disciples" at 10 percent.[14]

Yes, 10 percent.

And that's nationwide. In secular cities like Portland, where I live, the number is likely *much* lower.

While the church is not an ethnic minority (and it's important for me to clarify that), we are what sociologists call a cognitive minority. Meaning, as followers of Jesus, our worldview and value system and practices and social norms are increasingly at sharp odds with those of our host culture. We face constant pressure, from both the Left and the Right, to assimilate and follow the crowd.

Second, our place in culture is shifting *from a place of honor to a place of shame.*

Walk around the downtown core of any major American city, and just look at the buildings: carved into them is the language of Scripture. The Christian vision so penetrated our nation's early imagination that it was literally chiseled into the stone of our earliest architecture.

And while plenty of secular thought leaders gave shape to our nation as well, followers of Jesus were at the center of culture making. Many government leaders were Christians, most of the Ivy League started as pastoral training schools, and many intellectuals, scientists, and artists were believers in Jesus. Pastors were people of high standing. The church held a place of honor in the wider culture.

That time is a distant memory, if that.

Most people today want nothing to do with faith in the public square. The church is seen as part of the problem, not the solution. What's more, with the radical moral reversal around human sexuality, gender, and the life of the unborn, we now have the moral low ground in many people's eyes; Jesus's vision of human sexuality is perceived as immoral by a large swath of the population.

In a shocking twist, we are no longer the nice middle-class citizens wearing their Sunday best; we are the James Deans, the 1960s counterculture, the '80s Straight edge fringe.

Third is the tectonic shift *from widespread tolerance to a rising hostility.*

A growing number of our secular friends and neighbors think of us not just as weird—because we eschew premarital sex, give away a percentage of our income, and refuse to be held captive by a political party or ideology—but as dangerous. As a threat to secularism's alternative vision of human flourishing.

As the writer of Hebrews put it, "In your struggle against sin, you have not yet resisted to the point of shedding your blood,"[15] so I shy away from saying we face persecution. But there is a kind of cultural and socio-emotional persecution that we live under and carry the weight of. It's exhausting. The stigma. The slander. The wound to our hearts.

At the risk of mixing metaphors, the literary motif used by the writers of Scripture for this kind of a cultural experience is that of exile.

The apostle Peter opens his first New Testament letter with "To God's elect, *exiles* scattered . . ." and ends with "She who is in Babylon . . . sends you her greetings."

The writer Walter Brueggemann defined *exile* as "the experience of knowing that one is an alien, and perhaps even in a hostile environment where the dominant values run counter to one's own."[16] Wendy Everett and Peter Wagstaff added that this "sense of exile, or alienation, may result for the individual who is marginalised, cast adrift, by the inability or unwillingness to conform to the tyranny of majority opinion."[17]

Author Paul Tabori defined *exile* as "being an outcast within one's own country."[18] Meaning, you can be a citizen of America or the UK or Germany but still feel like you're an outsider.

The Barna Group called our cultural moment "digital Babylon."[19] In a predigital world, to experience the cognitive dissonance of exile, you had to attend a far-left university or live in the urban core of a secular city like Portland or LA (or London or Berlin). Now all you need is an iPhone and Wi-Fi.

We're all in Babylon now.

And Babylon is not an easy place to live; it doesn't feel like home. Hence, the moniker of *exile*. It's terrifying at times, even traumatic. We feel a dislocation and disequilibrium. An uncertainty over the future.

Every day can feel like war on our souls. A spiritual assault on our faith. A fight to just stay saved. Or at least to stay orthodox, to stay faithful to Jesus, and to stay sane, much less to stay happy and at peace.

When you're a cognitive minority under constant pressure to assimilate, you can't help but think, *Am I crazy to believe what I believe? To live how I live?* When these questions come to mind, remember Orson Welles. It's easy to laugh at *The War of the Worlds* fiasco now. Hindsight is twenty-twenty. But it's harder to admit that countless intelligent, educated Americans were swept up in a lie.

Or to realize that across the Atlantic, just as intelligent and educated Germans were rounding up Jews and feeding them into incinerators in concentration camps.

Or that politicians in the American South were forcing a young Rosa Parks to the back of the bus just because she was black.

Or that the Hollywood elite were smoking dozens of cigarettes a day because big tobacco companies paid them to endorse their products.[20]

Not to mention the many Americans who honestly thought there were aliens on Mars.

It's tempting to think, *What fools they were. So gullible and naive. Caught up in the fervor of lies.*

Not like us.

We're far too sophisticated to ever be fooled, far too enlightened to ever get that confused.

We would never let people in power like, say, politicians or the media, prey on our emotions, playing to our desires and fears to manipulate us to their desired end.

And we—individualists that we are—would *never* do something just because everybody else is doing it.

As if Welles's gullible listeners were Neolithic cave dwellers rather than our *grandparents,* less than a century ago.

This is a fine example of what C. S. Lewis called "chronological snobbery,"[21] the innate human bias to think we're smarter than people who came before us and therefore new ideas are naturally better or more truthful than old ones.

Add to that what sociologists call "the myth of progress," the quasi-religious Western dogma that human beings are evolving toward a utopian future, where we will at long last shed the tired constraints of religion and superstition (which are the same thing) and embrace our destiny as enlightened individualists, finally free to enjoy our lives, one flat white and Tinder date at a time (that is, if AI doesn't wipe us out before we develop the technology to upload our consciousness to the cloud and live forever in the singularity).

Of course, things aren't really getting better; there's a mountain of data to argue they are getting *worse*. And a short tour of Twitter will reveal that many people are simply freaking out.

When will the secular utopia arrive?

In my view, both the Left and the Right seem to have some insightful things to say. But they each possess a kind of willful naivete in their views of the human condition, and I find neither vision compelling.

I'm a pastor, not a pundit; I have zero political agenda here.

But I deeply believe this:

I have a soul.

You have one too.

And your soul, like mine, is locked in a war with lies.

And like the ancient Spartans who were born and bred to be soldiers, with no choice in the matter, we too have no choice but to fight.[22] Please hear my tone: I'm not angry or anxious. I chose the medium of a book because it's conducive to quiet, critical thinking. But make no mistake: I'm calling you, dear reader, to war.

Now, I could be delusional. Or worse, out to con you for book sales. (After all, writing about the devil is the best possible route to the bestseller list, right?) But I'm betting you can't help but ask yourself . . .

Why is my mind under so much duress?

Why do I feel inflicted by the ideologies of our time?

Why do I feel this tug-of-war of desires in my own chest?

Why do I keep coming back to self-defeating behavior?

Why is there a steady stream of bad news from across the world?

Why does injustice rage when so many of us decry it as evil?

Why can't we seem to fix the world's deepest problems, even with all our money and technology and political prowess?

And why do I even care? Why does it weigh on me so heavily?

Consider this: Could it be our souls are at war with another world?

And lest we start out on a negative note, consider a follow-up question: What if exile could be *good* for us? William Faulkner, widely considered one of the greatest novelists, once said, "It's hard believing, but disaster seems to be good for people."[23]

What if exile is something to fight but not to fear?

What if instead of coming apart, we came together?

What if instead of losing our souls, we discovered them?

This is a book about how (not) to lose your soul in digital Babylon.

This is a manifesto for exile.

This is a rally cry to the war on lies.

Part 1

The DEVIL

You belong to your father, the devil, and you want to carry out your father's desires. He was a murderer from the beginning, not holding to the truth, for there is no truth in him. When he lies, he speaks his native language, for he is a liar and the father of lies.

—Jesus Christ, in John 8v44

Be alert and of sober mind. Your enemy the devil prowls around like a roaring lion looking for someone to devour. Resist him.

—The apostle Peter, in 1 Peter 5v8–9

Nobody believed he was real. . . . That was his power. The greatest trick the devil ever pulled was convincing the world he didn't exist.

—Keyser Söze (as played by Kevin Spacey), in *The Usual Suspects*

The truth about lies

Late in the fourth century AD, a young intellectual named Evagrius Ponticus went into the desert of Egypt to fight the devil.

Like you do.

Evagrius had read the story of Jesus going out into the desert to face the devil head on and intended to follow Jesus's example.

Soon word got out: there was a monk out in the middle of nowhere at war with the devil. Apparently, rumor said, he was winning. He became a sought-after spiritual guide. Spiritual seekers would brave the dangers of the elements in an attempt to locate Evagrius and learn his tactics.

Before Evagrius's death, a fellow monk named Loukios asked him to write down his strategy to overcome the devil. As a result, Evagrius penned a short book called *Talking Back: A Monastic Handbook for Combating Demons.*

Best subtitle *ever.*

Recently, I got around to reading it; it blew my mind. In all honesty, I expected a list of Christian-style magic incantations, the incoherent ramblings of a premodern introvert who spent too much time under the North African sun. Instead, I found an erudite mind who was able to articulate mental processes in ways that neuroscientists and leading psychologists are just now catching up to.[1]

Evagrius generated the most sophisticated demonology in all of ancient Christianity. And the most surprising feature of Evagrius's paradigm is his claim that the fight against demonic temptation is a fight against what he called *logismoi*—a Greek word that can be translated as "thoughts," "thought patterns," your "internal narratives," or "internal belief structures." They are the content of our thought lives and the mental markers by which we navigate life.[2] For Evagrius, these logismoi weren't *just* thoughts; they were thoughts with a malignant will behind them, a dark, animating force of evil.

In fact, Evagrius organized his book into eight chapters, each grouped around a basic logismoi. Evagrius's eight thoughts later became the foundation of the "seven deadly sins" of antiquity.[3]

Each entry begins with the line "Against the thought that . . ."[4]

We'll come back to Evagrius at the end of part 1 because I think—over a millennium and a half later—after Jesus, he's still the most brilliant tactician we have in the fight to overcome demonic temptation. (And yes, I believe in demonic temptation. Keep reading . . .)

For now, let's open with his provocative idea: our fight with the devil is first and foremost a fight to take back control of our minds from their captivity to lies and liberate them with the weapon of truth.[5]

Can this idea be found anywhere in the teachings of Jesus himself?

Leading question. The answer: absolutely.

One of Jesus's most famous teachings is this:

> You will know the truth, and the truth will set you free.[6]

In context, Jesus had just told his followers that "if you hold to my teaching, you are really my disciples," and as a result, "you will know the truth, and the truth will set you free."

The Pharisees, the religious leaders of the day, immediately responded with antagonism: "We are Abraham's descendants and have never been slaves of anyone."

Which is a bit of an ironic statement considering the history of the Hebrew people. Read *Exodus*.

Jesus graciously explained that he's not referring to socioeconomic slavery so much as spiritual slavery, for "everyone who sins is a slave to sin."

That just made the Pharisees even angrier, and they pro-
ceeded to make a snide comment about how "we are not ille-
gitimate children." A not-so-subtle dig at Jesus's parentage.
(Except in the original Greek, it's not as milquetoast; it's closer
to "We're not bastards like you.") Full of contempt, they raged,
"The only Father we have is God himself."

Jesus didn't let that one slide. As feisty as he was tender, he
responded with a fascinating claim about who their "father"
actually was:

> You belong to your father, the devil, and you want
> to carry out your father's desires. He was a mur-
> derer from the beginning, not holding to the truth,
> for there is no truth in him. When he lies, he speaks
> his native language, for he is a liar and the father of
> lies.[7]

Right out of the gate, notice three things from Jesus's teaching about this enigmatic creature he called the devil.

Let's start with the obvious: for Jesus, **there is a devil.**

In Greek, the word Jesus used is διάβολος (*diabolos*), which is
from a verbal root word meaning "to slander" or "accuse." It
can also be translated "the accuser."[8] But this is just one of
many names for this creature. Scripture also calls him . . .

- the satan
- the evil one
- the tempter
- the destroyer
- the deceiver

- the great dragon . . . who deceives the whole world
- the ancient serpent . . . who leads the whole world astray

Notice, every example I just listed is a title, not a name.[9] Some biblical scholars argue this is a subtle dig from Jesus, a deliberate snub; his rival doesn't even get a name. Others read it as a sign of how dangerous he finds this creature—Jesus's equivalent of "he who must not be named."

But for Jesus, the devil is not a fictional villain from a Harry Potter novel; he is a real and cunning source of evil and the most influential creature on earth.

Three times Jesus called him "the prince of this world."[10] The word for "prince" is *archōn* in Greek, which was a political word in Jesus's day, used for the highest-ranking Roman official in a city or region. Jesus was saying that this creature is the most powerful and influential creature *in the world.* In another story, when the devil claimed that "all the kingdoms of the world" were his to give away, Jesus didn't disagree with him.[11]

Now, an in-depth biblical theology of the devil and his origins is beyond the scope of this book, but let's take just a minute and sketch out an outline.

For frame of reference, many scholars have compared the library of Scripture to a photo mosaic. Meaning, it's a collection of photos—poems, prophecies, stories, mythologies, histories, wisdom sayings, letters, etc.—that when put together form a composite image. If you apply that way of reading the Bible to the creature called the devil, you come up with the following contours:

- He was created by God.[12] This is key; he's not God's equal and opposite but a created being with a beginning. And an end.

- His original role seems to have been the spiritual formation of human beings through testing. Think of how a teacher tests children to bring them to maturity. But (as we see in the story of Job) he began to drift from his charter and used his skill set to *tempt* human beings into spiritual *de*formation.[13]

- He sat on God's divine council, a group of hand-selected spiritual beings whose job was to collaborate with God's rule over the world.[14] But he chose to rebel against God's rule, to seize the world's throne for himself, and to enlist as many creatures as possible in his violent insurgency.[15] Some scholars argue that Eden was created in a war zone, as a beachhead for God's kingdom.[16] But when humans later joined in the devil's rebellion, the earth fell under his dominion.[17]

- For thousands of years, he held sway as the "prince of this world,"[18] leading vast swaths of human and nonhuman creatures in their ongoing quest to seize autonomy from God and redefine good and evil as they saw fit (more on that soon).

- He was the animating energy behind many of the great atrocities of history and, some argue, even involved in the evolutionary process itself.[19]

- Jesus came "to destroy the devil's work."[20] To bind "the strong man"[21] and set humanity free.[22] He did this first through his defeat of the devil in the desert, then through his teaching and exorcisms, and finally through his death and resurrection and exaltation, in which he "disarmed the powers and authorities" and "made a public spectacle of them, triumphing over them by the cross."[23]

- Jesus's victory over the devil was like D-Day to World War II—the decisive battle that marked the beginning of the war's end. The devil's fate was sealed on the first Easter, as Hitler's was on June 6, 1944. But there are still many miles to cover to reach our equivalent of Berlin. In the interim, the devil is like a wounded animal, a dying dragon, more dangerous than ever. Contrary to popular artistic imaginings, the devil is not in hell; he's here, on earth. If Jesus's anthem is "On earth as it is in heaven," the devil's is "On earth as it is in hell."

- Jesus's kingdom was, and still is, nonviolent. However, Jesus likened the kingdom to a warlike assault on the "gates of hell."[24]

- In this ongoing war, harm—spiritual, mental, emotional, and even physical—is a very real possibility. Followers of Jesus are not immune. We bleed red; we suffer and die along with the rest of humanity; we're vulnerable to temptation and deceit. Though we know how the story ends, we are warned to stay "alert and of sober mind," for "the devil prowls around like a roaring lion looking for someone to devour."[25]

- Our great hope is in Jesus's return to finish what he started. On that day, the devil and his ilk will be

"thrown into the lake of fire" and all evil will be eradicated from God's good creation, forever. We will
then take our place as co-rulers with Jesus the king
over his beautiful world.

Now, I'm sure I'm missing some things in this sketch or even
getting some of the details wrong, but here's the key take-
away: for Jesus, the devil is *real.*

Not a myth.

Not a figment of an overactive imagination or a superstitious
hangover from a prescientific age.

And definitely not a red cartoon character on your shoulder or
Will Ferrell on *Saturday Night Live* shredding out B-level death
metal on his electric guitar.

No, the devil is an immaterial *but real* intelligence at work in
the world, with more power or influence than any other creature in the universe after God.

He is the evil *behind* so much of the evil in our souls and society.

For Jesus, the secular theories that attempt to explain evil as
simply a lack of education, inadequate wealth redistribution,
Marxist power analysis, or even the toxicity of religion gone
bad all fall short of explaining reality. The only way to make
sense of evil in all its malevolence—from large, global systems
of evil, such as systemic racism or economic colonialism, to
much smaller, human-scale evil, such as our inability to stop
our self-destructive drinking or hold back biting comments toward our friends—is to see an animating force behind it, add-

ing fuel to the proverbial fire. Dividing humanity against itself in a kind of societal suicide.

Now, if we're honest—and frequently we aren't—to many of us this sounds wonky.

A devil, really?

Come on.

We're back to Lewis's idea of chronological snobbery. It's the twenty-first century. We don't believe in talking snakes anymore, much less invisible demons behind current world events.

"Now we know better."

I regularly hear people cite the Flynn effect as justification for the ever-popular "now we know better" bias. James Flynn, a psychologist from New Zealand's University of Otago, asserted that IQ tests have been on the rise in Western industrialized countries since the 1950s by a growth curve of about three points per decade.[26] His original thesis: we're smarter than our grandparents. This phenomenon came to be called the Flynn effect, and for obvious reasons, it took off like a new single from Childish Gambino. It fit like a glove with the pervasive idea—or really, belief—that progressives are, by definition, ahead of the evolutionary arc of human history, the intellectual leaders (read, superiors) of humanity, and that conservatives are, by definition, behind on the Darwinian trajectory.

Like all good lies, this idea is full of truth.

I'm writing this chapter from the top of the world, in Iceland, which has got to be one of the most beautiful places on earth. Yesterday some local friends took me on a tour of Þórsmörk ("Thor's domain") and pointed out odd-shaped rock formations that ancient Vikings believed were trolls who turned to stone when they got caught in the morning light.

So, yes. We are a bit savvier today.

We now know that trolls are a myth and that odd-shaped rocks are created by geothermal forces and tectonic upheaval, not monsters with lousy time-management skills.

But people regularly cite the Flynn effect as proof we're getting smarter not just in some things but in everything. By this logic, people who believe in ancient ideas like the devil or, for that matter, Jesus himself are looked at with contempt and treated with the same intellectual incredulity as those who believe in trolls.

Never mind the fact that the Flynn effect has proven to be a fluke.[27]

Even Flynn himself eventually realized that his findings didn't give the whole picture. By his original calculation, high school graduates in 1900 would have had an IQ of about 70, but our great grandparents weren't mentally handicapped; they just thought differently than we do today (less conceptual, more concrete).[28] Not to mention, if the trend he found had continued, by now we would all be giving Bradley Cooper's character from *Limitless* a run for his money.

More recent data actually suggests that the average IQ level has been *falling* in the West—not rising—since the 1990s.[29]

Other research says that human beings are no more intelligent than we were thirty thousand years ago.[30] Our cumulative knowledge has grown by leaps and bounds, yes, especially around trolls and rock formations; but knowledge is not the same thing as intelligence, which is still not the same thing as wisdom.

All that to say, if your gut reaction to the idea of a devil is *That sounds like ancient nonsense,* I get it. No disdain here. At times, my own Western, quasi-secular mind finds Jesus's worldview incredulous.

But consider this: What if Jesus knew the true nature of reality better than we do? What if his perception was even more acute than that of Steven Pinker? Or Sam Harris? Or Stephen Hawking? What if he was the most intelligent teacher to ever live and his insight into the problems (and solutions) of the human condition is the most piercing to date?

What if our Western world is actually blind to a whole dimension of reality? Ignorant of what many consider to be common sense? What if we're attempting to solve the problems of the world without dealing with the root cause? What if, for all our science and technology and political theory, we're actually oblivious to—or worse, willfully ignorant of—the facts?

What if Jesus and the writers of the Scripture—not to mention many ancient luminaries outside Jesus's tradition (such as Socrates, Confucius, and the Buddha), most leading thinkers throughout history, and still most people outside the West—have eyes to see something we regularly miss?

What if?

As the Hollywood villain Keyser Söze (ironically, played by the accused sexual predator Kevin Spacey) once said, "The greatest trick the devil ever pulled was convincing the world he didn't exist."[31]

Our culture has a very high value for keeping an open mind. That's all I ask: that you simply consider the possibility that Jesus was right—the devil is real.

Second, for Jesus, *the devil's end goal is to spread death.*

Verbatim: "He was a murderer from the beginning."

What is a murderer? Someone whose intent is to end life.

Jesus went on to say, "The thief [another name for the devil] comes only to steal and kill and destroy; I have come that they may have life, and have it to the full."[32]

Steal . . .

Kill . . .

Destroy . . .

For Jesus, the devil is the archetype of a villain who is hell-bent on destruction. He just wants to watch the world burn. His motto: "Tear it all down." Wherever he finds life, he tries to stamp it out. Beauty? Deface it. Love? Corrupt it. Unity? Fragment it into a million pieces. Human flourishing? Push it to anarchy or tyranny; either will do. His anti-life, pro-death, pro-chaos agenda is an insatiable fire.

Jesus, on the other hand, is the author of life itself and an advocate for all that is good, beautiful, and true. Specifically, for love. God *is* love, and the devil is in rebellion against all that is God. Ergo, his intent is to wreck love: one relationship, one community, one nation, one generation at a time.

This is why our newsfeeds drip steady litanies of chaos and carnage.

This is why secular theories of evil simply don't add up to a valid explanation of human behavior.

And this is why following Jesus often feels like a war. It *is*. It's not easy to advance daily into the kingdom of God because there's opposition from the devil himself. (Or to be more specific, other spiritual beings under his sway.) We feel this opposition every day. In that nagging inner tension as we're torn between the opposing desires of love and lust, honesty and saving face, self-control and indulgence. In the struggle for faith in a secular age where so many cultural elites seem to have left faith behind, where scientism is the new superstition, and where, as the philosopher James K. A. Smith put it, "we're all Thomas now."[33] In the breakdown of a society losing its center and spinning out of control.

And there's no way out of this fight.

As a follower of Jesus, I see violence as incompatible with life in the kingdom, and I advocate for creative, nonviolent solutions to problems. But violence is not the same thing as force. And even I have to admit, to apprentice under Jesus is to become a soldier in a war. One where the long-term victory is assured, yes, but we still have many battles on the road to Berlin, with no Switzerland to hide away in. As C. S. Lewis wisely said, "There is no neutral ground in the universe: every square inch, every split second, is claimed by God and counterclaimed by Satan."[34]

But lest you think I'm rallying a digital militia to "take America back for God"—relax, really. That's not where we're heading. The devil is far too interesting and intelligent for a simple us-versus-them binary.

Here's my last observation from John 8: for Jesus, **the devil's means is lies.**

Did you catch that?

Jesus called the devil "the father of lies."

Translation: the origin point of deception.

Then Jesus has that great line about how "when he lies, he speaks his native language."

Okay, hold up.

This is not how most of us think about our fight with the devil or what has come to be called spiritual warfare. Sadly, much of what passes as a theology of spiritual warfare is at best conjecture, if not paranoia or superstition.

I can't tell you how often I hear people blame the devil for what is likely just bad luck, coincidence, or, frequently, their own tomfoolery. "My wife and I got in a fight on the way to church—it was the devil!"

The devil? The ruler of this world came to visit your minivan? Maybe. But isn't it more likely you were just in a hurry, a bit stressed out, and made a rash statement that caused your spouse deep pain?

Whenever people blame the devil for silly things, it makes it hard to not just write the devil off entirely. To throw the baby out with the bathwater, as the saying goes.

In C. S. Lewis's masterpiece of satire, *The Screwtape Letters,* he wrote,

> There are two equal and opposite errors into which our race can fall about the devils. One is to disbelieve in their existence. The other is to believe, and to feel an excessive and unhealthy interest in them. They themselves are equally pleased by both errors, and hail a materialist or a magician with the same delight.[35]

As easy as it is to poke fun at others, the danger for most of us is not that we "feel an excessive and unhealthy interest" in the devil; it's that we just ignore him entirely and go about our lives oblivious to his daily assault on our soul.

Let's say we keep our minds open and take the idea of the devil seriously; still, what comes to mind when we think of the devil or spiritual warfare is normally an exorcism, a mysterious disease, or a natural disaster like a tsunami or hurricane. Or maybe a horrifying poltergeist or a child's terrifying nightmare.

All those examples have legitimacy. In fact, after a cursory read of the four Gospels, this is what I would expect Jesus to talk about.

But ironically, in Jesus's most in-depth teaching on the devil in all four Gospels, *he doesn't mention any of it.*

There's no demon in his teaching, no illness, no tragedy.

Instead, it is an intellectual debate with the thought leaders of his day about *truth* and *lies.*

Reread Jesus's teaching one more time, and pay close attention:

> You belong to your father, the devil, and you want to carry out your father's desires. He was a murderer from the beginning, not holding to the *truth,* for there is no *truth* in him. When he *lies,* he speaks his native language, for he is a *liar* and the father of *lies.* Yet because I tell the *truth,* you do not believe me![36]

So, let's recap:

1. For Jesus, there is an invisible but real intelligence at war with God and all that is good, beautiful, and true.
2. The devil's *end goal* is to drive our souls and society into ruin. To decimate love.
3. But here's my main point: his *method* is lies. His primary stratagem—his go-to, signature move—is deception.

All the other stuff—demonization, illness, wreaking havoc in the natural order, scaring little kids with bad dreams—is biblical, and we need to take it seriously. It's all real. I could tell countless stories. But again, scope. That could easily fill the pages of a whole other book. But it's secondary.[37]

Jesus sees our primary war against the devil as a fight to believe truth over lies.

Which leads to the inevitable follow-up question, as ancient as Pontius Pilate and yet a staple of the modern psyche:

What is truth?

Ideas, weaponized

You up for a little philosophy? I know just enough to be dangerous, so go easy on me, but let's take a few minutes to explore the nature of truth and lies. This will feel like a content dump, but I know you have it in you.

Again: What is truth?

The best definition I know of truth is "reality, or that which corresponds to reality." It's easy to get lost in the metaphysical weeds, but for our nontechnical purposes, truth is what we can rely on as real. The chair I'm sitting on is reality. The air I'm breathing is reality. Jesus is reality.

And the best definition of *reality* I know is "what you run into when you're wrong."

If you say, "I believe I can fly!" and you walk off the top of a ten-story building, reality is what you hit a few seconds later. Hence, the cliché "a dose of reality."

When we call something a lie, we mean it doesn't correspond to reality.

For example, if I ask my boys (who share a bedroom) "Who left this wet towel on the floor?" and Jude says "Wasn't me," when Moto fires back "You're lying!" he's saying "Your claim doesn't correspond to reality."

(This is a hypothetical situation, I promise. It would never happen in a *pastor's* home . . .)

So, truth is reality.

Lies are unreality.

Pretty straightforward, but let's go a layer deeper.

We all live by what psychologists call mental maps of reality,[1] reference points in our minds by which we navigate the world. Neurobiologists talk about how the human mind is wired for story.[2] Sociologists talk about worldview. Followers of Jesus often talk about their faith.

Different terminology, same idea.

I really appreciate the language of mental maps. Think about it: we have literal mental maps, such as the route from our homes to our workplaces. *Take Burnside east over the river to 21st; turn left, cross over I-84, and turn right on*

Tillamook . . . If our mental maps are true, if they corre-spond to reality, then we get in our cars or step onto the bus and *x* minutes later we arrive at our destinations. But if our mental maps are *not* true, if they *don't* correspond to reality, we end up lost in the dystopian wasteland of bad cell coverage or glitchy Google maps (a terrifying experience for all).

Let's apply the metaphor: in the same way that we have men-tal maps for how to get to work or school or our favorite cof-fee shops, we have mental maps for all of life. Maps for our money. Our sexuality. Our relationships.

Our mental maps are made up of a collection of ideas. As long as we're in definition mode, the philosopher Dallas Wil-lard defined ideas as "assumptions about reality." They are working theories, usually based on some kind of evidence or experience, about how life actually works. Or in American lingo, what will make us happy.[3] Willard's work on trans-forming the mind in *Renovation of the Heart* changed the entire way I view spiritual warfare. Let me summarize: We live in a world of ideas, and every day we navigate this world by faith (more on that in a minute). Happiness is an idea. So is democracy, human rights, equality, freedom. Even theology, which this book is full of, is a collection of ideas about God and their far-reaching ramifications on us as human beings.

And our ideas coalesce to form a mental map by which we navigate reality.

We tracking? Great. Now, here's where things start to get in-teresting. The wonder of the human person is our ability to hold in our minds ideas that correspond to reality *and* ideas that don't correspond to reality.

Put another way, to envision what *is* and what *isn't.*

This is what separates us from animals. Even if you trust the evolutionary explanation of human origins (I still have a lot of questions there), all the recent research, as popularized in a book like *Sapiens* by Yuval Noah Harari, now says that the Portlandesque bumper-sticker view of evolution as a linear progression from monkey to *Homo erectus* to *Homo sapiens* to (naturally) progressive secular humanist is untrue. Many scientists now think that all sorts of hominin species were on the earth at the same time. (Fun fact: the average person of European ancestry is 2 percent Neanderthal.[4]) Harari makes the case that the reason *Homo sapiens* ended up as the dominant species wasn't our size or strength or even our opposable thumbs; it was our *capacity for imagination.*[5]

We are the only creatures who have the capacity to imagine what isn't but could be.

You see, there's a negative side to unreality—our capacity to believe a lie or illusion. But there's also a positive side—our capacity for imagination. This is what enables the miracle of human society. We can envision the unreality of an ideal society in our minds and then work together to bring it into reality. We can make a village. A city. A civilization.

In fact, this is what enables *all* human creativity, from writing a novel to baking a cake, programming an app, building a home, starting a business, or just playing a new riff on your guitar. We have the capacity to hold in our mental docks something that does not yet exist and then, through our bodies, bring that unreality to life.

And you thought you were just baking muffins. Actually, you were exercising your human capacity to take an idea in your mind and, using your body, create a new reality.

Pretty rad.

Here's the problem: our capacity to hold unreality in our minds is our genius, but it's also our Achilles's heel. Because not only can we imagine unreality, but we can also come to believe in it. We can put our faith in ideas that are untrue or, worse, that are lies.

As Willard once said, "We truly live at the mercy of our ideas."[6]

Because the ideas that we believe in our minds and then let into our bodies give shape to the trajectory of our souls. Put another way, they shape how we live and who we become.

When we believe *truth*—that is, ideas that correspond to reality—we show up to reality in such a way that we flourish and thrive. We show up to our bodies, to our sexuality, to our interpersonal relationships, and, above all, to God himself in a way that is congruent with the Creator's wisdom and good intentions for his creation. As a result, we tend to be happy.

But when we believe *lies*—ideas that are not congruent with the reality of God's wise and loving design—and then, tragi-

cally, open our bodies to those lies and let them into our muscle memories, we allow an ideological cancer to infect our
souls. We live at odds with reality, and as a result we struggle
to thrive.

Because reality does not adjust itself to our illusions.[7]

Let's broach a sensitive example but one we simply can't
skirt around, as it is the leading moral question of our
generation—human sexuality. And remember as you read
this, I'm a pastor, not a politician. My goal is to journey with
your soul on its way to healing in God, not to legislate anything. I don't expect secularists to live like Christians. As
Paul put it, "What business is it of mine to judge those outside the church?"[8] The move of the Spirit is inward to conviction, not outward to critique. I'm not trying to critique the
culture, much less control it; I'm trying to flourish a counterculture.

The sexual liberation revolution of the 1960s set in motion a
cascade effect: the reversal of the long-standing moral consensus around promiscuity (which separated sex from marriage) worked in tandem with the advent of birth control and
the legalization of abortion (which separated sex from pro-
creation), which moved on to the legalization of no-fault divorce (which turned a covenant into a contract and
separated sex from intimacy and fidelity), then to Tinder and
hookup culture (which separated sex from romance and
turned it into a way to "get your needs met"). From there it's
moved on to the LGBTQI+ revolution (which separated sex
from the male-female binary), the current transgender wave
(which is an attempt to separate gender from biological sex),
and the nascent polyamory movement (an attempt to move
beyond two-person relationships). Amid the revolution, the

questions nobody seems to even be asking are, Is this making us better people? More loving people? Or even happier people? Are we thriving in a way we weren't prior to our "liberation"?

Nobody is really even asking these questions, much less making a serious attempt to research the data.

It's just assumed.

Again, ideas are *assumptions about reality.*

But consider a few data points from the research:

Happiness levels have been in decline in the US since, interestingly, the '60s. While we know that correlation is not causation, you have to admit it's an interesting coincidence.

Some deeply disconcerting facts related to attachment theory are also worth noting. In spite of the cultural narratives that state otherwise, divorce is a traumatic event for children of all ages, and we're learning it's directly tied to the rising number of people who struggle to develop intimate, healthy relationships in adulthood.[9] Psychologists argue that the drop in those who identify as having "secure attachment" is wreaking havoc in our society.

Consider that divorce, while cited as an example of liberation from the patriarchy, has been shown to disproportionately benefit men.[10]

Or that those who cohabitate before marriage are less likely to marry,[11] are more likely to get a divorce if they do,[12] and often develop long-term trust issues.[13]

Or the research on oxytocin and vasopressin, the two chemicals released by our body during sex that bring our attachment system online and cause us to bond to another person. It seems that the more sexual partners you have, the *less* capacity your body has for intimacy.[14]

Or the much-documented but little-talked-about data on the effects of abortion on women's mental and physical health,[15] causing some to hypothesize the Left will eventually change its now hard-line view.

Or that 25 percent of children spend a portion of their childhood without a father in the home.[16] Overwhelming evidence indicates that this experience is damaging to both boys and girls.[17]

Or that sex reassignment surgery and hormone therapy for those who identify as transgender do not benefit their emotional health (which is the main rationale behind them).[18]

Or the stats on the epidemic of sexual addiction across the West.

Or the fact that porn is becoming increasingly violent, misogynistic, and cruel and is now a multibillion-dollar industry, intentionally targeting children.[19]

Never mind that while #metoo was dominating headlines, the *Fifty Shades of Grey* trilogy—a story about male sexual domination—was becoming the highest-selling book series of the decade and one of the highest-grossing film franchises of all time.[20]

Never mind that sexual abuse and sexual assault are getting worse, not better. Statistically, one out of every four women will experience sexual violence at some point in their lives.

Never mind that rape culture is a raging problem, even on the most liberal, progressive campuses of elite universities.

These facts are conveniently left out of the discussion, if there even *is* a discussion.

I'm a pastor in a city with no sexual boundaries. I deal with the fallout of Woodstock on a regular basis. I'm not angry; I'm sad. I care about the damage to people's souls, especially the vulnerable.

As Mary Eberstadt put it in her book *Adam and Eve After the Pill,*

> Contrary to conventional depiction, the sexual revolution has proved a disaster for many men and women; and . . . its weight has fallen heaviest on the smallest and weakest shoulders in society— even as it has given extra strength to those already strongest and most predatory.[21]

The "liberation" is starting to look more and more like enslavement.

The problem with the current carpet bombing of thousands of years of human wisdom around sexual desire is, well, *reality.* The secular world's dominant idea (read, working theory of reality) is that human beings are animals, simply aided by time and chance to evolve into the dominant species on our planet; monogamy is "not natural," as we rarely see it in "other animals." In fact, men evolved to spread their seed over as many women as possible for the survival of our species— evolutionary biology's way of saying, "Boys will be boys." In such an idea matrix, the prevailing consensus is "Sex is just play for grown-ups. What's the big deal? It's just an animal pleasure, no different from hunger or thirst. If you do pursue marriage, that's fine; be true to yourself. But you should at least live with your partner for a while to make sure you're a good fit. And if it doesn't work out, the important thing is to be happy." (After all, there's no meaning to life; it's just a glorious accident.) And of course marriage, sexual norms, and even gender itself are all social constructs, often created by elites to maintain power.

The secular view of sexuality and gender raises many good points. The patriarchy has done all sorts of horrendous things to women; to deny this is unconscionable. And it's nauseating the way LGBTQ people have been treated, often by Christians. The violence is real, and we must work to stop it. And gender expression *does* change from culture to culture. And sexual desire is a good thing, designed by God himself. And it is core to our humanity; we were sexual before we were sinful, and we must celebrate our sexual desire, not shun it.

But while I applaud our generation's advocacy for equality and human dignity, the problem with this interpretation of the data points of science and history is acute: overall, *it does not correspond to reality,* and reality does not conform itself to our desires, feelings, or incorrect thinking. Therefore, it does not lead to health and happiness. Nor can it. Ever.

The emotional/relational/familial/societal/political meltdown we've been living in for years now is daily proof of the fact that our mental maps are off, that we're drifting further and further into dangerous territory.

In my previous book *Garden City,* I made the point that the Christian tradition has understood the human vocation to be *to take chaos and make order.* To "make order" is to take the chaos of the planet and turn it into a garden-like city in which human beings can flourish and thrive in relationship to each other, to God, and to the earth itself. The word we use for this is *culture.*

We live in a fascinating moment of what the sociologist Philip Rieff called "anti-culture."[22] Very powerful cultural currents are actively working *to take order and make chaos.* To undo the order that was passed down to us by previous generations.

To clarify, the idea of "order" has been politicized recently, but please don't think I'm referring to the *abuse* of order as exemplified by systemic racism or police brutality; I'm not. I'm referring to the time-tested ways of being human that span cultures, continents, and generations and that have been passed down over millennia to enable each new generation to live in congruence with reality and thrive. Many of these have been thrown out the window, in just a few short decades, with little to no research or even an honest exploration of whether or not they are actually true.

Keep in mind that what we call traditional values were all radical when Jesus first introduced them. They were eventually adopted as the norm because they are based on a "highly sophisticated and deeply wise view of human nature" and, frankly, because they work.[23] When we live into Jesus's vision, we thrive.

Time will tell whether this anti-culture creates a better world or destroys an already fragile one. I fear the latter. Unfortunately, by the time the West is forced to face reality, most likely intractable damage will have been done to our society.

You simply cannot beat reality at its own game. As the philosopher H. H. Farmer put it, "When you go against the grain of the universe, you get splinters."

The "cold, hard truth" is our mental maps, the collection of ideas by which we navigate life, can be wrong. At times, horribly so.

Now, deep breath in . . .

Deep breath out . . .

Let's insert all this into Jesus and his teaching on the devil.

This is why Jesus called the devil "the father of lies." In fact, that whole section from John 8 is an allusion to Genesis 3, the story of Eve and the serpent. We'll go deep on this story in the next chapter. For now, let me just point out that the devil didn't come at her with an M16 or a predator drone.

He came at her with an *idea.*[24]

More specifically, with a *lie:* "You will not certainly die."[25]

M. Scott Peck, in his groundbreaking book *People of the Lie,* called the devil "a real spirit of unreality."[26]

When Peck came to faith in Jesus in his forties, it upended his view of reality. A well-known psychiatrist, he began to consider ideas he'd previously written off, such as the devil. He then applied his erudite mind and formidable research apparatus to the question of evil, specifically: How is it that some people seem to become pervaded by evil?

His first conclusion was that there are evil people in the world. The average person hears this and thinks, *Well, yes, of course. And the earth is round.* But to the scientific community, this was the breaking of a taboo. Science is supposed to be objective and unbiased; to claim someone is evil is to believe that good and evil exist. Again, common sense, but scientific heresy.

But his second and even more interesting conclusion was that the *way* people become evil is through lies. His basic thesis was that when we believe lies and then let those lies into our bodies, tragically, they often become a kind of upside-down shadow of the truth. As the psychologist David Benner put it, "It is not so much that we tell lies as that we live them."[27]

For example, suppose you believe the lie that you are unlovable—wherever you picked it up in your life journey, be it a broken relationship with your parents, a breakup, a failure, a demonic deposit into your mind, or anywhere. Then, if you let that lie into your body, into your neurobiology, you let that lie give shape to your behavior.[28] Because you don't believe you are worthy of love, you let people treat you in ways that are disrespectful or demeaning. Or you act in ways that are disrespectful or demeaning. If you live into this lie long enough, tragically, what was false *starts to become true.* You eventually become the kind of person that is not worthy of love and respect, and you alienate yourself from the very relationships you crave.

I do need to say, like all wounds to the soul, *this can be healed*—through loving relationships and truth. Ideally, through loving relationships with the God whom Jesus called Father and his family, the church, and through the truth of your identity as a daughter or son of God.

My point is this: lies distort our souls and drive us into ruin.

Cue the running debate right now in my country over free speech. A growing number of voices are calling for restrictions to the First Amendment. And while I'm firmly on the side of free speech over censorship, I do agree that words can cause harm; ideas can be weaponized.

A low-hanging-fruit example that's still fresh in our collective memory is Nazi Germany. What's easy to forget in the many parodies of twentieth-century Germany, from *Indiana Jones* to *Jojo Rabbit,* is that, at the time, Germany was the apex of Western civilization, on par with or ahead of England and far ahead of America. Pick your metric of choice: art, architecture, literature, poetry, academics, science and technology, even theology—Germany was the birthplace of Luther and the Reformation. And yet within a few short decades, the entire society was corrupted from the inside out by *ideas.* Ideas about race. About nationalism. About God. Ideas that drove Europe and the world into chaos.

So, yes, ideas can be dangerous. Willard said it right: "Ideas [are] a primary stronghold of evil in the human self and in society."[29] Ideas are more than synapses firing; as Evagrius long ago claimed, ideas are spiritual entities that enslave our souls.

Ideas—not tyrants.

For all the recent talk about the threat of tyranny, we forget that ideological tyranny is a far greater threat than political tyranny. In fact, the latter is based on the former.

The celebrated scholar Hannah Arendt, in her seminal 1951 book, *The Origins of Totalitarianism,* said, "The ideal subject of totalitarian rule is not the convinced Nazi or the convinced Communist, but people for whom the distinction between . . . true and false . . . no longer exist[s]."[30]

Around the same time, thinking about a post–Cold War world, Winston Churchill prophetically saw over the horizon and said, "The empires of the future are the empires of the mind."[31] He saw that the future would be a war of ideas, not bombs.

Foreign correspondent David Patrikarakos, in his book *War in 140 Characters: How Social Media Is Reshaping Conflict in the Twenty-First Century,* makes the case that wars are no longer about territory but about ideology.

This is why America can't win the war on terror. Jihad is an ideology. You can't fight an ideology with a tank. In fact, when you attempt to, it's often just gas on the fire.

It's also why so many outside the West are reacting against the attempt of Western elites to not only export but also enforce their new sexual vision on the rest of the world. Pope Francis has accused the West of "ideological colonization."[32]

There is finally an honest, in-depth conversation about the devastating aftereffect of colonization on minorities. In many ways, progressives have led the way in this conversation, and for that I'm very grateful. But many thinkers, from the pastor Timothy Keller to the novelist Zadie Smith, note that secularism and its emphasis on individualism, denial of God, and deconstruction of the traditional family is just as (if not more) destructive to indigenous cultures than nineteenth-century imperialism ever was.[33] My friend (and cultural analyst) Mark Sayers called it "Western supremacy." Imposing *whiteness* on the world is rightly shunned. But to some, imposing *westernness* (especially Western ideas about sexuality or gender) on the world is not only okay; it's virtuous.

You see the contradiction?

As a pastor, I get to sit with a fascinating array of people from across the sociopolitical spectrum. Over the last few years, I've watched so many people, on both the Left and the Right, be taken captive by ideology. It's grieved my heart. Ideology is a form of idolatry. It's a secular attempt to find a metaphysical meaning to life, a way to usher in utopia without God. The best definition I know of *ideology* is when you take a part of the truth and make it the whole. In doing so, you imprison your own mind and heart in lies that drive you to anger and anxiety. It promises freedom but produces the opposite. It does not expand and liberate the soul but shrinks and enslaves it.

But maybe I'm leading us down the wrong path. It's lowhanging fruit to point out the lies of ideology that play in the culture wars. Most of the lies we face don't make news headlines or end up in Twitter debates.

- It's the grown man who was berated by his father and comes to believe *I am only as good as I am successful at work.*

- It's the teenage girl who, comparing herself to the mirage of Instagram, comes to believe *I am ugly and unworthy of love.*

- It's the pastor who was a high-energy child, regularly scolded by her parents, who now believes *I'm a bad person.*

- It's the entrepreneur whose prior business failed after the betrayal of his partner, and who now believes *Everything I do will fail.*

- It's the middle aged woman who was raised by an angry perfectionist mother and decades later still believes *I have to be perfect to have peace.*

I've changed details for anonymity, but these aren't hypothetical examples. They are a small sampling of thousands of stories people have trusted me with as their pastor.

There is not a soul I know who is not living in, at some level, bondage to lies.

Facing the lies we have come to believe can be terrifying. As T. S. Eliot put it, "Human kind cannot bear very much reality." The illusions we cling to become part of our identity and, with it, our security. They make us feel safe even as they imprison us in fear. Ripping them out of the humus of our soul can be excruciating. As David Foster Wallace put it, "The truth will set you free. But not until it is finished with you."[34] It's only in coming face to face with reality as it *actually* is before God that we find peace.

All that to say . . .

Lies, that come in the form of deceptive ideas, are the devil's primary method of enslaving human beings and entire human societies in a vicious cycle of ruin that leads us further and further east of Eden.

This is why Jesus came as a rabbi, or teacher.

What is a teacher? A truth teller. A moral cartographer. Teachers give us mental maps to reality. In doing so, they set us free to live in congruence with how life actually works.

When Jesus said, "You will know the truth, and the truth will set you free," he was simultaneously saying that we're enslaved by lies. We're in bondage to the tyranny of false ideas about reality that hold our souls and our society in captivity to suffering and pain. As Paul later said, the devil has "taken [us] captive to do his will."[35] Jesus has come to liberate us with the weapon of truth.

This is how Jesus was able to overcome the devil without the use of violence. When he was standing trial before Pilate, Jesus was asked if he was a king. His answer was as brilliant as it was cryptic: "You say that I am a king. *In fact, the reason I was born and came into the world is to testify to the truth.*"[36]

In response, Pilate, in a view that would find its full flowering in twentieth-century French philosophers such as Michel Foucault, retorted, "What is truth?"[37]

Notice, for Jesus, truth was something that could be *known.*
"You will *know* the truth, and the truth will set you free." This
sounds a bit weird to us. Many of us have been taught that
following Jesus isn't about knowledge; it's about faith. And
knowledge and faith are opposites.

Right?

Not exactly.

Now we're getting into what Dallas Willard called "the disappearance of moral knowledge."[38] Published posthumously
after his unexpected death, his book by the same name was
his major contribution to philosophy.

Allow me to summarize Willard's thesis before we end this
chapter. As the West secularized, the locus points of authority
moved from God, Scripture, and the church to the
Enlightenment-based triad of science, research, and the university. This new seat of secular authority then redefined what
can be known (things like mathematics and biology and *not*
things like right, wrong, and God). In doing so, it conveniently
moved subjects like religion and ethics into the domain of belief, by which most people mean opinion, feeling, or just wish-
ful thinking.[39] As the world globalized and we became more
aware of other religious worldviews, Westerners began to view
religion as just a collection of opinions for private, therapeutic
purposes, not as the type of thing that can be known. Some,
following postmodernists like Foucault, went so far as to claim
that knowledge—or even truth itself—is a form of oppression.

In my country, this shift is nowhere more apparent than in the
separation of church and state. Originally intended to keep

the state out of the church, over the centuries this idea has mutated.[40] Most Americans now assume the point is to keep the church out of the state; that is, religion is a private matter and has no place in the public sphere. Tell that to the founders of our nation or of most universities who emblazoned their governmental and academic buildings with quotes from Scripture and Latin references to "truth" (*veritas*) and "virtue" (*virtus*).

This new framework assumes that things like theology, ethics, and the meaning of life, etc. can't be known. If we believed that our faith in Jesus was based on knowledge of reality, there would be no more talk of separation of church and state than there is of biology and state, algebra and state, or structural engineering and state.[41]

Now, don't misread me. I'm not remotely arguing for a Christian version of Sharia law or some cultish government-enforced Levitical code. My convictions run deep, yes, but I'm a firm believer in antidiscrimination laws. We live in a pluralistic nation, and I respect that, even enjoy it. Let me say it again: I don't have a political agenda here; my concern is for disciples of Jesus. My "agenda" is to strengthen your faith in Jesus's mental maps as reality.

My point is this: we've been taught—and at times, the church has aided and abetted secularism here—that religious ideas like good, evil, and God can't be known; they can only be taken on faith. But for Jesus and the writers of Scripture, *faith is based on knowledge.* It's a kind of deep trust in God that is grounded in reality.

This is not how many followers of Jesus in the West approach the Gospels or Scripture in general. Occasionally, we'll come across an article where research has proven the truth of something from the Bible, such as one I recently read on Jesus's line "It is more blessed to give than to receive."[42] (Short version: the more generous you are, the happier you are.) And we think, *Oh, cool, now we* know *it's true.* The assumption is that before we just believed, but now we know. In my teaching, I increasingly have to appeal to research from the social sciences because fewer and fewer people view the writings of the New Testament as trustworthy and true. I enjoy the social sciences and am happy to meet people where they are, but until we come to trust Jesus and his biographers as accurate guides to reality, we remain in a kind of intellectual stasis.

The writers of the Bible didn't view things like how we should spend our money, who we sleep with, or even the resurrection of Jesus from the dead as opinion or conjecture. They viewed them as reality. This is one of the starkest differences between the gospel of Jesus and other major world religions; more than any other form of spirituality, the New Testament is based on events in history. The Bible is full of times, dates, names, places. The four Gospels aren't mythology but history.

The Scripture writers constantly advocated for a faith that isn't *opposed to* knowledge but *based on* knowledge.[43]

Jesus defined eternal life as a form of knowledge: "This is eternal life: that they *know* you, the only true God, and Jesus Christ, whom you have sent."[44]

Paul wrote, "I *know* whom I have believed"[45] and prayed for us to "*know* the mystery of God, namely, Christ, in whom are hidden all the treasures of wisdom and *knowledge.*"[46]

We think of faith as something for religious people, but *all of us live by faith.* To have faith in something is simply to live as if it's true. It means to put your trust in something or someone and remain loyal to it.

The question isn't, Do you have faith? But *who* or *what* do you have faith *in*?

Jesus and the Scripture writers wanted you to have faith in Jesus and his teachings—a faith that is based on *knowledge* of reality.

Jesus and the writers of Scripture also recognized that the claim to have knowledge of reality does not imply arrogance or lead down the path to tyranny, contrary to popular opinion. I just got out of an Uber where my driver, a lapsed Christian, launched into a ten-minute diatribe on how he doesn't know what to believe anymore, ending with a sermonic appeal: "Who am I to tell somebody else that Jesus is the Son of God? As if I'm right and others are wrong? I would never want to force my view on others."

On one hand, I share his reticence to enforce a view of re- ality on other people; on the other, nobody would ever apply that logic to an idea that was considered a form of knowledge. No one would ever say, "Who am I to tell some- one else the earth is round? Or that five plus five equals ten? Or that smoking is bad for your health?" We actually have no problem telling people we love when we think they are wrong because we trust it will contribute to their happi- ness.

When people say, as they frequently do, "All religions are equal," what they actually mean is no religions have knowledge of reality. And by default, none of them should be taken seriously as a guide to life.

All religions are *not* the same. Yes, they agree on many things, and we should pay close attention to those common denominators, as they are likely signposts to reality. But they also differ wildly on many points.[47] To claim otherwise is to dishonor them and the cultures they were born in, practicing a form of Western supremacy that is simply the millennial update of old-school European imperialism.

Even the idea that God is love is not a universal idea. Followers of Jesus believe in God as a trinitarian community of self-giving love, while Muslims and Jews conceive of God as a single entity. Hindus have a vast pantheon of gods and goddesses, with all individuality an illusion; Buddhists don't take God to be any kind of a personal being at all but merely a state of consciousness we arrive at through the eightfold path; and indigenous people often see God in nature or even as nature.

These are very contradictory views of "God."

Yeah, but it's like the blind men and the elephant. Each religion just sees a different aspect of reality.

Well, sure, to an extent, but this is exactly my point: the overused blind-men-and-the-elephant metaphor *assumes that we're all blind.*[48] Jesus makes the opposite claim. That he is the "light of the world."[49] That he's come from the Father "to proclaim freedom for the prisoners and recovery of sight for the blind."[50] Light, then as now, is a metaphor for illumination over ignorance.

Jesus and the writers of the New Testament did not see faith as a blind leap into the dark. For them, it is a lifestyle of unswerving trust and loyalty to Jesus, based on his knowledge of reality.[51] As the Quaker intellectual Elton Trueblood so eloquently said during his tenure at Stanford, "Faith . . . is not belief without proof, but trust without reservations."[52]

All that to say, this is why Jesus came as a teacher and why he would regularly call for his apprentices to "repent and believe the good news."[53] To repent and believe simply means to rethink your mental maps of what you think will lead you to a happy life and trust in those of Jesus himself.

Ideas have power only when we believe them. We hear all sorts of ideas every day, some brilliant, others ridiculous; but they have zero effect on us unless we begin to trust them as an accurate map to reality. At that point, they are animated by a strange kind of energy and authority and begin to release life or death into our bodies.

Which means to apprentice under Rabbi Jesus is more than just to enroll as a student for a daily lecture in his master class of life; it's also to enlist as a soldier and join his fight to believe truth over lies.

So, dear reader, whose mental maps do you navigate reality by? Whose ideas do you trust? Are you currently believing any lies?

Lies about your body or sexuality?

Lies about whether or not you are the object of God's love and affection?

About your past?

About whether or not there is hope for your future?

But I'm getting ahead of myself. . . .

Before we can honestly answer these questions, there's one more problem we need to address, and it's a thorny one: the best lies are the ones we think are true.

Dezinformatsiya

Russia's in the news again.

As I'm writing this, a little-known app that ages your selfie a few decades has exploded in popularity. For a Warholian fifteen minutes (actually, about a week), it's all people were posting on Instagram. I now know what all my friends will look like in fifty years.

It turns out my buddy Dave is a leprechaun: he looks exactly the same at seventy.

Me, though, model handsome now, yes, but just you wait . . . It does not end well. (Note: I'm just kidding about the "model handsome" part.)

But then it comes out that FaceApp is actually run by Russians (and not just any Russians, *the* Russians). The app is harvesting mounds of data from users to some unknown, likely nefarious end.[1] Well, maybe. Nobody knows for sure.

The Russians have long been masters in the art of deception.

During the Cold War, the Russians coined the term *dezinformatsiya* to capture their new form of subterfuge, which entered our vocabulary as *disinformation.* The KGB began to flood the world with lies, half-truths, and propaganda, placing high-level spies in key roles in Western media, journalism, and entertainment, partially to advance their agenda but partially just to throw off the equilibrium of the West. To keep us chasing our tails, draining our energy, and, most importantly, blind to Russia's activity behind the Iron Curtain.[2]

Garry Kasparov, the former world chess champion and Russian democracy advocate who now lives in exile in Croatia, opined, "The point of modern propaganda isn't only to misinform or push an agenda. It is to exhaust your critical thinking, *to annihilate truth.*"[3]

I find Russia's recent foray into digital misinformation a fitting metaphor for the devil's assault on truth.

The term *spiritual warfare* wasn't actually used by any of the New Testament writers. That doesn't make it bad; it just makes it easy to import our own (at times, faulty) ideas into it. Case in point: When we hear *spiritual warfare,* most of us think of something like WW2, where two massive nation-state-based armies fought it out on land and sea and air. Even if we imagine an ancient war, we envision a J. R. R. Tolkien type of scene with two colossal armies meeting on a vast plane of battle—equal and opposite.

But this imagery doesn't remotely fit with what the Scriptures have to say about our fight with the devil. In a biblical theology of spiritual war, the devil has *already been defeated* by Jesus on the cross. Paul said it bluntly: "He made a public spectacle of them, triumphing over them by the cross."[4] In context, "them" is the devil and his horde of spiritual rebels. Our spiritual ancestors called this *Christus Victor* (Latin for "Christ the victor"), and many of them saw the devil's defeat as the primary, though not only, implication of the cross and resurrection.[5]

So, ditch your mental image of *Saving Private Ryan* or *The Lord of the Rings.* Instead, imagine a Russian hacker holed up in Saint Petersburg, programming bots and algorithms based on data harvested from Facebook, Google, and the corporate cadre of "surveillance capitalism."[6] These algorithms can work out when you are most emotionally vulnerable and susceptible to manipulation, then inject an emotion-loaded news story, alert, or link into your feed at just the right time to prey on your fear or desire and index you toward their desired behavior, opinion, or view.[7]

Or imagine the civil war in Syria—multipolar, more sides than I can even understand, key players constantly switching sides, countries like the US and Russia aiding and abetting from the shadows, insurgency tactics on the ground, fighting from house to house—leaving anarchy and a wave of refugees in its wake.[8]

Military theorists are calling warfare in the twenty-first century dirty war or asymmetric warfare. In the conventional wars of bygone eras, war was far more symmetrical, between relative equals. There was usually a clear winner and a clear end to the war. Those days are over. Now, it's between large nation-states like the US and small jihadist groups or online hackers. What good is an F-22 Raptor against a tweet? Or a Humvee with a .50-cal machine gun against religious extremism?

Dirty war is a far more fitting metaphor for our spiritual struggle. We're not up against the spiritual equivalent of the German war machine of the last century. It's more akin to bots, "deepfakes,"[9] insurgency IEDs, and opposing street rallies in Houston between "Stop Islamification of Texas" and "Save Islamic Knowledge" that was actually organized by Russian spies via Facebook ads.[10]

It's a war between truth and lies.

The meteoric rise of conspiracy theories like QAnon are tearing families and even churches apart. Fake news and grossly biased journalism (on both sides) adds to people's latent distrust of authority. The devil's assault on truth is creating havoc in culture at large, not just the church.

When President Obama sat down with David Letterman on *My Next Guest Needs No Introduction,* the line everybody was talking about was, "One of the biggest challenges we have to our democracy is the degree to which we don't share a common baseline of facts."[11]

He was referring, of course, to his successor President Donald J. Trump. *The Washington Post* (granted, a left-leaning newspaper and hardly an unbiased source) calculated that Trump made 2,140 false or misleading claims in his first year in office, an average of 5.9 per day.[12] That number went *up* over his term as president, turning into the Big Lie that gave way to the Capitol riot.

Whatever your political leanings, surely you can agree integrity is crucial to hold a nation together. And lest you think this is a not-so-subtle advocacy for left-wing politics, I promise you, it's not. Please don't make assumptions about me because I'm from Portland. People from across the political aisle were distraught over President Trump's lack of honesty.

Republican Senator Jeff Flake said the year he was elected "was a year which saw the truth—objective, empirical, evidence-based truth—more battered and abused than any other in the history of our country, at the hands of the most powerful figure in our government."[13]

The RAND Corporation, a right-leaning, pro-military, nonprofit think tank, coined the phrase *truth decay* to name our cultural moment.[14] *Alternative facts* has since entered the lexicon of America.

This is a cancer of integrity that's infected both the Left and the Right. In her leftist exposé of the Trump Administration, *The Death of Truth,* former chief book critic for the *New York Times* Michiko Kakutani was at least honest enough to admit that this war on truth did not start on the Right with President Trump or Breitbart News but much earlier with French philosophers like Foucault and Derrida. These left-leaning thought leaders spread the ideas of postmodernism and moral relativism deep into the nervous system of American academia. This began a university-based movement toward a post-truth society, as all truth became relative, or worse, a form of oppression in need of tearing down.[15]

Now our children are growing up in the fallout of deconstructionism.

Celebrated social critic David Foster Wallace, in a chilling interview before his tragic suicide, summarized our moment beautifully:

> What's been passed down from the postmodern heyday is sarcasm, cynicism, a manic ennui, suspicion of all authority, suspicion of all constraints on conduct, and a terrible penchant for ironic diagnosis of unpleasantness instead of an ambition not just to diagnose and ridicule but to redeem. You've got to understand that this stuff has permeated the culture. It's become our language; we're so in it we don't even see that it's one perspective, one among many possible ways of seeing. Postmodern irony's become our environment.[16]

Our new environment is one in which a battle is raging between truth and lies, and truth is losing. Disinformation—or in the language of Scripture, deception—is at the root of almost every single problem we face in our society and our souls.

Again, examples from the culture war can just trigger more tribalism; the far more common—and often more dangerous—lies are the ones inside our own heads.

- *I can't trust my wife; she'll cheat on me just like my mom cheated on my dad.*

- *Good things don't happen to me, so why even try to be successful?*

- *I can't say or do anything that will make people upset with me.*

- *My best days are all behind me.*

- *If anyone actually knew me, they would reject me.*

These types of lies prey on us indiscriminate of our political leanings; they are bipartisan and brutal.

And in this cultural moment of truth decay, I find Jesus's teachings on the devil and lies more plausible, insightful, and compelling than ever before. Jesus and the apostles warn us over and over again of the dangers of lies, deception, false doctrine, and false teachers who are wolves in sheep's clothing.

In one of his last teachings, Jesus warned his apprentices, "Watch out that no one deceives you." He then warned that "false prophets" would "deceive many people" and "because of the increase of wickedness, the love of most will grow cold,"[17] pointing forward to a reality we now inhabit.

The New Testament writers followed up Jesus's warning with upwards of *forty* more warnings of deception, especially in the areas of sexual immorality and false teaching. Here are just a few samples:

Do not be *deceived.*[18]

I tell you this so that no one may *deceive* you by fine-sounding arguments.[19]

Evildoers and impostors will go from bad to worse, *deceiving and being deceived.*[20]

At one time we too were foolish, disobedient, *deceived* and enslaved by all kinds of passions and pleasures.[21]

I am afraid that just as Eve was *deceived* by the serpent's cunning, your minds may somehow be *led astray* from your sincere and pure devotion to Christ.[22]

Dear children, do not let anyone *lead you astray.*[23]

Paul writes about those who "exchanged the truth about God for a lie" and people who "suppress the truth by their wickedness."[24]

Jude warns about false teachers who have "secretly slipped in among you . . . who pervert the grace of our God into a license for immorality."[25]

In Revelation, the unholy trinity of the apocalypse are masters of disinformation: the false prophet and antichrist "deceive" and "delude" and "lead astray" the nations.[26] The satan himself "deceives the whole world."[27]

Are you getting the picture? For Jesus and the early teachers of his way, deception was a major issue.[28]

And yet we rarely hear warnings like these today except from hard-core fundamentalists, who seldom engage the lies in a calm, rational way and expose them as unreality but instead shout into a bullhorn in rhetoric laced with contempt, rather than compassion.

You rarely see this angry tone in Jesus, and when you do, it's always directed at the religious leaders, who bore a unique culpability in Israel's spiritual state. You *do* see Jesus say hard things on a regular basis—uncomfortable things, unpopular things, the kinds of things that eventually got him killed. But most of the time, his tone was tender and wise. Still, unlike the West's popular definition of love as basically not disagreeing with people, Jesus disagreed with people constantly, *in* love.

That's because Jesus and the New Testament writers worked off this core conviction: deception is tied to temptation, temptation to slavery to sin, and it's the truth that will set you free.

Think about it: the devil can't make us do anything as followers of Jesus.[29] We have to choose it. To get us to choose evil, our enemy has to fool us into walking down a path other than the one Jesus laid down for us, *thinking it will lead us to happiness.* His primary way of doing this is through illusion.

One way to think about temptation is to see all temptation as the appeal to believe a lie, to believe an illusion about reality.

And now we're getting to the core thesis of this book.

Here it is again: the devil's primary stratagem to drive the soul and society into ruin is *deceptive ideas that play to disordered desires, which are normalized in a sinful society.*

Deceptive Ideas	▶	**Disordered Desires**	▶	**Sinful Society**
(the DEVIL)		(the FLESH)		(the WORLD)

I have thoroughly made the point that the devil is a liar.

Next, I need to make the point that he's a really good liar. The devil is a master manipulator. He's far more intelligent than we give him credit for; you can bet that if we know what makes for a good lie (an oxymoron if there ever was one), so does he.

He's well aware that . . .

1. the most effective lies are the ones that are mostly true. Here's a little free advice for those of you wanting to grow in the art of deception: spin a tale in which 95 percent of what you say is accurate; just make the 5 percent of inaccuracy the linchpin that undoes your mark.

2. the next most effective lies are those that are true but not the whole truth. They are one side of a two-sided conversation or an oversimplification of the complex reality of life. Cue the "Yes, *but* . . ." or "Yes, *and* . . ." retorts in a debate.

Even if we can accept that there is a devil and he's a master manipulator, this still doesn't explain how easily we fall for his lies *even when they are exposed as untrue.*

This conundrum is especially acute if you come from an Enlightenment worldview that claims human beings are rational, autonomous selves. Even though the social sciences have thoroughly debunked this assumption, it still lives on in the popular imagination. We prefer to think of ourselves as rational individualists rather than the emotional, relational, and easily manipulated social creatures we actually are.

The world's leading expert on deception is Dr. Timothy Levine. He's spent years conducting hundreds of interviews with everyone from police officers to CIA agents. His conclusion: even the most intelligent human beings are *terrible* at lie detection. Through his research, Levine developed the truth-default theory (TDT) to explain that humans default to truth. We assume someone is telling us the truth unless there's sufficient evidence to the contrary.[30]

The journalist Malcom Gladwell summarized TDT like this:

> We do not behave, in other words, like sober-minded scientists, slowly gathering evidence of the truth or falsity of something before reaching a conclusion. We do the opposite. We start by believing. And we *stop* believing only when our doubts and misgivings rise to the point where we can no longer explain them away.[31]

Okay, so we're easily deceived. That's helpful.

But that still doesn't explain *why* we choose to believe a lie even when so much evidence is stacked against it. Now it's time to touch on our disordered desires in the above thesis.

The reason the devil's dezinformatsiya campaign is so wildly successful, even when faced with the counterfacts of reality, is that it plays to what the New Testament writers called our flesh. We'll get into the flesh in part 2, but for now, just think of it as a placeholder for our animalistic, base drives.

The devil's lies aren't just random untrue facts with no emotional value.

Pssst. Hey you, Christian, Elvis is still alive. Believe it.

Okay, who cares. That has no emotional bearing on my life. A quick Google search and my mind can easily sort this into the lie category.

But what about this one?

Hey, you deserve to be happy, and let's face it: you haven't been happy in your marriage in years. Your wife just isn't the right fit for you. It happens. You married way too young, before you were self-aware, and this marriage just isn't what you hoped it would be. But if you were to divorce her, I'm sure there's someone else who would be a better fit and would make you happy.

This is just as flagrant of a con. A cursory Google search of the research on long-term relationships will expose the dark comedy of it;[32] but to be vulnerable, this one touches on some deep fracture in my own soul, where I'm torn. A part of me wants to honor my incredible wife and stay faithful to my wedding vows, to let the power of the marriage covenant shape me into a man who is increasingly free of my need to get what I want. But another part of me—my flesh—just wants to live a feel-good, easy life, chasing the fantasy of sex and romance over the horizon.

As you can imagine, only a few conspiracy theorists fall for the Elvis kind of lie, but many of us are vulnerable to the second.

As a pastor, I have front-row seats to watch the before and after of a lie's entrance into a soul, and not to scare you, but it's gut wrenching. I used the example of "You'll be happier if you get a divorce" because it's so common. I see it all the time. While every marriage is its own story, I watch so many people initiate a divorce in a desire to be happy but end up even more miserable. Many of them carry regret to their graves.

You see, nobody sins out of duty or discipline. Nobody wakes up in the morning and says, "Ahh, it's Tuesday, 7:00 a.m.—time to look at porn. I don't really want to, but it's just the right thing to do. I read *Atomic Habits* by James Clear, and I've made a commitment to become a lustful kind of person; habit stacking is the key if I ever want to work up to my long-term dream of serial infidelity and a low capacity for intimacy."

No, of course not.

We sin because we believe a lie about what will make us happy.

Ignatius of Loyola, the founder of the Jesuit order, is credited with defining sin as "unwillingness to trust that what God wants for me is only my deepest happiness." This is why the devil's primary target is our trust in God and his truth as it comes to us in Scripture. If he can get us to doubt God and instead trust in our own inner intuition as an accurate compass to the good life, he has us. In the ultimate irony, sin sabotages our capacity for happiness *by appealing to our God-given desire for happiness* via deceptive ideas.

But how do we sort fact from fiction as we navigate the dizzying bazaar of ideas that is the modern world?

This is where Jesus's teaching on the devil as the father of lies is incredibly helpful. What's easy to miss for a modern, non-

Jewish reader of the Bible is that when Jesus told the Pharisees, "You belong to your father, the devil," he was alluding to
a well-known story to make his case: that of the serpent and
Eve.

Unfortunately, many late-modern Westerners (especially
those, like myself, who are more skeptical by nature) find the
Garden of Eden story—and with it the Bible as a whole—all
too easy to write off as nonsense. After all, there's a talking
snake on page 3. But again, chronological snobbery. People
in the ancient Near East were just as aware as we are that
snakes don't talk. That's not something you need an advanced degree in molecular biology to deduce. They were
well aware something *else* was going on in that story.

Maybe you read the early chapters of Genesis as history, with
a literal talking snake and Eve speaking Parseltongue, or
maybe you read them as mythology, with the snake as a common ancient image for a spiritual being and Genesis as a subversive counterstory to ancient creation myths like the Enuma
Elish. Or maybe something else. But those are questions
about genre of literature, not about whether or not we can
trust Genesis as Scripture.[33] Whichever interpretation is right,
the garden story is *true.* For millennia, billions of people have
found it to be the truest and most insightful treatise of the
human condition in the history of the world.

Think with me about the truth of it for a few minutes.

In the story, the serpent, who is later identified as a personifi-
cation of the devil, came to Eve while she was deeply enjoying
her new life in Eden. The first descriptor of the serpent in the
Genesis account is that he was "more crafty than any of the

wild animals the Lord God had made."[34] The Hebrew word for "crafty" can mean "cunning" or "wily" or "deceitful."[35]

His first lie was a subtle one, posed as a question, not an angry diatribe: "Did God *really* say, 'You must not eat from any tree in the garden?' "[36]

Eve, caught off guard, seemed to say, "Well, yes, I think so."

The snake's next line was more forward: "You will not certainly die. . . . For God knows that when you eat from it your eyes will be opened, and you will be like God."[37]

Notice that the serpent came at Eve with a simple yet evocative *idea* (not a weapon): God's not as good or as wise as he claims to be. He's holding out on you. If you seize autonomy from God and do your own thing with me, you'll be better off.[38]

This is the lie underneath all other lies.

And notice how this lie played to Eve's (and our) disordered desires. Next line: "The woman saw that the fruit of the tree was good for food and pleasing to the eye, and also desirable for gaining wisdom."

Ooohh. Who doesn't want a little good food, beauty, and social status? Especially when it's so within our reach.

Tragically, she fell for it. As did Adam.

"She took some and ate it. She also gave some to her husband, who was with her, and he ate it."[39]

The rest, as they say, is history.

Adam, by the way, isn't a proper name in Hebrew; it's the word for "human."[40] Neither is Eve; it means "life."[41] That's why nobody else is named Adam or Eve in the Old Testament.

This is a story about how "human" and "life" got into their present state.

And this is the story Jesus is referring to in John 8 when he claimed the Pharisees "belong to your father, the devil." He was saying, "You claim you're descendants of Abraham, but actually you stand in the ancestral line of the snake."

Remember what I said about Jesus not always coming off as nice?

Here's why this is so helpful: the Genesis 3 lie is the paradigmatic *lie behind all lies.* The deception (or really temptation) is and has always been twofold: (1) to seize autonomy from God and (2) to redefine good and evil based on the voice in our heads and the inclination of our hearts, rather than trust in the loving word of God.

Here's another way to frame it. There are three great questions in life:

1. Who is God? (Or the gods? Or is there a God or gods?)
2. Who are we?
3. How do we live?

Put another way:

1. What is the meaning and purpose of life?
2. What does it mean to be human?
3. What is the good life?

These three questions are the driving force behind all religion, philosophy, education, art, and literature. They are the core questions of humanity.

We ask, "Who is God? What is he like? Can I trust him?"

The devil lies: *He's an unloving, jealous tyrant who is holding out on you. You can't trust him.*

We ask, "Who are we? What does it mean to be human? Am I just an animal or something more?"

He lies yet again: *You're not just a human being with a place in an ordered cosmos over the creation but still under the Creator. No, you can transgress your limitations and become whoever and whatever you want. Identity is self-defined. Morality is self-determined. Take control of your own life. "You will be like God."*

And we ask, "How do we live? What is the good life? How do I live it?"

Here the devil's lies are most salient: *You can't trust God, but you* can *trust yourself, your* own *wisdom and desires. Look at this bright, shiny thing—this tree that God said was off-limits. Eat it, take it, seize it, do it, experience it. Follow your heart.*

Your inner intuition is the most accurate map to the happy life you crave.

These are still the serpent's stock-in-trade lies. Lies about who God is, who we are, and what makes for a happy life.

The exact nature of the lies changes from generation to generation, culture to culture, and person to person, but they always run along these lines: Distance yourself from God. Do your own thing. Redefine good and evil based on your own gut and desire.

The most telling examples of this in my city come from the secular narrative and, increasingly, from the Eastern enlightenment narrative—a cocktail of selections from Buddhism, bits and pieces of Hindu self-actualization, and an infusion of American self-help.

The latter is less influential to cultural elites, though it's still on the rise, especially in coastal cities like Portland.

The basic answers of enlightenment chic are something like this:

"Who is God?"

All of us. The line of demarcation between the human and the divine is a Western illusion. The spark of god is in all of us.

"Who are we?"

Gods and goddesses. Authentic selves whose desires are the source of all wisdom and direction. Who must be free of all external authority to actualize our potential.

"How do we live?"

Be true to yourself. Speak your truth. Don't let anyone tell you what to do.

Does this sound at all familiar? Do you hear it in your own city? From your friends and family? Or even coming out of your own mouth?

Or maybe it's not appealing to you at all.

While the enlightenment self-actualization narrative is growing in popularity in the Portlands of the world, for most people, this way of life is still at the emerging level of self-help positivity.

Secularism, on the other hand, is far more deeply entrenched. For all the talk about being spiritual but not religious, I find that most of my fellow Portlanders are still mostly secular. What they mean by *spirituality* is usually that they practice yoga or they believe in wonder; it's not the more classical definition of *spiritual* as in a relationship with a spiritual being. Secular society is an attempt to answer the first question of "who is God?" with a negative.

"Who is God?"

There is no God. God is just a myth from the premodern, pre-scientific age. And a dangerous one at that—the cause of tribalism and war. Now we know better.

As one of my genuinely lovely secular friends said to me recently, "I don't believe in God; I believe in science."

This is the challenge of secularism—not that it has a high value for science (*that* I'm all for) but that it claims to be objective, based on facts instead of faith, when really it's an *interpretation* of the data points of science that takes just as much faith to believe as the gospel, if not far more.

Modern, secular society is the first to ever attempt to live as if there is no God. Which is a disaster waiting to happen, because the answers to the next two questions flow from the first. What we believe about the good life is based on what we think it means to be human, which in turn is based on what we believe about God.

Is there a Creator and creation?

Or is there just evolutionary theory, blind chance, and survival of the fittest?

Think about the implications of how we answer that question:

If there's a Creator, then there's design . . .

If there's design, then there's intent . . .

If there's intent, then there's morality . . .

But if there is morality, then there is accountability . . .

And *all human beings avoid accountability,* which makes this a vulnerability that is easily exploited.

Because if there's no Creator, if all this is just probability and statistics and Dr. Malcom was right in *Jurassic Park* and life just "finds a way,"[42] then there's no design . . . at least, not the design of a wise intelligence.

And if there's no design, then there's no intent other than the propagation of the species and, now that the earth is over-populated, we're free to jettison the intent of biology . . .

And if there's no intent, then there's no morality . . . Who are you to judge me? Tell me what to do? Limit my freedom?

And if there's no morality, then there's no accountability . . .

And we can do whatever we want.

Many intelligent and sophisticated people in our world simply do not want to be accountable to God or any kind of higher author-ity; instead, they want to be free to live as they please, with no guilty conscience from within or legal restraint from without. This is behind much of the West's rejection of God—as led by cul-tural elites, who often exemplify this heart posture en masse.[43]

But the problem is, if there's no accountability, *there's no reality.*

All we have left is Twitter feeds with alternative facts and French philosophers who deconstruct the world and leave it in chaos.

Or closer to home: broken relationships and a fog of confu-sion over the meaning of life. People living under the oppres-sion of false narratives about who they even are.

This is why even Nietzsche mourned rather than celebrated the "death of God" in Western culture.[44] He looked over the horizon to a post-God, post-truth world, and instead of liberation, he saw anarchy.

After all, what happens at the end of the *Genesis* story?

They die.

On that happy note, let's explore a potential way out of this conundrum.

And having done all, to stand

I grew up on *G.I. Joe.*

Yes, I know those toys are no longer politically correct.

No, I don't recommend violent toys for children.

But one of the (many) things I learned from *G.I. Joe* was that "knowing is half the battle."

For my readers who somehow missed the 1980s' glory of Duke, Scarlett, Flint, and Lady Jaye, each thirty-minute episode would end with a little vignette about safety for children. I remember one where two kids are riding their bikes near a downed power line, and Roadblock (one of my favorite characters) shows up to warn them about the dangers of live wires and electrocution.

It ends, as they all do, with the kids saying, "Now we know." Followed by Roadblock's iconic Joe line: "And knowing is half the battle."[1]

This idea—that knowing is half the battle—is a very recent, very Western idea. It comes out of a Cartesian worldview that sees humans as rational "brains on legs" rather than the ancient, more holistic view of humans as desire-based creatures. And we like this idea because (1) it allows us to justify emotional and desire-based decisions under the guise of rationality and (2) it doesn't require much from us. Just listen to a podcast, take an e-course, or read a book about, say, the devil. And *voilà,* you're halfway there. But the problem is, knowing something is not the same as *doing* something, which is still not the same as *wanting* to do something.

Laurie Santos of Yale called this the G.I. Joe fallacy. Santos is a professor of psychology and cognitive science, and her basic point is that simply knowing something is not enough to change. Change is hard. Knowing something is important, but it's not half the battle. It's more like 10 or 20 percent of the battle.[2]

For ideas, good or bad, to reshape our lives, they have to get into our *hearts*—the deep centers of our beings that integrate our thoughts, emotions, and desires—and from there into our *bodies,* our muscle memory. Or in more Christian language, into our souls.

We've been trafficking in ideas for the last few chapters (reminder: ideas are assumptions about reality). I've set out new (or really, very old) mental maps to reality derived from Jesus himself—maps where the devil isn't a myth or a premodern superstition but a real, intelligent force of evil who is hell-bent on the ruin of our souls and society and whose primary strategem is that of lies via a kind of spiritual dirty war.

Now that we've established a working grasp of the devil as the first enemy of our souls, we need to figure out how we actually fight this enemy. All we've done so far is unveil his strategy.

What's ours?

So, first a little theory; then we'll move on to practice.

Theory

Let's talk for a minute about spiritual formation. If you're new to that language, all I mean by *spiritual formation* is the process by which we are formed in our spirits, or inner persons, into the image of Jesus.

Or conversely, deformed into the image of the devil.

Spiritual formation isn't just a follower of Jesus thing; it's a *human* thing. We're all being formed every minute of every day. We're all becoming someone. Intentional or unintentional, conscious or subconscious, deliberate or haphazard, we're all in a process of becoming a person.

The question isn't, Are you becoming somebody? but *Who* are you becoming?

The question for us as followers of Jesus is, How do we become more like Jesus and not like the devil?

Teachers of spiritual formation, as well as leading experts in neuroscience, psychology, and the best of the social sciences, all agree that our mental maps play a key role. Again, this is why Jesus came as a luminary teacher: to give us new mental maps that congrue with reality.

But truth alone is not enough—cue the G.I. Joe fallacy. We need something more: relationship.

Or in the words of Jesus in John 4, we need "Spirit" and "truth."[3]

For years I puzzled over Jesus's language, but I've come to realize these are the *key* to spiritual formation. To change, to grow, to break free of our flesh and become like Jesus, we need Spirit and truth.

What is Spirit? Pentecostal scholar Gordon Fee defined Spirit as "God's empowering presence."[4] It's the animating energy we draw on through relationship to God.

And truth, as we already covered, is reality. Or words that we can rely on to find meaning in our lives.

Another way to say this is we become like Jesus through *relationships* and *reality.*

Let me give you a human example: Spirit (or relationship) without truth has no meaning. Imagine a time of suffering in your life—the death of a friend or family member, a brutal diagnosis, a lost job. Now, imagine it's caused you to seriously doubt God. A friend comes to visit with you. But she never says a single word. While that would still be comforting and make you appreciate your friend's love, it would likely not be transformative, as it would offer no truth or meaning to help you adjust your mental maps to reality in a healthy and healing way.

Or flip it around: truth without spirit is cold, even cruel. Think of the internet. It's full of truth, but without a human to help you navigate it—it's just a compendium of endless facts. Nobody's life was ever transformed by Wikipedia. Nobody who ever doubted God in tragedy discovered a set of *Encyclopaedia Britannica* in the basement that saved his soul. Or think of the vivid parody of a street preacher screaming truth into a bullhorn. Have you ever met anybody who repented at such preaching? I sure haven't. Why do we react with such emotional nausea to street preachers? Because it's truth without spirit; it's reality (kind of) without any kind of relational equity or loving presence.

So, we need *both* Spirit and truth—both the relational presence of Jesus and his community *and* the meaning-giving truth of our Rabbi's mental maps.

Are you tracking with me?

Great.

This is why Jesus comes as a human and a teacher. As a human being, he is able to offer *spirit,* or relational presence. To be with us in the pain of the human condition. The writer of Hebrews said Jesus was "tempted in every way, just as we are."[5] Meaning, he knows exactly what it feels like to be us. He knows what it feels like to be exhausted, worn thin, vulnerable, confused. To suffer. To doubt. To feel the pull of greed or lust or apathy. But as a rabbi, he is also able to offer *truth,* to point us to reality and give us meaning in our suffering. Human beings simply can't live without loving relationships and meaning to both our suffering and our existence as a whole. Jesus comes to offer both.

Spirit and truth.

Let me flesh this out with a real-life example: therapy. I've been in therapy for a decade straight, and God has used it to radically alter and heal me. And I'm not alone. Therapy, when done well, is spirit and truth.

When I sit with my therapist, a seventy-year-old, Jesus-loving PhD with decades of wisdom under his belt, I'm in the presence of a spirit—the presence of a relational being marked by compassionate love, not to mention a half a century of lived experience following Jesus and all the spiritual authority that comes with it. And I'm in the presence of truth—he speaks reality and meaning into the chaos and confusion of my life.

The psychologist M. Scott Peck, whom I mentioned earlier, called the devil "a real spirit of unreality"; he also defined mental health as "an ongoing process of dedication to reality at all costs."[6]

This is why bad therapy is so incredibly toxic and dangerous. (And sadly, there's plenty of bad therapy.) You're in the presence of an expert you come to trust, but then, in that vulnerable place, the therapist speaks unreality into your mind. After all, much of the therapeutic world is still Freudian in outlook, which is wildly at odds with Jesus's vision of the human person. And there's no community in the room to vet the therapist's words, to confirm or correct. And she has a degree on the wall. So, tragically, deceptive ideas often go uncontested into the soul.

Or let's apply this to an even more common example: parenting. Good parenting is a simple though hard-to-master combination of spirit and truth.

Spirit: the parent is present in relational love to the child. To borrow the language of the therapeutic world, the child "feels felt." And when we feel felt, we feel loved.

Then, truth: the parent speaks reality over the child. Reality about who God is, who the child is, and how the child is to live (the three core questions we covered in the last chapter).

There is no perfect parent (surely not this one), but when children are brought up in a loving relational matrix of trust and taught to live in congruence with reality, as a general rule, they thrive.

Bad parenting, on the other hand, is the exact opposite— absence and lies.

Absence: the parent is MIA, whether due to divorce, workaholism, or just walking out.

Lies: if or when the parent *is* around, the parent speaks lies.

Lies about who God is. "God is ashamed of you." Or "God doesn't care about who you sleep with. Have fun."

Lies about who the child is: "You'll never amount to anything. You're just like your old man. You're such a klutz."

And lies about how to live: "Look out for number one, kiddo. It's a dog-eat-dog world. A little white lie never hurt anyone."

Children who grow up in this kind of environment suffer damage to their souls. Is it treatable? Yes. But it's still painful, excruciatingly so.

This is why parenting is so incredibly important. And I'm convinced it's why the family itself is under a kind of demonic assault by the less-gracious wing of secular culture.

Now we come to a key point: It's by Spirit and truth that we're transformed into the image of Jesus, but the reciprocal is also true. *It's by isolation and lies that we're deformed into the image of the devil.*

Let's circle back to the garden story in Genesis 3. How did the snake bring about Eve's fall?

First, he got Eve *alone.* Away from God and her primary relationship, Adam. That way no other voice was in her head but his. No counterpoint of truth to mitigate his deceit.

Then he *lied.* He planted doubts in her mind about God's wisdom and good intentions, lies that played to her disordered desires for self-gratification, pleasure, and autonomy.

Alone and exposed to lies, she was easy prey.

And please don't read this story as a commentary on gender dynamics, as some have tragically done. I highly doubt Adam would have done any better. The point isn't that Eve was female and therefore easier to manipulate. It's that she was alone and away from community, and when humans are isolated, we are *all* easier to fool.

And while it's easy to laugh this story off—"I would never fall for the old talking snake routine"—the more sophisticated the person or culture, the more fine-tuned the devil's tactics. Again, he's far more intelligent than we give him credit for. *Crafty* is the word used in Genesis 3. But his tactic is the same basic formula on repeat: Isolate, then lie. Pick a lie that plays to a disordered desire. Get your mark to take a relational step away from God and to redefine good and evil for himself. Done.

This is *still* how the devil plies his craft.

As a pastor, I could tell you countless stories of people who have walked into sin or even walked away from God, and it *always* starts with drifting away from community with other solid followers of Jesus.

I mean, think about the worst things you've ever done. I'm thinking about mine as I type. For most of them, we were either alone or in the presence of someone who was a bad influence on us.

Any of you do something really, really bad—I mean, it wrecked your life forever—when you were having a coffee with your pastor from church? At 10:00 a.m. outside your local coffee spot deep in Bible study?

Or any of you make a thoroughly horrible decision when you were with your family on Christmas morning? You know, just decide to go rob a bank with Grandma Ruth and Aunt Mary?

No. In fact, just being in the presence of a good spirit, or relational being, is itself transformative. Because we become like the people we spend time with, for better, hopefully, but also for worse.

This is one of the things that made COVID-19 so devastating. Social isolation was a form of social justice, a way to care for the vulnerable, but its effect on mental health and human flourishing was lethal. The suicide rate spiked to an all-time high. We *need* community to thrive.

The devil is just as aware of our need for community as we are, if not more so, and he uses that awareness to gain the upper hand in the fight, doing all he can to cut us off from community with God's people and from God himself.

In the digital age, we make his job a breeze. Hurry, pathological busyness, distraction, smartphone addiction, the constant stream of alerts and interruptions—these all cut us off from community and feed our inordinate desire for autonomy. Cue the axiom, "When Satan cannot make you bad, he makes you busy."[7]

Speaking of digital overload and busyness, I find the current uproar over online privacy to be a fascinating social phenomenon. I'm always looking for areas where, for all the talk of political polarization, the Left and Right agree.[8] This is one. And while I completely concur that it's creepy for some megacorporation to know my Google search history, read my emails, or listen in to my conversations while I'm scrolling Instagram, still, I sometimes wonder, *What does everybody have to hide?*

As Supreme Court Justice Louis Brandeis once said, "Sunlight is . . . the best of disinfectants."[9]

My point here isn't to justify Facebook's dubious soft identity theft at all; that's a *major* problem. It's simply to say I think one of the reasons digital privacy is such a flash point is because of our Western obsession with autonomy, hyperindividualism, and privacy, which the devil manipulates for evil. If he can get us alone, staring at our screens in the dark, when we are most vulnerable to lies, we're quick pickings.

In his letter to the Corinthians, Paul explained the motivation behind his letter's sharp language: "That Satan might not outwit us. For we are not unaware of his schemes."[10]

Tragically, much of the time we *are* unaware of his schemes.

The past few chapters were my attempt to expose the devil's schemes, his not-so-secret plans to drive us to ruin via isolation and lies, and to offer an alternative from the Way of Jesus: Spirit and truth.

Now, to end, let's talk about practice.

Practice

By *practice,* I mean the disciplines by which we mitigate the isolation and lies of the devil in our secular society with the Spirit and truth of Jesus and his kingdom.

As followers of Jesus, we look to Jesus's own life as our template of how to fight the devil. What was his practice?

Jesus's first run-in with the devil was recorded by both Luke and Matthew, and right from the opening line of the story, what we find is surprising.

> Jesus, full of the Holy Spirit, left the Jordan and was led by the Spirit into the wilderness, where for forty days he was tempted by the devil. He ate nothing during those days, and at the end of them he was hungry.[11]

There's a lot going on here, but let me give you a brief synopsis:

- Within the scope of the larger story the Scriptures tell, Jesus comes as a second Adam, the one, true human being who comes to do what Adam was supposed to do all along but failed: face down the devil but not give in. Remember, Adam means "human." Like Adam, Jesus is tempted; unlike Adam, he is victorious over temptation.

- Instead of a garden, he's in a desert, symbolic of humanity's exile from the garden due to sin.

- Instead of eating from the tree of the knowledge of good and evil, he's fasting, feeding on the Spirit for power to defeat the devil's ploy.

- The devil starts in on Jesus the same way he did on Eve, by planting doubts in Jesus's mind about his identity as the object of God's love: "*If* you are the Son of God."[12] In the story literally right before, God said to Jesus, "*You are my Son,* whom I love."[13] For the erudite reader, it's the snake's update of "Did God really say?"

- The devil's threefold temptation is subtle, clever, and manipulative and has nothing to do with getting

Jesus to sin as we think of it. It plays instead to the undercurrents of desire in Jesus's heart. The desire to take his kingdom by an easier way. To get the right thing, the wrong way.

Three times the devil tempts Jesus. Each time, Jesus calmly responds with a quote from Scripture. He doesn't budge an inch.

Closing line:

> When the devil had finished all this tempting, he left him until an opportune time.[14]

This story is so different from what I would expect. It reads like a conversation. I can't really think of another word for it. There are no swords, no screams of fury, no Zeus-like battle cry, yet this is a *fight,* full on. But Jesus is calm, the epitome of a "non-anxious presence."[15] Exuding a quiet confidence in his Father's truth.

And notice, he's doing so via practices from his way, or what have come to be called spiritual disciplines.

He's all alone with God in the desert—in what has come to be called *silence and solitude.*

He's in *prayer.*

He's *fasting.*

His mind and mouth are full of *Scripture.*

And this is how we, as apprentices of Jesus, fight the devil.

Not via some emotional or spiritual frenzy. We simply stand in quiet confidence in God's truth via the practices of Jesus.

You could say it this way: *spiritual disciplines are spiritual warfare.*

The philosopher Steven Porter from Biola University has done some very interesting work around how we as material creatures interact with an immaterial Creator.[16] To summarize his conclusion, it's through spiritual disciplines. And while I prefer the language of *practices,* I love his definition of spiritual disciplines:

> The disciplines are embodied practices in a physical world whereby we present ourselves to the immaterial reality of the Spirit/presence and Word/ truth of Christ.[17]

Meaning, it's through the practices of Jesus that we present our minds and bodies before God and open our souls to his Spirit and truth.

There's no official list of the practices of Jesus. Technically, any habit you see in the life or teachings of Jesus is a spiritual discipline. But there are two anchor practices for our fight with the devil that Jesus put on display in the desert.

Quiet Prayer

Notice that Jesus is alone in the quiet with God in prayer. There are no other inputs into his mind. No chatter with his roommate, no reading the morning news, no popping online for a scroll through social media. Jesus literally goes into the wild of the desert not just to get rid of external inputs but also to face down his internal inputs—and sort the voice of his Father from the voice of his enemy.

A lot of people misunderstand silence and solitude (another name for this practice) as a place to relax and recharge. A kind of emotional break for introverts to catch their breath before they return to the fray of life.

But that is not the solitude of Jesus or the apostle Paul or Evagrius of Pontus. For them, it wasn't a break from the battle; *it was the field on which the battle was won or lost.*

Henri Nouwen said it this way: "Solitude is not a private therapeutic place." Rather, "solitude is the furnace of transformation. Without solitude we remain victims of our society and continue to be entangled in the illusions of the false self."[18]

It's in quiet prayer that the devil's lies—"the illusions of the false self"—are exposed and brought out into the open. We see what *logosmoi* or thought patterns dominate our minds. It's there that we face the decision: Will we give our attention to these thoughts or curate new ones? Will we trust the devil's lies or Jesus's truth? It's there, in the quiet, that we win or lose the battle for our minds' attention and hearts' affection.

This is why quiet prayer goes hand in hand with the next anchor practice.

Scripture

How does Jesus fight the devil's lies? By turning to Scripture. Three times the devil tempts Jesus with a lie; three times

Jesus quotes scriptures in reply. But please listen carefully: this is not the Christian version of a magic incantation. A quote from Scripture doesn't just make the devil fly away. In fact, in the story, the devil quotes Scripture back with great alacrity.

Something else is going on here.

Now we're ready to circle back around to Evagrius and his *Talking Back: A Monastic Handbook for Combating Demons.* I called it a book, but really, it's a handbook. There are a few pages of introduction—all brilliant—followed by just shy of five hundred entries. Each entry has a thought, emotion, or desire from a demon, followed by a scripture that speaks to that specific temptation.

Remember, for Evagrius, *logosmoi,* or our thought patterns, are the primary vehicle of demonic attack upon our souls. That might sound far-fetched to our skeptical Western ears, but think about it: Have you ever had a thought (or feeling or desire) that seemed to have a will to it? An agenda that was hard to resist? And not thinking it felt like fighting gravity? It seemed to have a weight or power over you that was beyond your ability to resist?

Could it be that the thoughts that assault your mind's peace aren't *just* thoughts? Could it be that a dark, animating energy is behind them? A spiritual force?

Could it be that this is about more than mental hygiene or positive thinking; it's about resistance?

And the stakes are high. As the writer Paul put it, "The mind governed by the flesh is death, but the mind governed by the Spirit is life and peace."[19]

Life or death, chaos or peace—these battles are won or lost in a mental theater of war.

If we give in to the *logosmoi,* the thoughts at war with life and peace, they become strongholds in our minds and hold us in captivity. But we can break free *if we set our minds on Scripture.*

Or in Evagrius's language:

> In the time of struggle, when the demons make war
> against us and hurl their arrows at us, let us answer
> them from the Holy Scriptures, lest the unclean
> thoughts persist in us, enslave the soul through the
> sin of actual deeds, and so defile it and plunge it
> into the death brought by sin. For "the soul that
> sins shall die." Whenever a thought is not firmly set
> in one's thinking, so that one can answer the evil
> one, sin is easily and swiftly handled.[20]

Evagrius was just riffing on Jesus's example here. You fight the devil's lies by simply choosing to not think about them. But as we all know, you can't think about nothing. So you give your mind something else to think about: Scripture. You replace the devil's lies with God's truth. You cut new neural pathways that eventually take root in the neurobiology of your body itself. You *become* what you give your mind to.

This is right in line with cutting-edge neuroscience. Dr. Jeffrey Schwartz, one of the leading experts on OCD, in his book *You Are Not Your Brain,* makes the case that your mind (which he defines as directed attention) can literally rewire your brain. When an unwanted thought comes into your conscious awareness, all you have to do is think about something else.[21]

This is a very simple idea and *a very hard discipline to master.*

But it's right in line with thousands of years of Christian tradition. For millennia, followers of Jesus have immersed their minds in Scripture, not just to gather data, memorize factoids, and get the right answers on a theology test. Doctrine does matter—very much—but not to "pass the test" and get into heaven. It matters because we become like our vision of God. The goal of reading Scripture is not information but spiritual formation. To take on the "mind of Christ."[22] To actually *think* like Jesus thinks. To fill your mind with the thoughts of God so regularly and deeply that it literally rewires your brain, and from there, your whole person.

There's no right way to read Scripture. Some people read slowly and prayerfully (a practice called Lectio Divina); others prefer reading large swaths of Scripture in one sitting. Some read it in the quiet; others out loud. Some alone; others with friends or family. Some like to listen to podcasts or read extra books to go deeper.

I'm a fan of all the above.

The key is not just to *think about* Scripture, but to *think* Scripture.

This simple practice has transformed my mind and, with it, my life. I was so impacted by reading Evagrius's take on the story of Jesus in the wilderness that I made my own monastic handbook for combating demons. Don't worry; this one won't see publication. It's not for others; it's for me. I spent months writing down in my journal every thought or emotion that came into my conscious awareness. I identified repeating thoughts that were lies from the devil.

Then I asked the Spirit to bring to mind a specific scripture to combat each lie. Sometimes a scripture would come immediately to mind; other times, I had to wait on God for days or weeks for just the right verse. Once I had it, I wrote it down beneath the lie, just like Evagrius. Against the thought, *Stepping out in faith to start this nonprofit will end in disaster for my family . . .*

"The LORD is my shepherd, I lack nothing."[23]

Against the thought, *My wife and I are a bad fit, and I would be happier if we got a divorce . . .*

"What God has joined together, let no one separate" and "Husbands, love your wives" and "be considerate as you live with your wives . . . heirs with you of the gracious gift of life."[24]

Against the thought, *I want to buy that new thing I don't need* or *If I had that thing, then I would be happy . . .*

"Be content with what you have, because God has said, 'Never will I leave you; never will I forsake you.' "[25]

Then I put each scripture to memory.

That was the *easy* part.

The harder challenge is the ongoing war to combat lies and curate my thoughts. Every time an identified lie comes into my conscious awareness, I don't fight it head on; I just change the channel. I bring the corresponding scripture to mind and direct my attention to truth. Then I go about my day. If the thought comes back three seconds later, I simply turn to the same scripture, again and again.

It's one of the hardest things I've ever done in decades of following Jesus.

And it has changed and is changing my life.

However you master the battle for your mind, my point is that it's through the spiritual disciplines that we make steady progress in our spiritual formation.

I love this from Willard's masterpiece *Renovation of the Heart:*

> As we first turned away from God in our thoughts, so it is in our thoughts that the first movements toward the renovation of the heart occur. Thoughts are the place where we can and must begin to change.[26]

And take note: it is *our* responsibility to curate our thought life. No one else can do it for us. Not even God. This may sound overwhelming in a culture where digital addiction is ubiquitous and the human mind is jumpier and more distractible than ever. But it's not.

You can do this.

It will take time—years, honestly—but you can rewire your neural pathways to organize your mind around God's Spirit and truth.

You *must*.

And it's a responsibility that we often don't take nearly seriously enough.

I grew up in a very conservative home. My parents were both first-generation followers of Jesus. My dad, who came to faith in his twenties, came out of the 1960s music scene in California, so when he started to follow Jesus, as you can imagine, his pendulum swung to the other side. We ended up in a soft-fundamentalist church culture that epitomized the quip, "The danger of premarital sex is it might lead to dancing."

And while there's much from my conservative upbringing that I remember as unhelpful, one thing I think they really got right, which I think a lot of people in my generation completely miss, is the power of lies on the mind and the need to curate your inputs as an act of apprenticeship to Jesus.[27] To think critically about what we take into our minds—what we read or watch or listen to or consume or let entertain us.

My parents used to say of entertainment, "Garbage in, garbage out." Usually, this motto was applied to TV or film, but it was used to discriminate against multiple other mediums— comic books, racy novels, certain news outlets, dirty language. And while it's easy to chuckle at the simplicity of such a saying or get angry about all the editions of *Spider-Man* I missed out on, still, now I regularly overhear people chatting after a church gathering about *Game of Thrones,* casually laughing about obscene sexual deviance and the epitome of gratuitous violence.

We've come a long, long way.

The prophet Habakkuk said God's eyes are too pure to even look on evil,[28] and yet we do it all the time for entertainment. We don't even stop to consider this could be a ploy of the father of lies to wreak havoc in our lives.

And while I'm not saying we need to boycott Hollywood, I am saying that everything we allow into our minds has an effect on our souls, for good *or for evil.* If you don't believe me, go do a little research on neurobiology, specifically how what we see affects our mirror neurons and how thoughts enter the mind, creating neural pathways in our brains, which create DNA proteins in our nervous systems, which are then disseminated throughout our bodies and become part of us and, some argue, are in turn passed on to our children in their genetic code.

Synopsis: what we give our attention to *will shape the persons we become.* What we think about we become. Or as Hwee Hwee Tan put it, "That's the profound truth: you are what your mind looks at. You are what you contemplate."[29]

This is why our entertainment choices, our reading habits, our screen time, and our news sources are all central to our spiritual formation into the image of Jesus. (Or our deformation into the image of the devil.)

Think about the simple math of it: the average American adult watches TV or videos online about five to six hours *a day;*[30] the average millennial is on her phone up to four hours a day.

That adds up to almost a *decade* of your life.[31]

Barna's recent research on millennials found they spend almost 2,800 hours a year consuming digital content, but only

153 hours of that is Christ-based content; the rest is an internet cornucopia of YouTube, Instagram, Netflix, Apple, and others.[32]

My point is this: many of us spend hours every day filling our minds with lies, cutting off our minds from God's Spirit and truth, and only a *few minutes* each morning, if that, filling our minds with truth and resting in the Spirit, or presence, of our Father.

Is it any wonder we often see the world more through the lens of secular theory than Scripture? Or that we often get sucked into our disordered desires and begin living just like everyone else because it's "normal"? Or that we stall out in our formation or even begin to deform into the devil's image by a strange kind of spiritual entropy?

Now, I'm not saying we need to close our ears and not give serious thought to secular ideas. I imagine Jesus would be the first to tell you that you must follow the truth wherever it leads. If Jesus really is the truth, as he claimed to be, then I'm confident an honest, open pursuit of truth—no matter what circuitous route it takes—will eventually lead you to Jesus. When you walk in the light, you need not fear the shadows.

But we must take great care to fill our minds with truth rather than open them to an unedited, endless stream of unreality.

I'm currently reading *Fall; or, Dodge in Hell* by Neal Stephenson. Part dystopian sci-fi, part social commentary, *Fall* traces the current trajectory of digital technologies into the near future and envisions an America torn apart by civil war. The internet has failed after reaching a tipping point where algo-rithmic false information (fake news) outweighs any accurate portrayal of reality. Humanity is divided into (1) those who are reality-based and approach the digital world only with the help of an editor to sift through their digital streams and sort fact from fiction and (2) those in "Ameristan" who live in the wild unreality of conspiracy theories, dangerous cults, and vio-lence.

Now, there are all sorts of nonsense in the novel. Naturally, the reality-based Americans are Northerners, secular progres-sives, and mostly live in coastal cities (Stephenson lives in Seattle); the crazy people are religious nut jobs in middle America and the South who read the Old Testament literally.

Sigh.

But still, I find his division of reality-based and nonreality-based eerily prescient, if pessimistic. (I don't think civil war is coming. After all, we're too busy watching Netflix.)

To live in reality we must edit our streams, digital or otherwise. We must filter our mental intakes. Just like we watch carefully what we put into our bodies—few of us pick up random gar-bage off the sidewalk and pop it in our mouths—we must take great care with what we allow into our minds. And we must take deliberate steps to set our minds on the reality of Jesus and his mental maps. This, and this alone, will lead us into the kingdom, where we will enjoy the deepest kind of life to be had.

The poet Mary Oliver once said, "Attention is the beginning of devotion."[33] The starting place of devotion to God and movement into his kingdom is simply to set our attention on his Spirit and truth.

And, again, *this is our responsibility:* to turn our attention to God all through our days and weeks. To think of him. To think deeply of him. And rightly of him, in line with Jesus's vision of God as the trinitarian community of self-giving, creative, generous, calm, loving joy and delight. To let Jesus's incredibly compelling vision of who God is give shape to who we become.

And this is not the drudgery of religion or onerous obligation; remember, we're already filling our minds with inputs all day long, and many of those inputs are creating in us hearts that are fractured, anxious, distracted, and angry. When we curate our attention on Jesus and allow the flow of his thoughts into our minds, we begin to experience his peace, his love and compassion for all, and his deep, pervasive joy. We become calmer, more loving, and plain happier. Just by abiding.

And we do this through the practices of Jesus.

Wait, after the last fifty pages of content, are you just saying find a quiet place to read your Bible and pray daily?

I can't help but laugh right now—*yes.*

I'm saying this: First thing upon waking, if at all possible, before you touch your phone or open your browser or touch the dial on your radio or TV, *spend time in quiet prayer and Scripture.* Soak your mind and imagination in Jesus's truth before they are assaulted with the devil's lies.

In the back of this book, I put a worksheet for you to write up your own monastic handbook for combating demons. It's there if you want it.

But however you pursue the "renewing of your mind,"[34] once you develop your practice, just stand, like Jesus did, in a heart posture of quiet confidence and faith in God.

In Paul's letter to the Ephesians, chapter 6, which is the most in-depth passage in Paul's writings on spiritual warfare, he likened the follower of Jesus to a Roman legionary. Notice how many times he used the word *stand.* (I've added italics for you.)

> Finally, be strong in the Lord and in his mighty power. Put on the full armor of God, so that you can *take your stand* against the devil's schemes. For our struggle is not against flesh and blood, but against the rulers, against the authorities, against the powers of this dark world and against the spiritual forces of evil in the heavenly realms. Therefore put on the full armor of God, so that when the day of evil comes, you may be able to *stand your ground,* and after you have done everything, to *stand. Stand firm* then.[35]

Or notice how Peter picked up on this same language in his advice on how to fight the devil.

> Be alert and of sober mind. Your enemy the devil prowls around like a roaring lion looking for someone to devour. Resist him, *standing firm in the faith,* because you know that the family of believers

throughout the world is undergoing the same kind of sufferings.[36]

This is how we win: we stand.

When confronted with false teachings, Jesus would simply call out the lies, almost always appealing to Scripture.

Said another way, he would *stand*.

And he never lost a fight.

Part 1 step sheet

Definitions:

- **Truth**—reality
- **Lies**—unreality
- **Ideas**—assumptions about reality
- **Mental maps**—a collection of ideas by which we navigate life
- **Spiritual formation**—the process by which we are formed from our spirits/inner persons to become like Jesus

Three implications of Jesus's teaching on the devil:

1. He is a real, immaterial, but intelligent being.
2. His end goal is to spread ruin in our souls and society.
3. His primary means is lies.

Key texts to meditate on: John 8; Genesis 1–3; and Luke 4

Working theory of the devil's strategy: deceitful ideas that play to disordered desires that are normalized in a sinful society

Working theory of spiritual formation: It's by spirit and truth that we are transformed into the image of Jesus and set free to live in line with all that is good, beautiful, and true. It's by isolation and lies that we are deformed into the image of the devil and enslaved in a vicious cycle of disorder and death.

Working theory of how we fight the devil: We practice the spiritual disciplines laid down by Jesus, such as silence and solitude, prayer, fasting, and Scripture—and continually set our minds before the Spirit and truth of God. When tempted, we stand in quiet trust in God's love and wisdom and bring our minds back to Scripture.

Key practices to overcome the devil: quiet prayer and Scripture

In summary: The devil's goal is to first isolate us, then implant in our minds deceitful ideas that play to our disordered desires, which we feel comfortable with because they are normalized by the status quo of our society. Specifically, he lies about who God is, who we are, and what the good life is, with an aim to undermine our trust in God's love and wisdom. His intent is to get us to seize autonomy from God and redefine good and evil for ourselves, thereby leading to the ruin of our souls and society.

Part 2

The FLESH

Very truly I tell you, everyone who sins is a
slave to sin. . . . So if the Son sets you free,
you will be free indeed.

—Jesus, in John 8v34, 36

You, my brothers and sisters, were called
to be free. But do not use your freedom to
indulge the flesh; rather, serve one another
humbly in love. . . . So I say, walk by the Spirit,
and you will not gratify the desires of the
flesh. For the flesh desires what is contrary
to the Spirit, and the Spirit what is contrary to
the flesh. They are in conflict with each other,
so that you are not to do whatever you want.

—Paul, in Galatians 5v13, 16–17

Men are qualified for civil liberty, in exact
proportion to their disposition to put
moral chains upon their own appetites. . . .
Society cannot exist unless a controlling
power upon will and appetite be placed
somewhere, and the less of it there is within,
the more there must be without. It is ordained
in the eternal constitution of things, that
men of intemperate minds cannot be free.
Their passions forge their fetters.

—Edmund Burke, in *A Letter from Mr. Burke,
to a Member of the National Assembly*

The slavery of freedom

"The heart wants what it wants," so the popular saying goes.

Yet very few of us remember who made it popular.

In 1992, the journalist Walter Isaacson was interviewing Woody Allen for *Time* magazine. The subject was Allen's notorious affair with Soon-Yi Previn.

There's debate as to what actually happened, but the basic story goes something like this: All through the 1980s, Allen was in an on-again, off-again relationship with Mia Farrow, an actress and model. Before she and Allen had begun dating, Farrow and her then-husband André Previn had adopted two children from Vietnam and then a seven-year-old girl from South Korea (Soon-Yi);[1] over the next few years, Farrow adopted two more children. Then she and

Allen had a son together. They were an eccentric brood, regularly gracing the covers of tabloids around New York and LA.

Years went by, and Farrow and Allen's relationship began to deteriorate. One day she found photos of her daughter, Soon-Yi, in the nude. *On Allen's fireplace mantel.* The truth came out—Allen and Soon-Yi had been sleeping together.

Allen was fifty-six; Soon-Yi was twenty-one.

And to clarify, Allen had been dating her *mom* for years and was her functional stepdad.

This was decades before #metoo. Hollywood was still in its transgressive glory days, reveling in its carte blanche cultural permission to overstep nearly any sexual boundary and take the rest of the country along for the ride. Allen went on to date and then marry Soon-Yi.

Isaacson's interview of Allen reads like a case study in postmodern ethics. Isaacson, one of the best interviewers of our day, calmly but persistently probed Allen's heart for some kind of regret, apology, or even moral uncertainty, but Allen simply refused to admit he'd done anything wrong.

At the very end of the interview, Isaacson asked why he did it. Allen paused, then proffered his iconic line, "The heart wants what it wants."[2]

This off-the-cuff saying has entered not only the vernacular but also the belief system of our generation; it's become a kind of self-perpetuating justification for anything from adultery to chocolate cake. A kind of get-out-of-jail-free card for any behavior that falls outside the lines of moral tradition. Yet very few people realize its origin story.[3] Even my most libertine friends would not approve of an affair between a college girl and a man more than twice her age, much less a sexual escapade where a dad becomes a brother-in-law and a sister becomes a stepmom. And yet, that's the story.

As we continue our exploration of the world, the flesh, and the devil, this story is a great illustration of our next topic. What Allen called the heart is closer to what the writers of the New Testament called the flesh.

To begin, have a look at Paul's language to the Ephesians:

> As for you, you were dead in your transgressions and sins, in which you used to live when you followed *the ways of this world* and of *the ruler of the kingdom of the air* [another name for the devil], the spirit who is now at work in those who are disobedient. All of us also lived among them at one time, *gratifying the cravings of our flesh and following its desires and thoughts.*[4]

Notice Paul's trifecta of enemies:

The world: "You followed the ways of this world."

The flesh: "Gratifying the cravings of our flesh."

The devil: "The ruler [*archōn*] of the kingdom of the air."

This is where early apprentices of Jesus picked up the framework of the three enemies of the soul. Ancient as they were, the first Christians were wide awake—much more so than many of us are today—to the fact that our fight "is not against flesh and blood," as Paul wrote a few chapters later.[5] It's not against Russia or ISIS or the Chinese digital kleptocracy, much less Republicans or Democrats; it's against a far more insidious axis of evil.

We spent part 1 thinking about our first enemy, the devil, and how he traffics in deceptive ideas. Next up on the docket is the flesh. Remember, we said the devil's primary stratagem is deceitful ideas that play to disordered desires. His lies aren't random: "Elvis is alive and hiding in Mexico." No, they play to some deep fissure in the human heart that is bent in the wrong direction: "Porn is a normal and healthy part of growing up, and sexual exploration is key to living a satisfying, happy life."

The word Paul and the writers of the New Testament used for this aspect of our inner being is the *flesh*.

Now, this is strange language to our modern ears. What exactly did they mean by the flesh?

The word Paul used in Greek is σάρξ (sounds like "sarx"). Similar to English, Greek words often have more than one meaning.

Think of the English word *squash.* It can mean a kind of vegetable, great in fall soups and salads; a quirky British game, similar to racquetball but weirder; or, used as a verb, to destroy or demolish, as in "to squash the bug."

In the same way, the Greek word σάρξ can mean at least three different things in the New Testament.[6]

It can simply mean the body, as in 1 Corinthians 6v16:

> Do you not know that he who unites himself with a
> prostitute is one with her in body? For it is said,
> "The two will become one *flesh.*"

Here, *flesh* is a synonym to *body.* We still use the word this
way in our expression *flesh and blood.*

And when it's used in the plural, it just means humanity, as in
1 Peter 1v24:

> All *people* are like grass, and all their glory is like
> the flowers of the field.

The word *people* is actually σάρξ in Greek. Older translations
have "All flesh is as grass."

So in this sense, your flesh isn't a bad thing at all, much less
an enemy; it's just a word for your physicality in all its fleeting
mortality and beauty.

In a similar vein, a second meaning of σάρξ is your ethnicity.
For example, Paul wrote to the Philippians:

> It is we who are the circumcision, we who serve
> God by his Spirit, who boast in Christ Jesus, and
> who put no confidence in the *flesh.*[7]

In context, Paul was writing about how his Jewishness didn't
give him a leg up in the kingdom, combating a form of Jewish
supremacy in the Philippian church.

So here, your flesh is simply your ethnicity: your racial, cultural, and/or national identity and history—the language you
speak, the food you eat, the thousands of little customs that

order your life in a particular time and place and distinguish you from other ethnic groups. Again, flesh in this sense isn't a pejorative in the least, though it can easily be contorted into evil by the heart's universal bent toward prejudice. Still, it's not a bad thing in and of itself.

But there's a third and final meaning. What we talk about when we talk about "the world, the *flesh,* and the devil" is not our body or our ethnicity; it's what Paul wrote about in Ephesians 2v3: "Gratifying the cravings of our flesh." Here he means the animalistic cravings of our body apart from God.

In Romans 7v5, he further defined it as our "sinful passions."

In fact, in the original New International Version translation (1978), scholars consistently translated σάρξ as "sinful nature." That did not go over well with theologians, so in the 2011 update, it was changed back to the older translation of "flesh."

To be fair, the biblical linguists and translators were just attempting to communicate this third sense of the Greek word—the sinful appetite in all of us that feels natural to our bodies and yet is wrong. After all, each of us is more than just a body; we are also a soul.

Peter later defined the flesh as "corrupt desire" and tied it to rebellion against authority.[8] He also wrote about the "corruption in the world caused by evil desires."[9]

The pastor and scholar Eugene Peterson, who translated the Bible into "American," defined the flesh as "the corruption that sin has introduced into our very appetites and instincts."[10]

Basically, it's our base, primal, animalistic drives for self-gratification, especially pertaining to sensuality (as in sex and food) but also to pleasure in general, as well as our instincts for survival, domination, and the need for control. Desires that are in *all* of us. In spite of the humanistic atmosphere all around us constantly telling us we're good, we all know we have these desires we don't know what to do with. Because they don't match the cultural messaging we hear all the time, we often feel terrified the truth will come out or we feel shame over our inner lives or even a kind of self-hate. But the New Testament is incredibly open about the dark underbelly of the human heart, and we're invited to explore it under the loving gaze of God's compassion.

Now, to be clear, this language is unique to Paul and early Christian theologians, but the *idea* is not a specifically Christian one at all. It's an ancient and cross-cultural insight into the problem of the human condition.

Five centuries before Paul, the Buddha said, "In days gone by this mind of mine used to stray wherever selfish desire or lust or pleasure would lead it. Today this mind does not stray and is under the harmony of control, even as a wild elephant is controlled by the trainer."[11] He was comparing his mind's attempt to rein in its desires for "lust or pleasure" to the challenge of riding an elephant, a giant beast.

Around the same time, Plato used the word picture of a chariot driver with two horses tied together, each fighting for domination. One horse he called "a lover of honor with modesty and self-control," while the other was "a companion to wild boasts and indecency . . . shaggy around the ears—deaf as a post—and just barely yields to horsewhip and goad combined."[12] Notice again, the word picture is of a rider trying to rein in an animal that is powerful and barely under control.

Some rabbis taught that each of us has not one but "two souls, waging war one against the other in the person's mind, each one wishing and desiring to rule over him and pervade his mind exclusively." Rabbi Zalman called them our "animal soul" and our "divine soul."[13]

More recently, the transcendentalist Henry David Thoreau, during his solitary, soul-searching time at Walden Pond, wrote, "We are conscious of an animal in us. . . . It is reptile and sensual, and perhaps cannot be wholly expelled."[14]

The psychologist Jonathan Haidt simply calls this part of our brain our "animal self."[15] Leading brain expert Jeffrey Schwartz calls it our "animal brain."[16]

Today this ancient idea continues to show up in everything from Joe Rogan and Elon Musk joking on a podcast about how humans are "all chimps," and chimps do terrible, nasty things to each other,[17] to Jordan Peterson writing about the mating dynamics of lobsters as a model for human behavior.[18]

My point is, for a very long time, humans of the more self-aware variety—from across ethnic, religious, and generational lines—have been conscious of a hierarchy of desires in our minds and bodies. Not all desires are created equal. Or at least, not all are equally beneficial. Some of our desires are higher or nobler and lead to life and freedom and peace; others are lower or more animalistic and lead to death and slavery and fear.

All healthy, free people self-edit this inner mix of desires. The wise recognize that pleasure is not the same thing as happiness. Pleasure is about dopamine; happiness is about serotonin. Pleasure is about the next hit to feel good in the moment; happiness is about contentment over the long haul, a sense that my life is rich and satisfying as it is. Pleasure is about want; happiness is about freedom from want.

Most ethicists define happiness as a kind of contentment, a soul-level satisfaction where you are grateful for what is rather than grasping for more, which means: happiness comes as the result of *disciplined desire.* In every area of life—from sex to diet to money—happiness, or the good life, is what happens *after* you discipline your desires. You have to curb some of your wants and cultivate others.

This is what the New Testament writers were referring to when they wrote about the inner tug-of-war between the spirit and the flesh. They recognized an invisible but real war in the deepest parts of our beings, raging on the battlefield of desire. As Dostoyevsky said in *The Brothers Karamazov,* "God and the devil are fighting there and the battlefield is the heart of man."

But tragically this ancient idea—which is central to the Way of Jesus—has become a bit of a foreign concept, if not a social pariah, in the late modern West.

Let's do a little history.

The philosopher Charles Taylor, in his seminal work *A Secular Age,* wrote about how the West changed from a culture of "authority" to a culture of "authenticity." Meaning, we used to live by what *external* authority structures (God, the Bible, tradition, and so on) *told* us to do, but now most Western people live from what their *internal* "authentic self" *wants* to do.[19]

The tipping point was Freud. While I'm no psychologist, most of my psychologist friends tell me that, savant that he was, Freud got pretty much everything wrong, and yet many of his ideas created the cultural air we now breathe.

Prior to Freud, most people in the West (whether they knew it or not) thought about desire through the lens of the fourth-century philosopher Augustine. Saint Augustine was actually a North African. But his ideas, while developed on African soil, gave shape to much of Western civilization for over a millennium.

According to Augustine, the basic problem of the human condition is that of disordered desires, or loves. In his view, human beings were created *in* love and *for* love. So, we're lovers first and thinkers second. We live primarily from desire, *not our rational minds.*

In the Augustinian view, the problem of the human condition isn't that we don't love; it's that we love either the wrong things or the right things *but in the wrong order.*

For example, it's not bad to love your job; I hope you do. But if you love your career more than your teenage son, that's a disordered love and will create major problems for both you and your child.

Another example: It's not bad to love your child; I do. But if you love your child more than you love God? That's disordered and will deform how you relate to both.

It's not even bad to love sex. God himself created us as sexual beings and commanded us to "increase in number."[20] But when sex becomes a pseudogod that we look to for identity, for belonging in a community, or for life satisfaction, when it becomes a soteriology (a doctrine of salvation) as it is for so many in the West, that's a disordered love. And it's not just that it's wrong in the moral sense; it's that it can't possibly satisfy the deeper ache of the soul for love, intimacy, acceptance, and generativity. After all, the body just wants an orgasm, but the soul wants more—communion and contribution.

So, in the pre-Freud West, human flourishing was about saying yes to the right desires, the higher desires for love, and no to the lower desires, the baser, more appetite kind of desires. And you would navigate your desires by the mental maps that were handed down to you by a trusted but *external* authority source—ideally, Jesus himself, as his teachings come to us through the New Testament—in order to not repeat the mistakes of previous generations and to carry forward those generations' cumulative wisdom. After all, you're not the first human to ever live. Why repeat other people's mistakes?

Freud's take was radically contrary. For him, our most important desire was our libido, which he defined as our desire not just for sex but for pleasure as a whole. But because libido without restraint would lead to anarchy, our parents and cultural structures forced us to repress our desire, and for Freud—and this is key—*repression of desire is the basis for all neurosis.* Translation: the reason you're unhappy is because other people are telling you you can't do stuff.

It doesn't take a private investigator to work out whose ideas won the fight for the West's view of reality.

Freud's ideas show up in the popular slogans and catchphrases of our day:

"The heart wants what it wants."

"Follow your heart."

"You do you."

"Just do it."

"Speak your truth."

And of course, "Be true to yourself."

Anybody remember Shakespeare from tenth grade? "Be true to yourself" is a quote from his play *Hamlet.* The original version was "This above all: to thine own self be true."[21]

Anybody remember who said that line? If not, don't feel bad; I had to look it up. It was Polonius, *the fool.* It's the fool who encourages us to live by the slogan "Be true to yourself," and yet we mouth his mantra like it's gospel. We just assume (remember, ideas are assumptions about reality) that the way to a happy, flourishing life is to follow our hearts, which we often misunderstand to be any authentic desire.

In the past, it was the responsibility of all people to restrain the desires of their flesh; today, it's the right of all people to follow the desires of their authentic selves.[22]

Jonathan Grant, in his excellent book *Divine Sex,* accurately summed up the tectonic shift:

> Modern authenticity encourages us to create our own beliefs and morality, the only rule being that they must resonate with who we feel we *really* are. The worst thing we can do is to conform to some moral code that is imposed on us from outside—by society, our parents, the church, or whoever else. It is deemed to be self-evident that any such imposition would undermine our unique identity. . . . The authentic self believes that personal meaning must be found within ourselves or must resonate with our one-of-a-kind personality.[23]

Happiness has become about *feeling* good, not *being* good. The good life has become about getting what we want, not becoming the kind of people who want truly good things.

The self—not God or Scripture—is the new locus of authority in Western culture.

The ethicist Robert C. Roberts, an expert on Freud's influence on the West, had this observation:

> We have been led to feel that the self is sacrosanct:
> just as in an earlier time it was thought never fitting
> to deny God, so now it seems never right to deny
> oneself.[24]

But listen to the perspective of the theologian David Wells on what happens when a society is given over to the flesh:

> Theology becomes therapy. . . . The biblical inter-
> est in righteousness is replaced by a search for
> happiness, holiness by wholeness, truth by feeling,
> ethics by feeling good about one's self. The world
> shrinks to the range of personal circumstances;
> the community of faith shrinks to a circle of per-
> sonal friends. The past recedes. The Church re-
> cedes. The world recedes. All that remains is the
> self.[25]

Self is the new god, the new spiritual authority, the new morality. But this puts a crushing weight on the self—one it was never designed to bear. It must discover itself. Become itself. Stay true to itself. Justify itself. Make itself happy. Perform and defend its fragile identity. As my Peloton instructor would say, "Validate your greatness." But what about the many days when we're not all that great? The pressure is exhausting. Cue the stats on burnout, anxiety, and mental health.

In this new religion of the self, what our ancestors called chastity is now called oppression if it's externally imposed or repression if it's internally imposed. What they called self-discipline or self-control, we call, honestly, sin. In a world-view where desire is sacrosanct, *the ultimate sin is to not fol-*

low your heart. As another theologian, Cornelius Plantinga, observed, "In such a culture . . . the self exists to be explored, indulged, and expressed but not disciplined or restrained."[26]

Like all the most powerful ideas in our world, this one is so lethal because it's assumed to be true. To even question it is a kind of cultural heresy; to raise the same doubt in others is a gross crime.

But the now-ubiquitous mantra of "Be true to yourself" raises a very interesting question:

Which self?

The spiritual director and psychologist David Benner, in his beautiful little book *The Gift of Being Yourself,* observed, "What we call 'I' is really a family of many part-selves."[27] This might sound like psychobabble, but it's not. He is noting the complexity of desire in each of us. We have all sorts of desires, many of them contradictory. When people tell us to "follow your heart," which heart do we follow? And what do we do when our hearts are fickle and our desires change by the hour and fluctuate with our moods?

Let me give you a very mundane, nonemotionally loaded example: the grocery store checkout line. About once a week, I have this experience: I stop by the market to pick up groceries for dinner, and while I'm waiting in line to pay, I face the ultimate case study in what my friend David Bennett called "a war of loves."[28]

To my right is a magazine rack covered with beautiful, thin, and/or muscular celebrities airbrushed to digital perfection.

Harry Styles is the new gold standard. Ryan Gosling is aging nicely. Timothée Chalamet is stealing the hearts of teenagers the world over.

To my left? Another magazine rack, but this one is covered in decadent photos of food. Enchiladas with guac and sour cream. "Top Ten Summer Beers." "Twenty Best New Restaurants in Portland." "Seven-Layer Dream Cake."

And over the top of both magazine racks? A shelf stacked with sugar, chocolate, and what is affectionately known in our home as "cancer gum."

Now, as I stand in line, I feel two deep, primal desires in my soul. On the one hand, I want to look like Ryan Gosling. But on the other, I want to go home and make the vegan cheese-cake with graham cracker crust and strawberry whipped cream. Ahem.

Both desires are "authentic" to my "true self." *But they are mutually exclusive.* As a forty-year-old guy with a type B metabolism, I can't have my cake and eat it too, literally.

So, what do I do with this great existential problem? Easy. I grab *GQ and* the chocolate peanut butter cups (they're or-ganic!) and munch on them while reading about Ryan's ab workout routine. I'll start tomorrow. Done.

That's a humorous experience from many of our regular lives, but the same is true of much more sensitive, more serious conflicts of desire.

I want to love my children well, be present as a father, and intentionally unfold them into their full potential, but I also want to close the door, watch TV, and let them sort out their own annoying problems.

I want to live deeply grateful and content with what I have, as well as practice radical generosity, but I also want to buy a new jacket I don't need and upgrade my perfectly good car.

I want to get up early and soak my mind and heart in Scripture and prayer, but I also want to stay up late watching *Long Way Up.*

We could go on for pages of this because it's the nature of the human experience. But what's easy to miss in the modern view of things is that our strongest desires are not actually our deepest desires.

Let me say that again: *our strongest desires are not actually our deepest desires.*

What I mean by that is, in the moment of temptation, the raging fire of desire that is your flesh—the desire to make a condescending comment about your coworker, buy another pair of shoes you don't need, overeat, overdrink, lust, ignore God, watch Netflix instead of reading your Bible—feels overwhelming and almost irresistible. But those desires are not actually the deepest, truest desires of your heart; they don't come from the bedrock layer in your soul.

Come to quiet before God . . .

Take a few deep breaths . . .

Let the deepest desires of your heart come to the surface of your heart.

What is it you want?

What do you *really* want?

My guess is, if you go deep enough, you ache for God himself. To live in his love. To yield to his gentle peace. To let your body become a place where his will is done "on earth as it is in heaven." That's a gift of the Spirit in you.

This is why for all the talk about how human beings are animals, how morality is a social construct, and how we need to be true to ourselves, it's still generally agreed upon that to live a good life, you must become a good person. I've never read an obituary that said, "He really got a lot out of his Tinder subscription." Or "This girl knew how to eat, drink, and be merry." Much less "This guy's commitment to sneakers was inspiring."

Of course not. When people die, we honor and celebrate the best parts of their character. Love, sacrifice, loyalty to family and friends, humility, joy, compassion. *All of which required their denial of fleshly desires.* So while our culture celebrates the gospel of self-actualization, the type of self you actualize into is still paramount.

My point is simply this: our deepest desires—usually to become people of goodness and love—are often sabotaged by the stronger surface-level desires of our flesh. This is exacerbated by a culture where the widespread wisdom of the day is to follow our desires, not crucify them. But in reality, "Be true to yourself" is some of the worst advice anybody could ever give you.

Here's why: giving in to the desires of our flesh does not lead us to freedom and life, as many people assume, but instead to slavery and, in the worst-case scenario, addiction, which is a kind of prolonged suicide by pleasure.

To that we now turn.

"Their passions forge their fetters"

In the days of intercontinental travel by sea, when you first came to America from the East, it was very likely that the first thing you saw was Lady Liberty. There she was, rising 305 feet out of New York Harbor on, tellingly, Liberty Island. An evocative symbol for the land of the free and the home of the brave.

It comes as no surprise that our founders gave us slogans like "Life, *liberty,* and the pursuit of happiness" and "*Liberty* and justice for all" or even Patrick Henry's rousing line, "Give me *liberty* or give me death!"

Never mind the tragic irony that we're also the nation that conducted a multicentury, transcontinental slave trade of over twelve million Africans (around two million of whom died before they even landed on the East Coast).[1] That as we were rebelling against the oppression of England, we were simultaneously developing a form of chattel slavery as barbaric as any the world had ever seen.

Hypocrisy aside, we Americans vaunt freedom as the ultimate good. In a wide-ranging study of our nation, a group of sociologists led by Robert Bellah discovered that for Americans, "freedom was perhaps the most important value."[2]

And yet something about this freedom seems to have gone awry. Systemic racism is the most evocative example, but there are so many more. Addiction in our nation is widespread, as is compulsive shopping, debt, financial fraud, obesity, alcoholism, and environmental damage. Anything that requires long-term fidelity is currently in decline: marriage, two-parent families, and so on. Add to that nationalistic xenophobia of the far Right and the anarchist impulse of the far Left.

We often scratch our heads at such realities and think, *How could this happen in the land of the free?*

The constitutional law professor Patrick Deneen from Notre Dame, in his book *Why Liberalism Failed* (a conservative book yet recommended by no less than President Obama[3]), made the point that the trouble with freedom didn't start in the 1960s with Foucault, Woodstock, and the sexual revolution. It started in the *1760s* with the Enlightenment, the founding fathers, and the US Constitution, which he called an attempt to make a whole new kind of human based on a new definition of freedom. This new definition of freedom is both crude and common: freedom is the ability to do whatever you want.

Few Americans realize that is not how Jesus, the writers of the Bible, and the great philosophers of history defined freedom.

To show you what I mean, let's spend some time in Paul's letter to the Galatians. There are a few go-to passages in the New Testament on the flesh; Galatians chapters 5 and 6 are my favorite. In Paul's theological framework, we find an alternate but compelling vision of freedom to that of our Western world.

It will take us more than one chapter to work through Paul's teaching, but let's start at the top of Galatians 5.

> It is for freedom that Christ has set us free. Stand firm, then, and do not let yourselves be burdened again by a yoke of slavery.

Now, at first glance, this reads like something a modern American would say. "Stay free! Don't let anybody or anything control you!" But if you keep reading, you quickly realize Paul did not mean what most of us mean by freedom. Verse 13:

> You, my brothers and sisters, were called to be free. But do not use your freedom to indulge the flesh.

Translation: Just because you're no longer under the Mosaic covenant, don't abuse your newfound freedom in Jesus; don't give in to your disordered desires. Instead, give yourself over to the relational constraints of love.

Paul used the word *freedom* here in the standard philosophical sense of self-determination. Philosophers argue that human beings are the only creatures with self-determining freedom. Unlike the animals, we don't just run off our primal, evolutionary drives for pleasure and survival. We *have* those drives—whether through evolutionary biology, the fall, or some combination of the two—but we also have self-determining freedom, the capacity to override those drives when they are disordered.

Think of an animal. A coyote doesn't decide to eat a rabbit or not. It doesn't see a rabbit and pause to consider, *Is this the right choice?* You won't find a coyote reading a book on veganism by PETA or queuing up a podcast by Michael Pollan on a plant-based diet. Of course not. It operates by a very simple formula: see rabbit; chase rabbit; eat rabbit. It's just run by instinctual drives for survival. This is why there are no ethics in the animal kingdom; all is amoral, causal, and drive based. It's why we don't hold a predator from the local zoo accountable for eating its prey.

But we're not coyotes. When we arrive at a restaurant, what does the server give us? A menu, not a live, wriggling rabbit that we fall on and consume raw. We read said menu and weigh our options, like cost, fat content, how this meal will make us feel or appear to our date, and so on. We consider the right wine pairing.

We can also decide whether or not to "eat" a fellow human being through gossip, a lie, injustice, or a subtle re-org of our company to inch our way up the corporate ladder.

This is what separates us from the animals—not our opposable thumbs or even our prefrontal cortices but our ability to choose our courses of action. A migratory bird, for example, has an uncanny, innate ability to fly south and hit Mazatlán right on the nose, every single winter. This is a magnificent ability. But it doesn't have the ability to say, "Ya know, I think I'll hit up Santa Fe instead this year or maybe pop by San Diego; I hear the art scene is interesting." Humans, on the other hand, *decide* where to spend their winters, even if, for most of us, it turns out to be wherever our rent checks are due. This is because we have an enormous amount of self-determining freedom.

But—here's the rub—freedom is very easy to abuse. And when we abuse freedom, we negate love. Notice Paul's next line:

> Rather, serve one another humbly in love. For the entire law is fulfilled in keeping this one command: "Love your neighbor as yourself." If you bite and devour each other, watch out or you will be destroyed by each other.[4]

Interesting. For Paul, the opposite of "indulge the flesh" was "love your neighbor." This is a bit weird sounding at first, because in our culture, we often confuse love with lust. Or more broadly, love with desire.

When we say, "I love chocolate cake," what we mean is, "I want to *eat* it. Indulge in it. Consume it."

And when we say, "I love my boyfriend or girlfriend," we often mean the same thing.

I'm not saying that sexual or romantic desire is bad; it's a beautiful, God-given joy. But love as defined by Jesus, Paul, and the New Testament is a very different phenomenon. The Greek word they used for love wasn't *eros* (where we get the word *erotic*) but *agape.* Here's my best shot at a definition of *agape* love:

> A compassionate commitment to delight in the soul
> of another and to *will that person's good* ahead of
> your own, no matter the cost to yourself

Love is the desire not to *take* but to *give.* It's the settled intention of the heart to promote good in the life of another. To see the beauty inherent in another soul and help them come to see it as well.

Notice: if to love is to will the good, this means that to love people you need knowledge of reality—to know what is *really* good for them. Remember that; we'll come back to it later.

Paul's point is that our flesh is anti-love. The flesh runs off our animal drives for self-gratification and survival, which, as Dr. Schwartz of UCLA accurately observed, perceive "fellow sentient, suffering beings as nothing but objects of, or obstacles to, your desires."[5]

My wife, T, uses the adjective *fleshy* in our home. When someone in our family is in a lousy mood, grouchy, and thinking only about their wants and needs, she will say, "(So and so) is being *fleshy.*"

It's never me, I promise . . .

While Bible translators might not pick this up in their next edition, she's right on target. When we're "in the flesh" (fleshy), we're out of love. That's because love—as defined above—

is hard work and full of pain as well as joy. The flesh is lazy and self-indulgent. It just wants to feel good in the moment.

Augustine called sin "love turned in on itself." Likely playing with that idea, Martin Luther later called the one who lived for one's own pleasure and sensual gratification *homo incurvatus in se,* or "man curved in upon himself."[6]

Now, with that in mind, look at what Paul says next:

> I say, walk by the Spirit, and you will not gratify the desires of the flesh. For the flesh desires what is contrary to the Spirit, and the Spirit what is contrary to the flesh. They are in conflict with each other, so that *you are not to do whatever you want.*[7]

Note: "do whatever you want" is exactly what we're told by our culture.

As the pop icon Billie Eilish said in an interview for *Vogue:* "My thing is that I can do whatever I want. . . . It's all about what makes you feel good."[8] She was defending her wearing a revealing corset for the photo shoot—a symbol many feminists associate with misogyny.

But just because something feels good, doesn't mean it is good. And if there's anything we should not do, it's whatever we want. This is as blatant of a demonic idea as they come.

To be fair, those who advocate the "just do what feels good" philosophy regularly clarify "as long as it doesn't harm anybody." From international pop stars to our local baristas, many of our secular neighbors are deeply good, noble people who simply want their fellow citizens to be happy. They still recognize the need for law and order. In fact, they often have a higher standard for human rights than we Christians do. I hate to admit that, but it's true.

The problem with the "as long as it doesn't harm anybody" rubric is *it requires an agreed-upon definition of harm.* Something that, in the secular, pluralistic world we inhabit, we don't have. We no longer have a transcendent moral authority such as God or the Bible to appeal to. We don't even have the Enlightenment idea of the laws of nature anymore. All we have is the self and the state. The problem is, all sorts of things are legal that do not lead to human flourishing.

This debate over harm is really a debate over ethics. To define an act as "love" or "hate" requires an agreed-upon definition of good and evil, which again, we don't have. Since ethics have been individualized in the new religion of self, Harm with a capital *H* is difficult to define.

Think about the uproar over immigration and border patrol in my country and the call to "abolish ICE" from the Left and "Make America Great Again" from the Right. Some see illegal immigration as a grave threat to the economic opportunity of the working class and the cultural heritage of our nation; others see opposing undocumented citizens as a form of racism toward people of color, cruelty toward children, and a lost opportunity for diversity.

Clearly, they don't agree on what constitutes harm.

Or think about one woman who wears a thin-line bikini to the beach and sees that as her right and celebration of female empowerment, but she's sitting next to a Muslim woman in a hijab who sees a bikini in public as an assault on female dignity, the propagation of a suffocating cultural definition of beauty, and sexual desensitization. They both experience the encounter as harm—one feels oppressed; the other feels ostracized.

Or I think about Nkechi Amare Diallo (legal name, Rachel Anne Dolezal), who served as the president of the NAACP in Spokane, Washington. After she presented for many years as black, a national story broke in 2015. In turns out, she has zero non-European ancestry (that is, she's white) but she "identifies as black." As a result, she was not only fired from her job as an instructor of Africana Studies at Eastern Washington University; she was charged by the State of Washington for perjury and felony theft by welfare fraud.[9] But rather than recant, she continued to claim she was born with white parents but is actually black in her mind and experience (interestingly, using the exact same logic as transgenderism). So, who is harmed here? The black community by a white woman claiming she is black and is the victim of race-related hate crimes? Or Nkechi/Rachel for being fired on account of her self-determined racial identity?

These are all current, real-life examples of the challenges presented by postmodern ethics and the lack of an agreed-upon definition of either harm or good.

But note carefully that Paul described not one but two categories of desire: the flesh *and the Spirit.*

If the flesh is our shallow, animalistic drive for self-pleasure, the Spirit is our higher and even deeper desire for love and goodness. It's the empowering presence of God deep in the marrow of our bones, gently coaxing us into greater levels of self-giving *agape*.

And which set of desires we give in to will shape the trajectory of our souls and society.

Look at where Paul said the flesh will take us:

> The acts of the flesh are obvious: sexual immorality, impurity and debauchery; idolatry and witchcraft; hatred, discord, jealousy, fits of rage, selfish ambition, dissensions, factions and envy; drunkenness, orgies, and the like. I warn you, as I did before, that those who live like this will not inherit the kingdom of God.[10]

Any of this sound familiar?

"Sexual immorality, impurity and debauchery"—Tinder, hookup culture, your local bar or club scene.

"Hatred, discord, jealousy, fits of rage"—Twitter, cancel culture, and most of the news.

"Selfish ambition, dissensions, factions"—politics, from office gossip to Washington DC.

"Envy"—the internet, the mall, advertising, and the great envy generator that is Instagram.

"Drunkenness, orgies, and the like"—Netflix, HBO, and others.

Of course, I'm harping on the negative aspects of our culture and these apps; there are still many wonderful things about the West: human rights, freedom of religion, freedom of speech, material well-being, science, medicine, education, the arts, and so on. But we can't ignore the dark side of culture. Paul's point is, *this is the kind of soul and society that is created when given over to the flesh.*

To compare and contrast, look at where the Spirit will take us.

> The fruit of the Spirit is love, joy, peace, forbearance, kindness, goodness, faithfulness, gentleness and self-control.[11]

This sounds like a pipe dream to many of us because it's so far removed from our experience, but this is the kind of "fruit" that is grown in the soil of the Spirit. When people walk in the Spirit, this is the kind of people they become—loving, joyful, unanxious, unhurried, helpful, deeply good souls.

Paul ends with this summary:

> Those who belong to Christ Jesus have crucified the flesh with its passions and desires. Since we live by the Spirit, let us keep in step with the Spirit.[12]

We'll come back to Paul's invocation to crucify—that is, put to death—our flesh. For now, I just want you to see one thing: Paul's definitions of freedom and slavery are radically at odds with those of our Western world.

A short word on each. First, freedom . . .

I'm not sure any word in the Christian vocabulary has been more misunderstood than *freedom.*

Philosophers parse out two different types of freedom: negative and positive. Negative freedom is freedom *from;* it's the removal of any and all constraints on our choices. Positive freedom is freedom *for*—not just the permission to choose but the power to choose what is *good.*

Let's take them one after the other. First, negative freedom.

Negative freedom is best exemplified in the following poetic masterpiece from that great Scandinavian intellectual, Princess Elsa (yes, from *Frozen*):

> No right, no wrong
> No rules for me
> I'm free!

Ahh . . .

And you thought I was gonna quote Søren Kierkegaard or Dag Hammarskjöld.

A more serious example comes from the majority opinion of Justices Sandra Day O'Connor, Anthony Kennedy, and David Souter in *Planned Parenthood of Southeastern Pa. v. Casey* (1992):

> At the heart of liberty is the right to define one's own concept of existence, of meaning, of the universe, and of the mystery of human life.[13]

This view of freedom arises out of a postmodern worldview that has no belief in moral absolutes or any ultimate meaning to life beyond personal happiness.[14] In this view, the opposite of freedom is constraint—whether it comes from an external authority source, a sacred text like the Bible, or a binding commitment (such as marriage or parenting). Freedom, in this take, is the "liberation" to do whatever the hell we want. (My word choice is deliberate here.) To define the good for ourselves. To pursue and enjoy and buy and sell and sleep with and do and say whatever we desire, of course, "as long as it doesn't harm anybody."

This has become the dominant view of freedom in the West. Our children are being educated into this view, one Disney movie at a time.

But that's not Paul's view of freedom. Or Jesus's. Or most luminaries of the human condition prior to the modern era. They put more emphasis on positive freedom. Freedom not just to choose but to choose *the good.* For them, freedom isn't about autonomy from authority but about liberating loving relationships from sin. And positive freedom means we need a kind of power from outside ourselves (think, the "higher power" of Alcoholics Anonymous) to overcome our (strong) desires for self-gratification and fulfill our (deep) desires for self-giving love.

Now let's talk about slavery. I hear the word *slavery* and cringe. As an American, it draws to mind the horror of chattel slavery and the open wound of a nation that four hundred years later has still never had a moment of national repentance. Much less reparations. And to be clear, despite empty attempts by a select few to use the Bible to justify slavery, Scripture teaches the exact opposite. Racial discrimination, dehumanization, and oppression are wrong. Full stop.

Honestly, sometimes I hesitate to even use the word *slavery* in my writing and teaching. But Jesus and the New Testament writers used it constantly. As the descendants of slaves, it was a provocative metaphor for them to employ. Yet they used it for a kind of spiritual slavery—to the devil or simply to one's own flesh.

Peter, in another masterful passage on the flesh that's worth your time to read, wrote about false teachers who "promise . . . freedom, while they themselves are slaves of depravity." Then he had this great line: "People are slaves to whatever has mastered them."[15]

For the Scripture writers, anything that has control over you—be it an autocratic tyrant, a slave owner, a self-defeating behavior, or an addiction to drugs or alcohol or even your phone—*is your master.* This is why the Hebrew wisdom literature includes sayings about how the wicked are "trapped by evil desires."[16] It's why New Testament theologians portrayed our pre-Jesus life as one where we were "foolish, disobedient, *deceived and enslaved* by all kinds of passions and pleasures."[17]

And it's not just the Scripture writers. Most ancient luminaries would have agreed. Here's Andrew Sullivan, in a piece for *New York* magazine:

> For most of the Ancients, freedom was freedom from our natural desires and material needs. It rested on a mastery of these deep, natural urges in favor of self-control, restraint, and education into virtue. . . . They'd look at our freedom and see licentiousness, chaos, and slavery to desire. They'd predict misery not happiness to be the result.[18]

The therapeutic word for this kind of enslavement is a *compulsion,* which is defined as "a very strong feeling of wanting to do something repeatedly that is difficult to control."[19] Compulsion, left unchecked, turns into addiction, which is a form of slavery to desire.

Gerald May, a spiritual director and psychiatrist I love, said it this way:

> Regardless of how a compulsion appears externally, underneath it is always robbing us of our freedom. We act not because we have chosen to, but because we have to. We cling to things, people, beliefs, and behaviors not because we love them, but because we are terrified of losing them. . . .
>
> In a spiritual sense, the objects of our attachments and addictions become *idols*. We give them our time, energy, and attention whether we want to or not, even—and often especially—when we are struggling to rid ourselves of them. We want to be free, compassionate, and happy, but in the face of our attachments we are clinging, grasping, and fearfully self-absorbed.
>
> This is the root of our trouble.[20]

Notice his language: "We want to be *free*." He's using freedom in the positive sense—not freedom to do whatever we want but freedom from our disordered desires to sate our animal appetites in order to be happy.

This is the main form of bondage in the democratic West. For all the talk about the danger of tyranny from the Right or illiberalism from the Left or the rising specter of China's digital censorship, most of that is fear mongering and a red herring.

Slavery to our flesh is the more pressing danger. Maybe even more so than the devil. As the saying goes, "If the devil died today, you'd still sin tomorrow." The devil can only trick or tempt us, not coerce or control us.

Of course, many Westerners have recently started to use the word *oppression* in a much broader sense. Oppression has been redefined from its original rendering (things like chattel slavery, codified misogyny, and legal discrimination against gay people) to mean any and all forms of external authority or constraint. Be it a law or doctrine or social norm or parent or even God—anything that keeps us from doing what we want.

Now, just to be crystal clear: much external authority *is* oppressive, toxic, and cruel. North Korea comes to mind or ISIS or, closer to home, systemic racism, police brutality, or stifling, 1950s-era gender roles. There is a time and a place to oppose external authority. The uprising of Black Lives Matter in 2020 was a great example. But the problem isn't external authority per se but the *abuse* of external authority.

As near as I can tell, in biblical theology, external authority is one of the main roles of government in the public sphere and parents in the private. Their job is to restrain the flesh in those who can't self-restrain—be that a criminal on a bank-robbing spree or simply a two-year-old being, well, two.

In fact, for those of us who follow Jesus, we *choose,* of our own free will, to place ourselves under external authority—that of God himself, as mediated through Scripture, and, to a degree, our church. We do this because we believe authority is not inherently oppressive but, similar to parenting for children, a training ground for us to learn how to master our flesh and grow into people of love. Through trusted sources of authority, we get access to reality. And when authority is used well, with wisdom and compassion, we grow and mature into the kind of people who live in congruence with reality and, as a result, have the capacity to handle even more freedom.

This is why we don't give gun permits to ten-year-olds, alcohol to teenagers, or drivers' licenses to people with too many DUIs. It's not because those freedoms are bad necessarily but because you first have to become the kind of person who is free *internally* so you can enjoy and express your freedom *externally.*

This is also why the founders of our nation envisioned America as a republic, not technically as a democracy. True democracy has been tried at least twice before, in ancient Greece and Rome. In both attempts, it degenerated into mob rule and from there into tyranny. Anxious to avoid a repeat of history, Edmund Burke laid out the logic behind the American architecture in a letter from 1791:

> Men are qualified for civil liberty, in exact proportion to their disposition to put moral chains upon their own appetites [read: flesh]. . . . Society cannot exist unless a controlling power upon will and appetite be placed somewhere, and the less of it there is within, the more there must be without. It is ordained in the eternal constitution of things, that men of intemperate minds cannot be free. *Their passions forge their fetters.*[21]

Because freedom without self-mastery is a disaster waiting to happen. Saint Augustine said it well: "Free choice is sufficient for evil, but hardly for good."[22]

All that to say, much of what our world calls freedom is what the Way of Jesus (and many others) calls slavery, and vice versa. Or in Orwellian terms: freedom is tyranny; tyranny is freedom.

Timothy Keller, after decades of living in the secular mecca of New York, astutely summed it up like this:

> We see . . . that freedom is not what the culture tells us. Real freedom comes from a strategic loss of some freedoms in order to gain others. It is not the absence of constraints but it is choosing the right constraints and the right freedoms to lose.[23]

The ultimate example of this is love. Is there a greater constraint than a loving relationship? To gain intimacy, we have to give up autonomy. As a mentor said to me just the other day, "Intimacy only resides in the safety of commitment."[24]

I think of the constraint of my marriage, of my responsibility as a father, or even of New Testament ethics. I can fight these constraints. I could even run from them; but my self would never let me escape. I hear Gustave Thibon's haunting warning in my mind: "You feel you are hedged in; you dream of escape; but *beware of mirages.* Do not run or fly away in order to get free. . . . If you fly away from yourself, your prison will run with you."[25]

On the other hand, if I stay in my constraints and let them do their work, if I consider that my duty to follow through on my commitments is just as "authentic" as my feelings or desires, then my constraints have the potential to set me free from the tyranny of my own flesh and forge me into a person of love.

Of course, the original source for this vision of freedom and slavery is Jesus himself, who said both "Very truly I tell you, everyone who sins is a slave to sin" and "You will know the truth, and the truth will set you free."[26]

Jesus was incredibly free. As the Oxford theologian Michael Green said, "In this age which values freedom almost more than anything else, Jesus confronts us as the most liberated man who ever lived."[27]

Another Oxford professor, C. S. Lewis, once said, "The *main* work of life is to *come out* of our selves, out of the little, dark prison we are all born in," and warned of the danger of "coming to *love* the prison."[28]

This is the human journey—the exodus from slavery to freedom, with Jesus as our new Moses. Jesus's offer was, and still is, to rescue and deliver us from the prison of sin and self, to lead us to a new land, a new life.

Which begs the question, How do we become free?

The law of returns

In her searingly honest memoir, *The Recovering,* Leslie Jamison wrote about how addiction is a kind of ghost haunting the Western world. In her struggle to write a memoir about addiction that was original, she realized it was an impossible task because addiction *is* the human condition: "Addiction is always a story that has already been told, because it inevitably repeats itself, because it grinds down—ultimately, for everyone—to the same demolished and reductive and recycled core: *Desire. Use. Repeat.*"[1]

It turns out that sin makes people the same. When we give in to our flesh, we devolve to a remarkably unoriginal baseline.

Desire.

Use.

Repeat.

We call it addiction; Jesus and Paul called it slavery.

And Paul was not done. He continued his train of thought on freedom in the Spirit versus slavery to the flesh with a final warning for the Galatians.

> Do not be deceived: God cannot be mocked. A
> man reaps what he sows. Whoever sows to please
> their flesh, from the flesh will reap destruction; who-
> ever sows to please the Spirit, from the Spirit will
> reap eternal life. Let us not become weary in doing
> good, for at the proper time we will reap a harvest if
> we do not give up.[2]

Recognize this? I'm guessing you do. It's a well-known passage, especially the end where Paul wrote about not growing
"weary in doing good." That line is regularly quoted in a sym-
pathy card or an encouraging word from a friend or family
member in a rough season of life. And while that's a perfectly
legitimate use of the passage, Paul was not actually writing
about getting through a hard time; he was writing about fighting our flesh. And in his often-quoted warning, we get a key
insight into the mechanism by which we are either enslaved
by our flesh or set free by the Spirit.

Notice how our working theory of the three enemies' strategy
shows up yet again in Paul's theology:

> Do not be deceived.

> *Deceitful ideas . . .*

Whoever sows to please their flesh . . .

That play to disordered desires . . .

Will reap destruction.

Paul upped the ante here from slavery to full-fledged destruction, connecting the dots to argue that slavery isn't static but dynamic; it leads, in the end, to a kind of ruin.

Thankfully, *the same is true for the Spirit.*

Whoever sows to please the Spirit . . . will reap eternal life.[3]

Many people think that eternal life refers to a *quantity* of life after death, but for the New Testament writers it also meant a *quality* of life that starts *now* for the apprentice of Jesus, grows in scope over a lifetime of apprenticeship, and then continues into eternity.

All because "a man reaps what he sows"—whether that's freedom and life, or their counterparts, slavery and death.

Now, outside the Bible, this idea is called the law of returns. It's less of a distinctly Christian doctrine and more of a truism about the human condition. We hear it in all sorts of sayings:

"What goes around comes around."

"You get what you pay for."

"You get back what you put in."

"No pain, no gain."

"Garbage in, garbage out."

Karma, poetic justice, "It's been a long time coming"—all are statements of the law of returns.

Jesus himself taught it with sayings like "Give, and it will be given to you. A good measure, pressed down, shaken together and running over."[4] Or "With the measure you use, it will be measured to you."[5]

It's a very simple yet profound idea that basically has two parts:

1. *Every cause has an effect.* When you hit a baseball with your bat, the ball goes forward. And it's just as true of the spiritual world as it is of the "nonspiritual" world. Most of us get this from a pretty young age. But the less intuitive part is this:

2. *The effect is often disproportionate to the cause.* There's a kind of amplifying effect where our actions yield far more than we expect over time.

Paul wrote to readers living in an agrarian economy, so he used the word picture of sowing and reaping. I'm no farmer, but most of us are familiar enough with the basics of horticulture to get his drift.

1. Sow a rose seed, and you get what? A rose. Sow poison ivy, and you get a noxious weed. But more importantly . . .

2. Sow a *seed*—rose, ivy, apple, grain of wheat—a tiny, black dot smaller than your fingernail, and over time, you get a plant or a tree or even a full-on harvest.

Had Paul been writing to readers in a knowledge economy like ours, my guess is he would have expressed this concept with the word picture of compound interest.

Have you ever sat down with a financial adviser to plan out your long-term financial goals and retirement? No worries if not; I'm aware this is a very middle class example. But I have this vivid memory from my early twenties when I landed my first-ever salaried job. What a great feeling! It wasn't much, but we had enough each month to pay the bills and a little left over. One of the elders at our church worked as an investment banker, and he was kind enough to sit down with T and me and offer us free financial planning. It was all pretty basic—spend less than you make, invest in a Roth IRA for retirement, and so on. But the part I still remember the most was when he explained compound interest to me. My eyes bulged, not when he explained the theory of it, but when he calculated my finances over the next forty-five years and turned it into a graph.

The balance rises slowly over time. Assuming you don't start investing until postcollege or your early twenties, there's not much to get excited about up through your thirties. In your forties, okay, looking better. Then in your fifties, the miracle of compound interest kicks in and, *boom,* all those monies you've been patiently stashing away begin to multiply at an exponential rate.

And I remember our elder/adviser (thanks again, Steve) giving me the absolute best piece of advice. He said, "It's less about how much you invest each month and more about how early you start." The stats are crazy. Let's say you invest 5K a year starting from the age of eighteen, and then you stop after ten years (a total investment of 50K). You will still have more money at retirement than if you were to invest 5K a year starting from the age of twenty-eight and not stopping until retirement (a total investment of 200K).[6] With a little sacrifice, even those who live paycheck to paycheck can accumulate modest wealth over a lifetime.

This is the miracle of compound interest, which—and here's my point—is not only a financial reality but also a *life-as-a-whole* reality.

The theologian Cornelius Plantinga said this about Paul's words to the Galatians:

> No matter what we sow, the law of returns applies. Good or evil, love or hate, justice or tyranny, grapes or thorns, a gracious compliment or a peevish complaint—whatever we invest, we tend to get it back with interest. Lovers are loved; haters, hated. Forgivers usually get forgiven; those who live by the sword die by the sword. "God is not mocked, for you reap whatever you sow."[7]

This is just how things are in the universe. "God cannot be mocked. A man reaps what he sows" isn't a command but a statement about reality. Trying to cheat the law of returns is like trying to defy gravity. Good luck with that.

And Paul applied the law of returns not to a retirement nest egg for people with privilege but to our spiritual formation. By way of reminder, spiritual formation is the process by which we are formed into a certain kind of person, good or evil.

Every time we sow to the flesh—or put another way, every time we give in to our flesh's desire to sin—we plant something in the soil of our hearts, which then begins to take root, grow, and, eventually, yield the harvest of a deformed nature.

Thankfully, the same is true of the Spirit. Every time you sow to the Spirit and invest the resources of your mind and body into nurturing your inner man or woman's connection to the Spirit of God, you plant something deep in the humus of your central fulcrum, which, over time, takes root and bears the fruit of a Christlike character.

Again, this is just the way things are.

The popularized idea of Hebb's law (named after Dr. Donald Hebb) from neuroscience states that "cells that fire together wire together." Translation: every time you think or do something, it becomes easier to think or do that same thing again, and the more you repeat this process, the harder it is to break the self-perpetuating cycle. Through repetition, thoughts and actions get into your brain's habit system, the basal ganglia, which is either your best friend or your worst enemy depending on what you sow into it, and are then encoded into the wiring of your brain.[8]

This is why riding a bike is such a breeze. Can you remember the first time you tried to ride a bike? My guess is, it was really hard. You felt clumsy, awkward, and out of control. But the more you practiced, the easier it got. Now, if you're a good Portland urbanite and regularly ride your bike rather than drive, you don't even think about it anymore. It's been encoded into your muscle memory through repetition.

This is also why a few nights ago, while driving to our friends' new home for dinner, I got into a stimulating conversation with T, only to realize I'd driven in the completely wrong direction, toward their former home. Because I'd driven there a hundred times.

This is the miracle of the human brain, as designed by God. With our self-determining freedom, we point our mind and body in the right direction, and eventually, *it directs us,* automatically.

Unfortunately, this is also why it's so hard to stop sinning. Because every time we sow to the flesh (that is, sin), we etch a neural pathway into the grooves in our brain, and from there, it begins to shape our muscle memory until we end up squarely in the New Testament's definition of slavery, or what Saint Augustine called the "shackles of gratification."[9]

While recent neuroscience has helped us understand the technical aspects of how this works, the combination of the law of returns, spiritual formation, and slavery to sin is an ancient one.

Saint Augustine wasn't always a saint; he spent decades of his life as a kind of fourth-century playboy, chasing sex, money, and power. Later, in his *Confessions,* a kind of memoir-meets-theology exposé, he said this about his slavery to lust before he became an apprentice of Jesus:

> By servitude to passion, habit is formed, and habit
> to which there is no resistance becomes necessity.
> By these links . . . a harsh bondage held me under
> restraint.[10]

And by "harsh bondage," he was referring not to Caesar or a
North African slave trader but to sin. This simple mechanism—of
mind to thought to action to habit to character to either slavery
or eternal life—*is at the very heart of apprenticeship to Jesus.*

Here's Plantinga to say it better than I can:

> A fuller statement of the great law of returns would
> therefore go something like this: sow a thought,
> and reap a deed; sow a deed, and reap another
> deed; sow some deeds, and reap a habit; sow
> some habits, and reap a character; sow a charac-
> ter, and reap two thoughts. The new thoughts then
> pursue careers of their own.[11]

The cycle of spiritual formation (or deformation) begins to feed
off its own energy and either spiral out of control or culminate
in Christlikeness.

Now, to get a little more clarity, let's run this idea through the
lens of psychology, philosophy, and theology. While we tend
to think of these as separate disciplines, that was not always
the case. And while I'm grateful for experts in each field, I
can't help but feel something is lost when the human experience is siloed into academic subdisciplines. For most of
human history, psychology, philosophy, and theology were all
studied as a unified whole and fell under the rubric of spirituality and the domain of the priest or pastor.

So let's do our best to put them back together . . .

First, let's dig into a little psychology.

The journalist Charles Duhigg, in his bestselling book *The Power of Habit,* popularized what psychologists have been saying for years: that our choices become our habits, our habits become our characters, and, as the Roman poet Heracleitus said five hundred years before Christ even walked the earth, character is destiny.

The things we do, *do something to us.* They shape the people we become.

This idea of the power of habit is an exciting, playful concept when applied to our workout routine, email hours, or workflow, but all too often it's a sobering reality when applied to our spiritual formation.

Well-respected psychologist and researcher Dr. Erich Fromm lived through both world wars and lost his Jewish faith on the other side of that trauma. After researching Nazism for years, he came to the conclusion that no one starts out evil;[12] instead, people become evil "slowly over time through a long series of choices."[13]

His book *The Heart of Man,* which is an exploration of evil and the human condition, is worth quoting at length:

> The longer we continue to make the wrong decisions, the more our heart hardens; the more often we make the right decision, the more our heart softens—or better perhaps, becomes alive. . . .

Each step in life which increases my self-confidence, my integrity, my courage, my conviction also increases my capacity to choose the desirable alternative, until eventually it becomes more difficult for me to choose the undesirable rather than the desirable action. On the other hand, each act of surrender and cowardice weakens me, opens the path for more acts of surrender, *and eventually freedom is lost.* Between the extreme when I can no longer do a wrong act and the extreme when I have lost my freedom to right action, there are innumerable degrees of freedom of choice. . . .

Most people fail in the art of living not because they are inherently bad or so without will that they cannot lead a better life; they fail because they do not wake up and see when they stand at a fork in the road and have to decide.[14]

It's our daily, seemingly insignificant decisions that eventually sculpt our characters and harden them into stone or free them to flourishing.

Take the all-too-common example of an affair, one of the few sexual taboos that's still generally recognized (though that's changing). In all my years as a pastor, I've never known anyone who just woke up one morning in a happy, healthy marriage and had an affair that night. In every case, the affair started not with the act of infidelity but with a thousand earlier acts. The choice to skip date night, to quit couples counseling, to make a flirtatious comment to a coworker, to allow a certain kind of film into the entertainment queue. The affair itself was the result of not one but a thousand choices, made over a long period of time, which all built to a head and brought ruin from the substrata to the surface of a life.

Or take a less dramatic and far more humdrum example like, say, negativity. I can speak to this one as an expert. With every decision we make to complain, criticize, play the victim, focus on the negative, and so on, we become more and more the kind of person who is *by nature* negative, grouchy, unhappy, and unpleasant to be around, until eventually we lose the very capacity to live happily, gratefully, and full of wonder at our lives in God's good world.

Here C. S. Lewis's insight is devastating:

> Hell . . . begins with a grumbling mood, and yourself still distinct from it: perhaps criticizing it. . . . But there may come a day when you can do that no longer. Then there will be no *you* left to criticize the mood, nor even to enjoy it, but just the grumble itself going on forever like a machine.[15]

But again, the reciprocal is true as well. The daily decision to rejoice—to cultivate a way of seeing our lives in God's good world, not through the lens of our phones, news apps, or flesh, but through gratitude, celebration, and unhurried delight—will over time form us into joyful, thankful people who deeply enjoy life with God and others. What starts as an act of the will eventually turns into our inner nature. What begins with a choice eventually becomes a character.

Trust me, I've spent years undoing neural pathways of perfectionism, cynicism, and negative rumination I laid down in my college years and early twenties. And with each passing year of apprenticeship to Jesus, my mind is further and further from hell and closer to the place where God's will is done.

This is the power of our choices, decisions, and habits. For good or for evil. To index us toward freedom or slavery.

We make our decisions, and then our decisions make us.

In the beginning we have a choice, but eventually, we have a character.

On that note, let's move on to philosophy.

One of the long-standing questions of philosophy is that of free will. What exactly is free will? How does it jibe with God's sovereignty, nature's laws, and our genetic programming? Cue the running debates in both academia and the church.

But most philosophers agree that human beings have self-determining freedom, a type of freedom that goes beyond instinct and impulse. We're not run by our primal, evolutionary drives or animal brains. When Darwinian materialists claim that human beings are animals or primates, they are right in that we are very much like the animals, particularly the order known as primates. We eat, sleep, mate, fight, fear, get sick, and die. But the Darwinists have to admit that, unlike the animals, we have the capacity to *override* these drives.

Animals can't turn the other cheek or love their enemies. They can't restrain their sex drives out of care for their mates' emotional conditions that day. They have no way to interrupt the cycle of "hungry feeling" straight to "eat." Or "horny feeling" straight to "mate."

Humans can override these drives. We can decide to eat a salad for lunch or not have an affair. Or at least, we can decide that at first. But here's the contribution of philosophy to our conversation: our level of self-determining freedom *does not stay the same over a lifetime;* it goes up or down depending on the choices we make.

We become freer to love or more enslaved to our flesh with each choice.

Have a look at this from Greg Boyd, educated at Princeton and Yale. His book *Satan and the Problem of Evil* is the best case I've ever read against the ever-popular "God is in control" mantra. In his section on philosophy he wrote this about spiritual formation:

> Self-determining freedom ultimately gives way either to a higher form of freedom—the freedom to be creatures whose love defines them—or the lowest form of bondage—the inability to participate in love. We either become beings who are irrevocably open or irrevocably closed to God's love. The former is eternal life; the latter is eternal death.[16]

C. S. Lewis, another brilliant mind who lived through both world wars but unlike Fromm became a Christian as a result, said it this way:

> Every time you make a choice you are turning the central part of you, the part of you that chooses, into something a little different from what it was before. And taking your life as a whole, with all your innumerable choices, all your life long you are

slowly turning this central thing either into a heavenly creature or into a hellish creature. . . . To be the one kind of creature is heaven: that is, it is joy and peace and knowledge and power. To be the other means madness, horror, idiocy, rage, impotence, and eternal loneliness. Each of us at each moment is progressing to the one state or the other.[17]

He went on to say we are all becoming either "immortal horrors or everlasting splendors."[18] Of people who refuse Jesus's invitation to follow him into love, he said, "First they will not, in the end, they cannot."[19]

The insight of philosophy is this: *our freedom expands or shrinks with each decision we make.*

This is why the older you get, the harder it is to change. Think of the saying "You can't teach an old dog new tricks." Who says that? Not young people. Young people tend to think of human nature as more pliable, less fixed. That's because when you're younger, it is. When you're in your twenties, you have this nagging sense of *Who will I become?*

To my readers under thirty, please listen carefully: that feeling goes away.

By the time you're forty, you're more likely to think, *Well, this is who I became.*

All my grandparents have passed away, but my wife has a ninety-eight-year-old grandmother, Evelyn, a devout Catholic who's been following Jesus far longer than I've been alive.

Last Thanksgiving, I sat with her for about thirty minutes before dinner. She had just taken a bad fall, spent time in the hospital, and was sitting in a wheelchair in pain. On top of that, she deeply misses her husband of fifty-eight years, who died ten long years ago. But try as I did, *I could not get her to complain.* She was joyful, grateful, present to the moment. The worst thing I could coax from her was this fantastic line: "Getting old is for the birds."

She's free.

Free from the slavery of an emotional state that's dependent on her circumstances. Free from the need to be young or beautiful or married or wealthy to enjoy her life in God's world.

Evelyn is a flesh-and-blood example of what philosophers argue for in the abstract: the longer we choose a habit or even just a disposition—like negativity, gratitude, worry, or joy—the less likely we are to ever change.

Finally, theology.

One of the great questions of theology is over hell. What is it, exactly? What does the Bible *actually* teach on the matter, and what is speculative? Who goes there, or is that even the right language? Does it last forever or just for a time?

And of course, the perennial question, How could a loving God send anybody to hell?

Without doubt, there are all sorts of goofy and, frankly, ridiculous ideas about hell. They go back at least as far as Dante's *Inferno* (as a book of poetry, spirituality, and social critique, a masterpiece; as a biblical theology of hell, a misleading work of conjecture) and lead all the way up to interstate billboards with blue clouds behind the word *heaven* and red flames behind the word *hell,* overlaid with the piercing question, "If you were to die tonight . . ."

(No, I'm not making this up. They've been along Interstate 5 in Oregon for years.)

I've zero desire to get into the debate over eternal conscious torment (ECT) versus annihilationism versus second-chance Christian universalism versus Unitarian universalism versus Catholic purgatory. . . . Deep breath. But let me just make one observation: what's often missing from the long-running debate over hell and how a loving God could send people there is the rather simple observation that, for some people, *heaven would be a kind of hell.* Whatever the kingdom of heaven turns out to be in all its fullness, it will be, for sure, a community of people who live under King Jesus's rule.

It's dishonest and disrespectful to people's human dignity to just assume that everyone would want that.

Most of my secular friends seem quite content to live without God. They aren't sitting around in existential angst, pining away over the God-shaped hole in their hearts. Many of them seem very happy to live without God and by their own moral vision. To marry, raise children, do something meaningful with their lives, and then face death when it inevitably comes. They don't give off the "I'm miserable" vibe. It's more the "where are we going to brunch this Sunday?" vibe. And many of them are good, intelligent, lovely people that I respect and enjoy.

But I have little reason to believe that people who have zero desire to live with Jesus and his community now would want to be conscripted into that forever.

Now, you might say, "That's because they don't realize what they're missing. Once they see reality for what it actually is, once the demonic deception is cleared away for good, everyone will want to live with Jesus in his new world."

That may well be true, in which case this next bit is a red herring. But let me offer another perspective by way of an analogy: Florida.

Yes, Florida.

To all my readers from Florida, I apologize for the next few paragraphs, but keep reading; you come out on top by the end.

I'm West Coast born and raised: temperate weather, low humidity, third wave coffee, #westcoastisthebestcoast.

None of which exist in Florida.

My first trip to Florida was in the month of June. Humidity was 80 percent. Daytona Beach. The aesthetics of the city, as you would imagine, fit the home-of-NASCAR stereotype. There was no single-origin coffee shop for a hundred miles. The heat was *stifling.* This was a few years ago, when skinny jeans were extra skinny, and I just remember trying to walk from my hotel, across the parking lot, to an event center where I was speaking.

Squeak, squeak, squeak.

I must have looked like a warm-weather penguin waddling across the road.

Oh, don't forget there are alligators. That eat people.

Now, I'm told by my East Coast and Midwestern friends that many people's dream is to retire to a golf course in Florida. There are literally people right now slugging it out through winter in west Michigan, taking the overtime shift at the plant and forgoing the car payment just to save their pennies to someday move to the Floridian green and take it easy. For some people, that would be a kind of heaven on earth.

Not for me.

It would be much more like the other place.

I wilt in humidity. I can't stand golf. Lest you golfers judge me, I tried to like golf. Several of my best friends are obsessed with the sport. I love the idea of spending days with them walking a beautiful, green course, talking about life. But I found it tedious and infuriating. In fact, I remember a decision point where I thought to myself, *Self, you could become the kind of person who likes golf, but it would take thousands of hours of practice, dedication, money, and time.*

Nah . . .

The reality is, through a long series of decisions made over many years, some by me and others by my ancestors who immigrated to California, I have not become the kind of person for whom living on a golf course in Florida would be heaven on earth. I would not even have the capacity to enjoy what other people have been tirelessly working for their entire lives.

You see where I'm going with this. Willard used to say, "Hell is just the best God can do for some people."[20] I think he meant a blatant racist or a pathological liar or a vehement God hater would be just miserable in the kingdom of heaven.[21]

Could it be that death simply seals the trajectory a soul is already on, toward slavery and death or freedom and life? Timothy Keller defined hell as "one's freely chosen identity apart from God on a trajectory into infinity."[22]

Again, Lewis: "It's not a question of God 'sending' us to Hell. In each of us there is something growing up which will of itself *be Hell* unless it is nipped in the bud."[23]

I grew up in a Protestant home, so I always assumed the Catholic idea of purgatory was nonsense. (To my Catholic readers, please forgive my crassness.) "Where is *that* in the Bible?" I asked.

And yet I always wondered over the conundrum of free will. The way *Genesis* tells the story, the main reason evil is in the world is because humans are free, but we've abused that freedom and used it for evil. But in *Revelation,* there's no more evil in the world even though humans are there. Does that mean we're no longer free?

The evangelical view seems to be that upon death some kind of switch is flipped and we become incapable of doing evil anymore yet somehow retain our free will. I never really read this in the Bible but simply assumed something like it must be the plan.

It quite possibly is.

But a few years ago, I read an essay by Ronald Rolheiser (my favorite Catholic writer) on purgatory that blew my mind. He made the most compelling case for it, not based on the Bible—he was very honest that this idea *isn't* in the Bible—but based on logic and common sense. To become the kind of people who (1) will even enjoy the kingdom of heaven and (2) will steward our self-determining freedom for good and not evil, we must be "purged" (hence the name *purgatory*), set free from sin's hold on our souls, so we can actually live free in God's new world.[24] It's the best explanation of purgatory this Protestant has ever heard.

Now, I'm not arguing for purgatory. I'm just saying, regardless of who is right about how free will works in eternity, it seems like the time to start down this path is *now.* What if fighting our flesh is a kind of voluntary purgatory in the present life? And what if following Jesus is training now for life forever, a sort of school where we become the kind of people who are so free that we are fully capable to "reign forever and ever"?[25]

This is the power and potential of freedom. And the danger.

Again, it's bad news or great news depending on what we sow. Every thought, every desire we follow, every choice we make is an investment in our future, in the kind of people we want to become. How do you grow a forest? One seed at a time. How do you grow a life? One tiny, unglamorous decision at a time.

So, take care what you sow, dear friend. Give careful thought to what you think about, what you say, what you do, whom you do it with. You are becoming who you will be forever.

Character is destiny.

So I say, live by the Spirit

Growing up, I was a sensitive child. I can relate to the opening line of Ruth Burrows's autobiography, "I was born into this world with a tortured sensitivity."[1] I was also a bit wild, so I regularly got in trouble and afterward felt very bad.

I had a lot of kind people, including my kind parents, attempt to assuage my guilt.

"Guilt is from the devil, not Jesus."

Jesus "paid it all" and took my place, they said. "You don't need to feel bad about your sin."

"You're a good person."

Yet this always felt a bit off to me. It was appealing, yes, but was it true?

The New Testament writers never claim that all guilt is bad. In fact, many scholars argue that a number of Greek words translated into English as "sin" or "debt" or "fault" would be better translated as "guilt."[2]

This is borderline heresy in the modern West where, for a generation raised on a steady diet of self-esteem, the ultimate evil is to feel bad about yourself. But near as I can tell, there are two types of people who no longer feel any guilt:

Saints—people who have achieved John Wesley's "Christian perfection" and sin so infrequently they live a kind of guilt-free existence.

And *sociopaths*. Sociopaths sin with impunity. They do whatever the heck they want and don't feel bad afterward. Those of the mild variety lie about coworkers to angle for their jobs and then go out for a beer. Those of the more extreme type murder someone and then . . . go out for a beer. No guilt. No lingering bad feeling. No tossing and turning in bed that night. As Paul would say, their "consciences have been seared as with a hot iron,"[3] and "they have lost connection with the head."[4]

I would argue a more helpful way to frame the dichotomy is to delineate between guilt and shame.

Guilt is about the *what;* shame is about the *who.*

Guilt says, "What I did was bad."

Shame: "*I* am bad."

Guilt thinks to itself, *What I did was unloving, and I need to make it right.*

Shame thinks, *I am unlovable, and there's no hope for me.*

Shame is almost never helpful, and most of the time it's toxic.[5] We all live from an identity, or a sense of self, to give us belonging in a community and a purpose in life. Shame says our identity is bad, unlovable, or irredeemable. So as a result, we live out that identity, which is a lie, and—surprise, surprise—we live badly.

But I would argue that guilt can actually be a good thing. There are times and situations when guilt is the emotionally healthy, mature, loving response to our own sin. Guilt is to the soul what pain is to the body. A kind of moral discomfort. Pain is bad only when it goes on indefinitely; in the short term, it's a gift from God to our bodies, a messenger whose job is to tell us we need to fix something and fast.

Guilt is unhealthy only when we wallow in it. When it lingers in the back of our minds, a kind of permanent fixture in our thought lives, playing the role of the accuser. But it's just as unhealthy to ignore or suppress it through self-talk, a well-meaning but misguided friend, or simple distraction via our cultural narcotics of choice.

All healthy people experience occasional guilt. Because all people, even the healthy ones, make mistakes. We tear the moral fabric of our world. Guilt is a gentle hint we need to repair something. It's also a part of how we mature into people of love.

All parents know this. All parents secretly (or not so secretly) look for an appropriate level of guilt when their kids mess up and let that set the tone of their discipline.

The Comers are pacifists in theology but not always in practice. We have two wonderful boys, and I won't name names, but recently one of them hit the other. A heated debate over which brother owned a certain Lego turned physical. It happens. Brothers! But when I sat down with the offending brother, as a loving father I *wanted* him to feel guilty. Not because I'm sadistic and enjoy watching him feel miserable but because I love him and want him to grow and mature into a person of love.

In fact, a secret that parents keep from their children is that our discipline is often commensurate with the level of guilt we intuit from the child. If children feel horrible and are berating themselves for their mistakes, we tend to go really easy on them and play the role of compassionate comforter and identity truth teller more than the parental version of judge and jury. But if they blame shift and downplay and don't really seem to care that they hurt somebody, we up the level of our discipline, with the goal not of punishment but of purgation.

We do this not because we're cruel but because we're loving. And we know that if they pick up the habit of guilt suppression (which is based in self-deception), they could master the art of drowning out their consciences' persistent but quiet voices, dulling their sensitivity to moral pain, and that could usher ruin into their lives and our world.

All that to say, if all this talk about the flesh has you feeling bad, give careful thought to what you do with that feeling. If a certain habit, entertainment choice, budget line item, or relationship has been itching at the back of your mind, I invite you to pay attention to it. Not to wallow in it or muzzle it but to open your heart to however the Spirit of God is coming to you in it.

Saint Thérèse of Lisieux's beautiful line comes to mind: "If you are willing to serenely bear the trial of being displeasing to yourself, then you will be for Jesus a pleasant place of shelter."[6]

So, if we're feeling any of the healthy kind of guilt right now, let's do something about it.

On that note, one final question remains: *How?* How do we fight our flesh?

Again, this is where Paul's work is incredibly helpful. We skipped over his language at the end of Galatians 5 about how to fight our flesh, and now we're ready to circle back:

> Those who belong to Christ Jesus have crucified the flesh with its passions and desires. Since we live by the Spirit, let us keep in step with the Spirit.[7]

Step one: we are to "crucify" our flesh

In Paul's world, crucifixion was the most brutal, visceral, and emotional form of execution known to man. It's how Jesus died. And it's how we fight our flesh. We don't coddle it, baby it, or placate it—we *crucify* it. My Calvinist friends use the word *mortification.* It's a fourteenth-century word from the Latin root *mors,* meaning "death." (*Mors* is also the root of the noun *mortal.*)[8] We are to mortify our flesh, as in, kill it.

As we saw in the last chapter, the gospel of sin management doesn't work because the flesh isn't a static reality but a dynamic one. In Genesis 4, the story about Cain killing his brother Abel in the wake of Adam and Eve's sin, God described sin as a beast within,[9] and that beast shrinks or grows depending on whether we starve or feed it.

Again, this is where I find neurobiology's idea of an animal brain helpful, secular as it may sound. Dr. Jeffrey Schwartz, whom I quoted earlier, in a letter to a fatherless young man he was mentoring, said it this way:

> Neither should the body be indulged and catered to, because the more you pamper and submit to its desires, the more they grow into insatiable cravings. (A potato chip—or an orgasm—tends to make you want another one.) And that way lies being nothing more than an animal.[10]

Every time we sow to the flesh, we feed that animalistic part of us. As it grows, it takes more control over our freedom and attempts to eat us alive from the inside. This is why Peter, writing about "those who follow the corrupt desire of the flesh" said that, in time, they become like "unreasoning animals, creatures of instinct . . . and like animals they too will perish."[11] Harsh as his language sounds, he wasn't being mean, just honest—and loving. The more people indulge their flesh, the more it takes over their whole beings and turns them into brutes, however socially sophisticated they may remain.

This is why Paul didn't mess around. You don't manage your flesh or simply keep it in check—you launch a militant campaign to kill it.

But still, the question remains, How?

Step two: "let us keep in step with the Spirit"

Now, this, my friends, is gold.

This command to "keep in step with the Spirit" is the last of three synonymous commands in Galatians 5, which come at the beginning, middle, and end of Paul's teaching on the flesh.

1. "Walk by the Spirit" (v16).
2. Be "led by the Spirit" (v18).
3. "Live by the spirit" and "keep in step with the Spirit" (v25).

This is Paul's unique contribution to our subject matter. As I said before, all sorts of other religious, philosophical, and even scientific traditions have a similar category to the New Testament idea of the flesh versus the Spirit. Non-Christian and even nonreligious people all recognize a hierarchy of desires, many of which are in conflict with each other and many of which need to be denied. This is not a Christian problem or a new problem but a human and ancient one.

What was new was Paul's solution. For Paul, the way we fight the flesh and win is not through willpower but through the *Spirit's power.*

He urges us not to white-knuckle it, slap our faces, or pull ourselves up by our own bootstraps, but simply to "live by the Spirit."

Now, willpower is not a bad thing at all. In fact, as we follow Jesus, our capacity to choose the good should grow and expand with each passing year. Things that once were excruciatingly difficult and required high-touch accountability and constant vigilance should hopefully become easy—the natural outworking of Christlike character formed in us over time.

But most of us aren't there yet; I'm sure not. So here's my strategy: when willpower works, I use it.

It just doesn't work as often as I'd like. At least not on my deepest problems.

Willpower versus a second cookie is one thing.

But willpower versus triggered trauma? Or willpower versus addiction? Or willpower versus a father wound? *It doesn't stand a chance.* As long as a temptation is just interfacing with the prefrontal cortex, willpower is a great resource to draw on. But the moment we're dealing with the amygdala, with the part of the brain or soul that is deeply wounded or hardwired in sinful ways of being, we are outmanned and outgunned by the flesh.

If you're trying to use willpower against your self-defeating behavior that's rooted in trauma or past pain and you feel like you're failing, don't beat yourself up; change your strategy. Willpower is not the answer to your problem.

Leslie Jamison said of overcoming her addiction,

> I needed to believe in something stronger than my willpower. . . .
>
> This willpower was a fine-tuned machine, fierce and humming, and it had done plenty of things—gotten me straight A's, gotten my papers written, gotten

me through cross-country training runs—but when
I'd applied it to drinking, the only thing I felt was
that I was turning my life into a small, joyless,
clenched fist. The Higher Power that turned sobri-
ety into more than deprivation was simply *not me.*
That was all I knew.[12]

To win, we need access to a power that is beyond us. We
need an ally in the fight to come alongside us and turn the
tide. That power is the Spirit of Jesus.

And how do we access this power?

Simple: via the practices.

Willpower is at its best when it does what it *can* (direct my
body into spiritual practices) so the Spirit's power can do what
willpower *can't* (overcome the three enemies of the soul).

We've been working under the hypothesis that spiritual disciplines are spiritual warfare. Put another way, the practices of
Jesus are how we fight the world, the flesh, and the devil.

Think of the work we did in the last chapter on the power of
habit and how the things we do, do something to us. The
practices of Jesus are effectively counterhabits to those of our
flesh. They are habits based on the life and teachings of Jesus
that resist the habits of our flesh. Every time you practice a
habit of Jesus, your spirit (one way to think of your spirit is as
your inner willpower muscle) gets a little stronger and your
flesh (your inner animal) gets a little weaker.

But, that said, the practices aren't *just* counterhabits to work
out our willpower muscles. They are the means by which we

access a power from beyond us. They enable us to live from an animating energy and pneumatic force that is far more powerful than any inner resource we could possibly draw on. That's why many call them *spiritual* disciplines—they are spiritual in that they open us to the Spirit, whom the respected Pentecostal scholar Gordon Fee defined as "God's *empowering* presence."[13]

In Romans 8, another passage on the flesh, Paul connected the dots between Jesus's death and resurrection and our new capacity for victory in our struggle against the flesh. He wrote that, prior to Jesus,

> the law was powerless . . . because it was weakened by the flesh.[14]

Meaning, humans could not live out God's commands because their will-to-good was sabotaged by their flesh. But God saved us

> by sending his own Son in the likeness of sinful flesh to be a sin offering . . . in order that the righteous requirement of the law might be fully met in us, who *do not live according to the flesh but according to the Spirit.*[15]

I added the italics to show you the synergy in Paul's thought. The solution to our flesh's control over us isn't to buck up but to rely on the Spirit. Paul then went on to say we live "according to the Spirit" through the simple act of setting our minds on God:

> Those who live according to the flesh have their minds set on what the flesh desires; but those who live in accordance with the Spirit have their minds

set on what the Spirit desires. The mind governed
by the flesh is death, but the mind governed by the
Spirit is life and peace.[16]

It's as simple as that: small, regular habits/practices/disci-
plines that open our minds up to the Spirit and close them off
to the flesh.

Let me highlight two I think are especially important as pertaining to the flesh: fasting and confession.

First, fasting

No practice of Jesus is more alien or neglected in the modern
Western church than fasting. In the post-Enlightenment intellectual landscape, where human beings are viewed as *res cogitans,*[17] or "thinking things," the idea of drawing on the Spirit's
power not through your mind but through your *stomach*
sounds absurd. Few followers of Jesus regularly fast anymore.

And yet, until recent history, fasting was one of the core practices of the Way of Jesus. For hundreds of years, the church
would fast twice a week: Wednesdays and Fridays. That was
just what you did if you were a Christian. In the fourth century,
when the church developed the practice of Lent, it was originally a fast similar to Islam's Ramadan. As a lead-up to Easter,
followers of Jesus would wake and go without food until sun-
set. For forty days. Every year.

Please note: go without *food.*

I regularly hear people use the term *fasting* for other forms of
abstinence, such as "I'm fasting from social media/TV/online
shopping."

That's great, but it's not fasting; it's abstinence, and it's still a helpful practice with a long-standing tradition in the Way of Jesus. I'm all for it. But fasting is a practice by which you deny your body *food* in an attempt to starve your flesh. It is a psychosomatic act, in the true sense of the word, that's built around a biblical theology of the soul as your whole person. Contrary to what many Western Christians assume, your soul isn't the immaterial, invisible part of you (a better word for that is your spirit or your will); it's your *whole* person, which includes all of your body—your brain, nervous system, and stomach.

Now, just to make sure we're clear, your body is not evil. This is where the medieval monastic movement got it wildly wrong. Your body is a gift, as is pleasure in the right time and place and way. But your body, like the rest of your soul, has been corrupted by sin. As a result, your body often works against you in your fight with the flesh, via your sex drive, fight-or-flight system, or survival instincts.

Fasting is a way to turn your body into an ally in your fight with the flesh rather than an adversary.

If you don't believe me, just try it. See what happens.

Now, by way of warning, at first, fasting likely won't feel like this great access to power. Richard Foster astutely observed, "More than any other Discipline, fasting reveals the things that control us."[18] Very few practices have the capacity to humble us as does fasting. When you begin fasting, it's common to feel sad, even anxious, or just plain hangry. With regular practice, these feelings (mostly) go away and are replaced by joy, contentment, a sense of intimacy with God, and spiritual power. But it takes a while to wean your soul off its addiction to the Western gods of pleasure, instant gratification, and sensory appetites. The first thing it normally does is reveal where you are still in bondage.

Fasting trains our bodies *to not get what they want.* At least, not all the time.

This is yet another reason why, in a culture so run by feelings and desire, fasting is a bizarre idea even to Christians. We assume that we must get what we want to be happy, and by *want,* we often mean what our flesh wants.

This simply isn't true.

With fasting, we decide of our own accord to not give our bodies what they want (food); as a result, when somebody else decides to not give us what we want (or life circumstances decide, or even God decides . . .), we don't freak out, rage, or go ballistic on Twitter. We've trained our souls to be happy and at peace, *even when we don't get our way.*

This is why fasting—far from a medieval form of self-hate— when done rightly is a pathway to freedom. Fasting is practicing suffering; it's teaching our bodies to suffer. Suffering is unavoidable in life; joy is not. In fasting we're learning how to suffer with joy.

What Scripture reading is to our fight with the devil (a way to fill our minds with truth to combat his lies), fasting is to our fight with the flesh (a way to starve our flesh and weaken its hold over us).

I occasionally give spiritual direction, and whenever I'm sitting with a spiritual friend who is struggling with any kind of habitual sin, I recommend he take up regular (ideally weekly) fasting. *Especially* if the sin is sexual in nature. Not because fasting is a silver bullet; it's not. I'm well aware that most addictions and most any form of self-destructive behavior that is impervious to our attempts to change are rooted in trauma. Wickedness is tied to woundedness. We all need healing. Much could be said about that. But still, through fasting, perhaps more than any other practice, the power of the Holy Spirit to break the chains of sin is released into our bodies themselves.

I just had breakfast (yes, the irony) with a dear friend who recently began fasting every Wednesday. He's a foodie, type seven on the Enneagram, wine aficionado, fun-loving kind of personality, so when I asked him how it's going, I was expecting a negative report. Instead, he gushed that it's one of the most transformative things he's ever done.

I should not have been surprised.

Is it any wonder that when Jesus went toe to toe with the devil, he was fasting? In fact, it was after forty days of fasting. It's easy to misinterpret this story; I did for years. I took it to mean the devil waited until Jesus was exhausted and weak to make his move. But this is a gross misunderstanding of the reciprocal relationship between fasting and spiritual power. Forty days in, Jesus was at the *height* of his spiritual power and was able to wisely discern the devil's lies and dismiss his temptations with adroit skill.

Such is the potential of fasting.

Second, confession

For us Westerners in the Protestant stream of the church, this is perhaps the second most neglected of the practices of Jesus. Similar to fasting, confession was abused by the Catholic church in the late Middle Ages (and still is in parts of the church today). It was contorted into a private, therapeutic thing between you and the priest, not the community, with a screen to shield your identity, and essentially functioned as a get-out-of-jail-free card for the penitent. In its worst form, it was a means for spiritual abuse or for funding a corrupt clergy. As you would imagine, it was one of many things that drew the ire of Martin Luther and the Reformers, and as a result, many Protestants just threw it out entirely.

Yet it was the *abuse* of the practice the Reformers were reacting against, not the proper use.

What's left of the practice in the Protestant church is usually around the Lord's Supper, where people say sorry to God in their minds before they receive the bread and the cup at church. The problem with this way of practicing confession is similar to that of the medieval church—it's private. For confession to yield not just forgiveness but *freedom,* it must drag our sins into the light, not keep them in solitary confinement.

Dietrich Bonhoeffer said it so well:

> Sin demands to have a man by himself. It withdraws him from the community. The more isolated a person is, the more destructive will be the power of sin over him. . . . Sin wants to remain unknown. It shuns the light. In the darkness of the unexpressed it poisons the whole being of a person.[19]

That's a quote from *Life Together,* widely considered one of the best books ever written on community. Based on Bonhoeffer's experience of living at Finkenwalde, an intentional community he set up to resist the Third Reich's cancerous influence on the church, he came to see confession as a crucial aspect of community or, for that matter, any relationship.

Because we find our deepest intimacies in our greatest vulnerabilities.

Jesus's brother James commanded us to "confess your sins to each other and pray for each other so that you may be healed."[20]

Notice: *to each other.*

A raw power and genuine freedom come when you name your sin in the presence of loving community. Just the act of naming your sin out loud to people you know and trust has the power to break chains.

This is why saying sorry to God in your mind as you receive the Lord's Supper (as it's practiced in most churches today) does not have nearly the power to set us free as an AA meeting, where you sit down, often in a dingy church basement full of ordinary people drinking bad coffee and struggling with sin, and say, "Hi, my name is ____, and I'm an alcoholic. Last night I got drunk."

The latter is far closer to the New Testament practice of confession than most of what we do in church. It comes as no surprise that "the Big Book of AA was initially called *The Way Out*"—not just out of drinking, but out of "the claustrophobic crawl space of the self."[21]

My agenda here isn't to devalue communion *at all;* it's to move you toward the practice of true confession in community.

But here's the main thing I hope you take away from this chapter: the way we fight and overcome our flesh isn't through willpower but through the Spirit's power. And we get access to that power via the practices of Jesus. Fasting and confession are just two especially helpful practices in our war with the flesh, but there are many more you can experiment with. The key is to find ways of living in reliance on the Spirit's presence and power in your ordinary life.

If you hear nothing else, hear this: we all face a war with our flesh. It's inescapable. *But it doesn't have to be a tug-of-war* where both sides are equally matched and, no matter how hard you fight, you just remain in a kind of stasis, exhausted and resigned to mediocrity.

To circle back to the line we began part 2 with, "The heart wants what it wants." There's truth in this statement for sure. Specifically, we can't control our hearts' desires. The heart has a mind of its own, literally. But what this statement completely misses is that while we can't control our desires, we can *influence* them and come to the point where *they no longer control us.*

Desire is a sibling to emotion and functions in a similar way. There's no switch for emotion. When we're sad, scared, or angry, we can't just flip on the happy switch and make all our unwanted feelings disappear. But that doesn't mean we have no say (or responsibility) over our emotions. As a general rule, our feelings follow our thinking, so if you want to augment your emotions, change your thought life. We can't change what we feel, but we can, within reason, change what we think about.

Desire works along the same lines. We can't control what we desire, but we can control what habits we give our minds and bodies to and, in doing so, index our hearts away from the flesh and toward the Spirit. This is under our power and therefore a form of responsibility before God and our fellow humans.

This is why the writer James was careful to note that while desire itself is not necessarily a form of sin, we still bear culpability before God for the kinds of desires we engender.

> When tempted, no one should say, "God is tempting me." For God cannot be tempted by evil, nor does he tempt anyone; but each person is tempted when they are dragged away by their own evil desire and enticed. Then, after desire has conceived, it gives birth to sin; and sin, when it is full-grown, gives birth to death.[22]

James was both warning us of the danger of desire left unchecked and calling us to train our desires to love and want what the Spirit loves and wants. This is what the library of Scripture calls guarding your heart. Like a sentry, we are to police the flow of traffic into our inner beings. The heart, in biblical literature, is the trifecta of a person's thinking, feeling, and desire. Or in other language, the mind, the emotions, and the will. We must guard all three.

Henri Nouwen wrote, "The heart is the seat of the will . . . the central and unifying organ of our personal life. Our heart determines our personality and is, therefore, not only the place where God dwells but also the place to which Satan directs his fiercest attacks."[23] This is why we must guard against fleshly desires "which wage war against your soul"[24] and the "many foolish and harmful desires that plunge people into ruin and destruction."[25]

And we do this through the practice of habits. Through our regular acts of mind and body we either sow to the flesh and in doing so further entrench our slavery to it, or we sow to the Spirit and increase our capacity to live freely and joyfully with God in his world.

Therefore, we must run every habit, every thought, every relationship—*everything*—through this simple grid:

Does this sow to my flesh or my spirit?

Will this make me more enslaved or more free?

More beastly or more human?

Remember, the key to spiritual formation is to change what we *can* control (our habits) to influence what we *can't* control (our flesh).

In closing, I'm struck by one of the last things Paul said in his *Galatians* passage on the flesh:

> Let us not become weary in doing good, for at the proper time we will reap a harvest if we do not give up.[26]

Notice again that Paul's exhortation isn't to not quit a hard job or to keep following your dream to start a small business. In context, the "doing good" he's referring to is the fight against our flesh.

The first application of this beautiful line is to not give up in our struggle to get free of our animal natures. Because—and here's the most beautiful thing—"at the proper time we will reap a harvest." Again, in context, he means the harvest of Christlike character and freedom. Back to the compound-interest metaphor, if we keep depositing our resources, it's only a matter of time . . .

As I write this, I just came off a pretty rough week. A few interpersonal things had me really stressed out, and by the time my Sabbath rolled around, I was really feeling it. I've had an adulthood-long struggle with anxiety that, while better than it's ever been, still rears its ugly head on a regular basis. Sitting there on my Sabbath, on my back deck on a beautiful day, I would love to tell you I was just basking in the shalom of God, deeply happy and at peace. I wasn't. I was stressed out, mad at a friend, and feeling tension all over my body. As a nice addition, I was feeling anxiety over my anxiety, and a deep shame over my inability to just let go. And in that moment of discouragement, when I was literally thinking, *Will I ever mature past anxiety's hold on my soul?* I felt the Spirit bring to mind my friend Steve's graph of compound interest and then apply it, not to my retirement, but to my peace.

Here's John Mark and peace in his twenties . . . Not much to look at. A very anxious young man with a "tortured sensitivity."

Here's John Mark and peace in his thirties . . . Better, but still a long way to go.

Forties . . . Wow, I see a noticeable uptick. But still a lot of road ahead.

But by the time I'm in my sixties? *Deep shalom, friends, deep shalom.* Come what may, my soul is at peace in God.

So, with that vision of my future self in my mind, I practice Sabbath every week. I can't flip a switch and control my anxiety, but I can turn off my phone. I can rest and trust that, in time, God will utilize the practice of Sabbath to fill me with more of his Spirit, set me free from anxiety, and yield a harvest of peace in my soul. I'm practicing the Way of Jesus, as best I can, and playing the long game.

My father has been a pastor for longer than I've been alive. On his desk is a little frame with one simple sentence, a daily reminder: *Take the long view.*

What are you facing right now? Where do you need a way out? A thought pattern you just can't break free of? A compulsion or addiction that's killing your joy? A character flaw that leaks out in embarrassing ways, despite your best efforts to nip it in the bud?

How do you feel about it? Sad? Defeated? Resigned?

Are there areas of your life and character where you've lowered your expectations? Settled for the tug-of-war rather than victory? Grown numb?

Don't.

Don't grow weary in doing good.

It will come, in time.

Take the long view.

Part 2 step sheet

Definitions:

- **The flesh**—our base, primal, animalistic drives for self-gratification, especially as pertains to sensuality and survival
- **The Spirit**—God's empowering presence in us
- **Freedom in modern Western use**—the permission to do whatever we want
- **Freedom in the New Testament**—the power to want and do what is good
- **Love in the modern Western use**—desire; often sexual desire
- **Love in the New Testament**—the compassionate commitment of the heart to delight in the soul of another and to will that person's good ahead of your own, no matter the cost to yourself
- **The law of returns**—every action has a reaction, and those reactions are often disproportionate to the action.

Key texts to meditate on: Galatians 5–6; Romans 8v1–13; and 1 Peter 2v9–22

Working theory of the devil's strategy: deceitful ideas that play to disordered desires that are normalized in a sinful society

Working theory of the law of returns applied to spiritual formation: sow a thought, reap an action; sow action, reap another action; sow some actions, reap a habit; sow a habit, reap a character; sow a character, reap a destiny, either in slavery to the flesh or freedom in the Spirit.

Working theory of how we fight the flesh: We feed our spirits and starve our flesh by practicing habits laid down by Jesus, specifically fasting and confession of sin. As we do this over time, we not only grow our own willpower muscles but, more importantly, we open our minds and bodies to a power that is beyond us—that of God's Spirit.

Key practices to overcome the flesh: fasting and confession

In summary: The devil's deceitful ideas are not random; they appeal to our disordered desires, or what the New Testament writers call the flesh. The flesh is our animal side, the primal, instinctual drives of self-gratification and self-preservation. The solution is not to white-knuckle our way through but to live by the Spirit via practices that enable us to draw on the power of God to live in freedom.

Part 3

The WORLD

My prayer is not that you take them
out of the world but that you protect
them from the evil one. They are not
of the world, even as I am not of it.
Sanctify them by the truth; your word
is truth. As you sent me into the world,
I have sent them into the world.

—Jesus, in John 17v15–18

Do not love the world or anything in
the world. If anyone loves the world,
love for the Father is not in them.
For everything in the world—the lust of
the flesh, the lust of the eyes, and the
pride of life—comes not from the
Father but from the world. The world
and its desires pass away, but whoever
does the will of God lives forever.

—John, in 1 John 2v15–17

A friend of mine shared it with me.

—Shawn Fanning

The brutal honesty about normal

September 7, 2000, the MTV Video Music Awards. Celebrity presenter Carson Daly is on stage, about to introduce Britney Spears. But first, he has a surprise for the audience. Enter stage left: Shawn Fanning, the creator of Napster. Along with his era-expected baggy jeans, he's wearing a black Metallica T-shirt.

Daly says, "Nice shirt."

Fanning: "A friend of mine shared it with me."[1]

Now, for you digital natives who are too young to remember either Napster or Metallica, here's the backstory: A few months before, the heavy metal rock gods were in the studio working on a song called "I Disappear" for the upcoming Mis-

sion: Impossible movie. They woke up one morning to find their song being played on radio stations across the country. Here's the thing: *they hadn't released it yet.* It wasn't even mixed. Somebody stole it and released it, unfinished, into the digital ether. They traced the theft back to a then-fledgling file-sharing program called Napster, where they found not only "I Disappear" but their entire catalog available for download. For free.

Thus began one of the most infamous street fights in music history.

Metallica filed a lawsuit for copyright infringement and racketeering for the not-small sum of $10 million. They won in the US District Court but lost in the court of public opinion. Metallica fans—many turned ex-fans—the media, music critics, and others all lambasted them as greedy thugs. The controversy spawned one of the first-ever viral videos, a cartoon parody of Metallica as former heavy metal kids who sold out for gold Lamborghinis.[2]

Napster's basic case was this: "Metallica is rich! Filthy rich. We're poor college kids. We don't have the money to buy their record. What's the big deal about skimming a little off the top?"

Metallica's retort was simple: "It doesn't matter if you steal from the rich or the poor; stealing is illegal and wrong. Plus, we want to keep control over our art."

Now, to state the obvious, this was not a moral gray area. No ethicists were called in to discuss the matter or debate various points of view. In pretty much every culture sociologists have ever studied, stealing is a moral taboo, a kind of a moral baseline for people to live together in community. And Napster was no Robin Hood, as much as they tried to position their business model as such.

(Napster later sold for $121 million. So, they weren't *that* poor . . .)

Napster, of course, was one of the first piracy sites, first for music, then later for TV and film, that spread lightning fast via the internet to culture at large. Within a matter of months, "everybody's doing it."

Remember those antipiracy commercials that would play before movies?

> You wouldn't steal a car . . .

Followed by shots of people stealing stuff, including a dude at a video store slipping a DVD into his leather jacket.

> Downloading pirated films is stealing.
> Stealing is against the law.
> Piracy. It's a crime.[3]

(In a shaky white-on-black typeface that wasn't actually that old but looked like it was made in 1991.)

Now, this is kindergarten-level ethics, but these commercials played before everything for years. Why? Because even though legally and ethically right and wrong were crystal clear, still *most people moved the moral line* to make piracy socially acceptable.

Why would they do that?

Again, you digital natives have no memory of a pre-Spotify or Apple Music world; I do. In 2000, when this all hit, I was in college myself, but my passion was playing guitar in my indie rock band. After Jesus, music was my life. I made $6.50 an hour working part time as a barista after school, and a CD was normally around $18 at Music Millennium on Burnside. That meant, post taxes, it was three to four hours of work for just one record. Now, it was one thing to drop a half day's work for Coldplay's *A Rush of Blood to the Head,* but what about some new band nobody had ever heard of? Sigur Rós? That was a lot of time and money to risk on the unknown.

So, naturally, Napster was well received among my friend group. All my indie rock mates would pass around burned CDs with the name of some new band scrawled in Sharpie across the top (in the post-CD world, Sharpie has gone into an economic tailspin . . .), and, not gonna lie, I imbibed multiple times.

Yes, I, John Mark Comer, used to listen to burned CDs.

Eventually, though, I came to the conviction that I was stealing and the right thing to do was to stop receiving (or giving) burned CDs. But here's what I'm getting to: from then on, whenever I would turn down friends' offers for free CDs, it would usually spark instant ire—they would get really angry with me. Now, this could have been from my immature, self-righteous personality saying something offensive and lame like "Sorry, *I* don't steal." But no matter my tone, I would regularly end up on the receiving end of contempt: "Who are *you* to judge *us*?"

Because we now lived in a moral ecosystem where "judging" your friends for burning CDs was seen as wrong but stealing was seen as just fine. Right and wrong had been redefined along the lines of popular opinion—or better said, popular *desire*—and the moral line moved, in just a few short years.

And that, my friends, is a great example of what Jesus and the writers of the New Testament call the world.

Finally, we arrive at our third enemy of the soul.

No, not burning CDs.

The world.

I began part 3 with the dated-but-nonemotionally loaded story of Napster (few of us have triggers around file sharing) to ease our minds into our final category—our fight with the world.

Now, what exactly do we mean by *the world*? Well, let's begin with what Jesus had to say about it . . .

Perhaps his best-known saying on the world is a warning to not fall under its spell:

> What good is it for someone to gain the whole
> *world,* and yet lose or forfeit their very self?[4]

Yet Jesus saw the world not just as a temptation to avoid but as a threat to be on your guard against:

> If the *world* hates you, keep in mind that it hated
> me first. If you belonged to the *world,* it would love
> you as its own. As it is, you do not belong to the
> *world,* but I have chosen you out of the *world.* That
> is why the *world* hates you. Remember what I told

you: "A servant is not greater than his master." If
they persecuted me, they will persecute you also.[5]

He's warning his apprentices that the world, which eventually
crucified him, would treat them very similarly. The relationship
is hostile.

Which makes sense if you follow Jesus's logic. He saw the
world as under the rule of the devil, not God, and saw his upcoming death and resurrection as the liberation of humanity
from the devil's tyranny:

Now is the time for judgment on *this world;* now
the prince of *this world* will be driven out.[6]

But in spite of the semihostile relationship between Jesus and
the world, Jesus's intent was never for his apprentices to ab-
dicate their responsibilities in the world. As much as I love the
monastic movement, Jesus was no monk. He didn't abscond
to or hide away in a cell. He went to the desert, yes, but then
he *came back.* That's the template. Listen to some of Jesus's
last words, in a prayer to the Father for his apprentices:

I have given them your word and *the world* has
hated them, for they are not of *the world* any more
than I am of *the world.* My prayer is not that you
take them out of *the world* but that you protect
them from the evil one. They are not of *the world,*
even as I am not of it. Sanctify them by the truth;
your word is truth. As you sent me into *the world,* I
have sent them into *the world.*[7]

This is a small sampling of what Jesus had to say about the
world. There are dozens more. As you would expect, this

major theme in Jesus's work was picked up and further developed by the writers of the New Testament. Here's the writer John with a deeply insightful warning about the world and its gravitational pull on our hearts' desires:

> Do not love the world or anything in the world. If anyone loves the world, love for the Father is not in them. For everything in the world—the lust of the flesh, the lust of the eyes, and the pride of life—comes not from the Father but from the world. The world and its desires pass away, but whoever does the will of God lives forever.[8]

The world, while possibly a newish idea to modern followers of Jesus, is a central idea running all the way from Jesus through the New Testament.

Now, let's combine all these sayings into some kind of a definition. What exactly do these writers mean by *the world*?

The word is κόσμος in Greek, where we get the English word *cosmos*. And similar to the Greek word for "the flesh," it has more than one meaning.

By way of reminder, think of the English word *ball*. It can mean (1) a round object you play a number of games with, (2) a dance party where you dress up in formal attire, or (3) to have a good time, as in, "to have a ball."

In the same way, the Greek word κόσμος has at least three meanings in the New Testament.[9]

Sometimes it just means the universe or, more specifically, planet earth, as in Romans 1v20:

> Since the creation of *the world* God's invisible
> qualities—his eternal power and divine nature—have
> been clearly seen, being understood from what has
> been made, so that people are without excuse.

Clearly, the world here isn't an enemy at all. It's a theater to display God's "power and divine nature," meaning, it's a daily signpost to God's reality and his wise, generous, creative intelligence and love. As I'm writing this chapter, I'm down in Melbourne, Australia, one of my favorite cities on earth. I just finished a long morning run through Yarra Bend Park, and it was stunning. With each stride, I felt my soul wake up to God's glory.

But other times, the word κόσμος refers not to the beauty of the Yarra River or planet earth but to humanity, as in the iconic line from John 3v16:

> God so loved *the world* that he gave his one and
> only Son, that whoever believes in him shall not
> perish but have eternal life.

While I'm sure God loves the Rocky Mountains or the Austrian Alps a lot, too, this is clearly referring not to our planet but to the mass of humans who populate our planet and, as part of his creation, draw the loving eye of the Creator's compassion.

Again, the world here is a positive thing, not negative. An object of love, not angst or acrimony.

But what we talk about when we talk about "the world, the flesh, and the devil" is a third sense of the word κόσμος, colored in a far more pejorative shade.

One Greek lexicographer defines it simply as

> the system of practices and standards associated
> with secular society.[10]

(Remember, we defined a secular society as one that attempts to live as if there is no God.)

The world is a place where, in the language of Abraham
Joshua Heschel, people believe that

> man reigns supreme, with the forces of nature
> as his only possible adversaries. Man is alone,
> free, and growing stronger. God is either non-
> existent or unconcerned. It is human initiative
> that makes history, and it is primarily by force
> that constellations change. Man can attain his
> own salvation.[11]

But the world is more than just no-God; it's *anti*-God.

I appreciate Dallas Willard's kind but blunt definition of *the
world:*

> Our cultural and social practices, that are under the
> control of Satan and, thus, opposed to God.[12]

My theological mentor Gerry Breshears put it this way:

> The world is Satan's domain, where his authority
> and values reign—though his deception makes that
> hard to realize. If you are of the world, then it all
> seems right.[13]

I rarely read political books, but I can't stop thinking about Patrick Deneen's *Why Liberalism Failed.* In context, he's writing about the social crisis of modern America, but honestly, I can't think of a better one-paragraph biblical theology of the world:

> In this world, gratitude to the past and obligations to the future are replaced by a nearly universal pursuit of immediate gratification: culture, rather than imparting the wisdom and experience of the past so as to cultivate virtues of self-restraint and civility, becomes synonymous with hedonic titillation, visceral crudeness, and distraction, all oriented toward promoting consumption, appetite, and detachment. As a result, superficially self-maximizing, socially destructive behaviors begin to dominate society.[14]

In layperson's terms, the world is what happens when a lot of people give in to their flesh and base, animalistic desires are normalized.

Perhaps the best example of the world that most of us can agree on is the systemic racism of chattel slavery—what many have called America's original sin. More than just an idea, a feeling, or even a sin, racism became inextricably woven into the fabric of the social, moral, legal, economic, and, tragically, in some circles, spiritual arenas of American society. First, it was practiced by a few, then by many. Then it was accepted as a necessary evil by society, codified by law, written into the Constitution,[15] and even justified in some circles of the church (though fiercely opposed in others). In time, it just became "the way things are." As a result, a barbaric, heinous evil was normalized. An evil that, though we have come so very far, is still like a multigenerational trauma in America's collective soul.

But the world is more than just a system that's out there in the sociopolitical ether. It is, as Eugene Peterson pointed out, "an atmosphere, a mood,"[16] that's crept into us like a cancerous rot. An airborne emotional pollutant we inhale every day, an anti-God impulse we circulate in our bodies' lungs. It's "the society of proud and arrogant humankind that defies and tries to eliminate God's rule and presence in history."[17]

In summary, I would define *the world* as

> a system of ideas, values, morals, practices, and social norms that are integrated into the mainstream and eventually institutionalized in a culture corrupted by the twin sins of rebellion against God and the redefinition of good and evil.

By *twin sins,* I'm referring to our earlier work on the Garden of Eden and the devil's paradigmatic temptation of Adam and Eve. Remember, his temptation had essentially two parts: (1) to rebel or seize autonomy from God, to secularize their lives and live apart from God, and (2) to redefine good and evil based on the voice in their heads (personified as the snake, who was later identified as the devil) and the disordered desires of their own hearts.

The world is what happens when Adam and Eve's sin goes viral and spreads through a society. The result? The distorted becomes normative. Sin is recast as any number of things— freedom, human rights, reproductive justice, "the way things are," nature, science, "boys will be boys"—anything but *sin.*

And the key insight for us is this: it all has an effect on our moral and spiritual reasoning or, to be more precise, *lack* of reasoning.

Long before the controversy around Netflix's *13 Reasons Why,* people were up in arms over Johann Wolfgang von Goethe's tragic novel *The Sorrows of Young Werther,* in which the hero commits suicide. Upon its publication in 1774, a rash of suicides spread across Europe.[18] It was almost as if suicide was behaving like a contagious disease and had to be quarantined, irrational as that may sound. Multiple countries banned the book, which was anathema to the burgeoning Enlightenment value for free speech.

And yet an emerging field of research by social psychologists into social contagions has confirmed their intuition: behaviors, both good and bad, spread through networks of friends, family, and acquaintances in a very analogous way to a virus.

The classic example of this is yawning. When somebody near you yawns, what do you do? Likely yawn. This is a well-documented phenomenon. Yet it's true not only of physical behaviors—yawning, shivering, smiling, etc.—but of *moral* behaviors as well. Smoking, not smoking, healthy eating, junk food, temperate drinking, alcoholism, civility, rudeness—pretty much any behavior you can think of has the potential to spread through a society person to person, and it behaves oddly like a disease. Consumer psychologist Dr. Paul Marsden noted that "sociocultural phenomena can spread through, and leap between, populations more like outbreaks of measles or chicken pox than through a process of rational choice."[19]

The key insight here is that these phenomena spread, not through an expensive marketing campaign, government legislation, or even through rational choice, but by some other less logical, more insidious motivation. "The empirical research has tended to confirm . . . the hypothesis that human behavior clusters in both space and time even in the absence of coercion and rationale."[20]

Translation: monkey see, monkey do.

The herd mentality is literally woven into our brains. Buffalo all walk on the same side of a field; teenagers all wear the same sneakers. People in coastal cities tend to vote Left; people in the heartland, Right. We're created by our relational God to live in community, but under the fall, we devolve back into pack animals. This is often how the devil's deceptive ideas keep such a strong hold on societies for so long. "I want it" and "everybody's doing it" have overwhelming power by themselves; put together, they are well-nigh irresistible.

As Renée DiResta, technical research manager at the Stanford Internet Observatory, summarized postmodern ethics: "If you make it trend, you make it true."[21] But the widespread social acceptance of an idea or behavior does *not* make it true, much less cause it to lead to flourishing. If history teaches us anything, it's that the majority is often wrong. "Crowds lie. The more people, the less truth," as Eugene Peterson put it.[22] Crowds are often more foolish than wise.

Dr. Jeffrey Schwartz wrote about the "ecosphere" and the "ethosphere," the latter of which he defined as a "shared realm of attitudes, behavior, and ethics." He made the point that our generation races against time to preserve our polar ice caps, glaciers, and endangered species yet tragically sits idly by as our even more important moral and spiritual resources are rapidly disappearing.[23]

Thankfully, social contagion goes both ways. The research of social scientists Nicholas Christakis and James Fowler showed that "staying healthy isn't just a matter of your genes and your diet, it seems. Good health is also a product, in part, of your sheer proximity to other healthy people."[24]

While it's nice to cite a scientist or two, this is not remotely a new idea. Two millennia ago, Paul quoted what was likely an already-ancient wisdom saying: "Bad company corrupts good character."[25]

In the East, in the Buddha's list of thirty-eight "highest blessings in life," the first is "to avoid the company of fools." The second? "To associate with the wise."[26]

Point being, you don't need to be a follower of Jesus to believe this; it simply *is.* We become like the relationships we cultivate and the culture to which we belong.

But especially for us as followers of Jesus, who want to stay true to Jesus's mental maps in a culture falling into a kind of moral orbital decay, this is a crucial insight.

The midcentury prophet/pastor A. W. Tozer once said, "The cause of all our human miseries is a radical moral dislocation."[27] He used the analogy of a sailor and his sextant; as a sailor once navigated his place in the world by the stars, we once navigated our place in the world by the true north of God and his vision of good and evil. But in the world, especially in the secular, (mostly) progressive West, we no longer get our bearings from God.[28] The old moral absolutes have been called into question. The new authority is, as we explored earlier, the authentic self, defined as desire and feelings. As a result, we've completely lost a sense of direction other than our own inner emotional rudders, which all too frequently lead us astray.

Yuval Noah Harari, the popular historian and leading atheist of our time described the crux of the problem quite well:

> In earlier times, it was God who could define goodness, righteousness and beauty. Today, those answers lie within us. Our feelings give meaning to our private lives but also [to] our social and political processes. Beauty is in the eye of the beholder, the customer is always right, the voter knows best, if it feels good do it, and think for yourself: these are some of the main humanist credos.[29]

As nice as many of these aphorisms sound, they don't really give us a North Star to live by.

The ever-insightful David Foster Wallace, as he watched many of his secular friends age, noted, "This is a generation that has an inheritance of absolutely nothing as far as meaningful moral values."[30]

But while this may seem like an especially acute problem in the late-modern West, it's as old as the garden.

Notice the writer John's trifold definition of the world we read a few minutes ago:

> Everything in the world—the lust of the flesh, the lust of the eyes, and the pride of life—comes not from the Father but from the world.[31]

His word choice of *lust* is telling. Lust is perverted love; it's desire turned in on itself.

John warned against three lusts of the world:

"The lust of the flesh"—clearly, he had in mind sexual temptation, the epitome of love deformed, where an image bearer we were made to give sacrificial love to becomes an object of desire we *take* pleasure from, even if it's consensual. But this includes more than just sexual desire; it's any desire of our flesh—for food, drink, instant gratification, control, domination over others, and on down the list.

"The lust of the eyes"—clearly, greed was in John's crosshairs, but also envy, jealousy, discontentment, and the "cancerous restlessness" of our age.[32]

Finally, "the pride of life"—the human bent in all of us to go our own way, rebel against authority, and think we know better than our forebears. "Who are you to tell me?" is the anthem of project self.

These are the three great temptations Jesus himself faced in the desert. The language is different, but the devil's offer was the same. Think about it . . .

"The lust of the flesh"—the temptation to turn stones into bread, to give in to his body's desire for gastrointestinal satisfaction and his flesh's craving for pleasure.

"The lust of the eyes"—the temptation to bow down and worship the devil and in turn receive "all the kingdoms of the world and their splendor";[33] to have it all, desire with no boundaries.

And "the pride of life"—the temptation to throw himself down from the high point of the temple and, in doing so, to receive the glory and awe of humankind; to turn his life into a spectacle, to become a celebrity.

You see the parallels?

These are the three paradigmatic temptations of the world. And they are very, *very* old.

New Testament scholars point out that both John and the gospel writer Matthew alluded to the garden temptation in Genesis 3. Remember the language?

> When the woman saw that the fruit of the tree was good for food and pleasing to the eye, and also desirable for gaining wisdom, she took some and ate it. She also gave some to her husband, who was with her, and he ate it.[34]

Can you see how the three line up?

> "The lust of the flesh" = "good for food" = stones to bread

> "The lust of the eyes" = "pleasing to the eye" = the kingdoms and their splendor

> "The pride of life" = "desirable for gaining wisdom" = the temple spectacle

They hearken back to the garden story because it's the archetypal *human* story. They warn us to keep our eyes open because, in the world, the lust of the flesh, the lust of the eyes, and the pride of life are not only tolerated—they are *celebrated.* You're more likely to find them in a parade than in a stinging rebuke.

Theo Hobson, in his book *Reinventing Liberal Christianity,* has this syllogism to sum up the three marks of modern moral revolution:

> What was universally condemned is now celebrated.
> What was universally celebrated is now condemned.
> Those who refuse to celebrate are condemned.[35]

Interesting: in his book, he's *pro* revolution. He's trying to articulate a working progressive morality. Today, these three marks are what most people, at least in my city, call progress. And in some areas, I agree. Especially in the progress we've made toward equal rights for women and minorities. But in other areas, what we call progress is what *Ephesians* calls "the ways of this world." Note: as *opposed to* the Way of Jesus.

Paul wrote about "the wisdom of this world." Meaning, what the world thinks is smart, clever, or even virtuous "is foolishness in God's sight."[36] This echoes Jesus's earlier words, "What people value highly is detestable in God's sight."[37]

Now, Jesus and Paul weren't saying that *everything* people value highly is detestable; many of the things people value, even in our secular society, are wonderful. Nor did they mean there's no wisdom to be found outside the Christian sphere. But they did seem to be saying that there are *some* things that many people value, promote, celebrate, and parade that God has a radically different take on. Jesus, in particular, seems to be operating off a different set of moral calculi.

We would be wise to slow down and honestly seek out Jesus's wisdom on the moral issues of our day—the wisdom that arises from his unparalleled intelligence, discerning insight, and loving intentions. But were we to do so, we would inevitably find at least a few examples of jarring difference between Jesus and *both* the Left and the Right's visions of human flourishing.

The late Dr. Larry Hurtado, historian of early Christianity, in his wildly celebrated book *Destroyer of the Gods,* told the story of how a tiny Jewish sect of Jesus followers overcame the bastion of paganism and won over the Roman Empire in only a few centuries. His thesis was that it wasn't the church's relevance or relatability to the culture but its difference and distinctness that made it compelling to so many. The church was marked by five distinctive features, all of which made it stand out against the backdrop of the empire:

1. The church was multiracial and multiethnic, with a high value for diversity, equity, and inclusion.

2. The church was spread across socioeconomic lines as well, and there was a high value for caring for the poor; those with extra were expected to share with those with less.

3. It was staunch in its active resistance to infanticide and abortion.

4. It was resolute in its vision of marriage and sexuality as between one man and one woman for life.

5. It was nonviolent, both on a personal level and a political level.

Now, if you plot those five features onto the map of modern American politics, the first two sound like liberal positions, as they are dealing with race and class; the second two sound like conservative positions; and the last one doesn't jibe with either.

No political party or intellectual ideology outside the church of Jesus—that I'm aware of—holds all five together.

Yet all five positions are basic, historic Christian orthodoxy. *Nothing* in the five is fringe or off center for a disciple of Jesus.

If you lean Left in your politics, you will likely feel an overwhelming pressure to prioritize the first two and ignore the rest; and if you lean Right, to prioritize the third and fourth. But if we capitulate to either side, we let the name of Jesus become chaplain to the world rather than stand as a compelling alternative to the status quo.

As far back as the 1970s, Lesslie Newbigin—a seminal thinker on post-Christianity from the UK—predicted (or maybe prophesied?) that as the West secularized, religion would not go away; it would redirect to politics. He warned of the rise of the political religions.

We're living in his vision; our nation is more divided than it's been since the Civil War. Right and Left are no longer two opposing sides that keep each other in balance; they are two rival religions locked in holy war with zealots fighting it out on-line and, increasingly, on the streets of cities like Portland or the halls of DC.

As David Brooks put it in a *New York Times* op-ed, "Over the last half century, we've turned politics from a practical way to solve common problems into a cultural arena to display re-sentments."[38]

People import a religious-like devotion and frenzy onto poli-tics. *The Economist* called it "America's new religious war."[39] And in this sweeping craze, so many people have been taken captive to ideology, which is a form of idolatry. A growing number of people are more loyal to their ideology or political party than they are to Jesus and his teachings. I feel this tug in my own heart, and we must resist it. It takes us into territory outside the kingdom of God and demagnetizes our moral compass, pointing us in a direction that does not lead to life and peace.

Followers of Jesus need to come back to the reality that bap-tism is their primary pledge of allegiance,[40] contempt has zero place in the heart of those who claim to apprentice under Jesus, and the litmus test of our faith is the degree to which we love our enemy.

My point is this: Jesus's vision of a flourishing life is often 180 degrees apart from the moral norms of our day.

I think of John Milton's famous line from *Paradise Lost,* "Evil, be thou my good."[41] Milton put that line into the mouth of the devil, but it's an echo of the prophet Isaiah's dirge from the eighth century BC: "Woe to those who call evil good and good evil."[42]

Woe is a fascinating word choice. It's not actually a word. It's just a vocal expression of emotion. *Ohh* is the positive version, the way we express surprise or delight when confronted with unexpected good. *Woe* is the negative version, the sigh of the heart. For years, I read this in a hellfire-and-brimstone tone of voice, the bullhorn turned up to eleven—"Woe to those who call evil good!" And, honestly, that could be right. But the more time I spend around the Father, the Son, and the Spirit and experience their love and compassion, the more I hear it in the tone of a weeping parent, heart rent open by the child's folly and the consequences it will inevitably reap.

I can only wonder at God's emotional response to the redefinition of good and evil in our society. A society where . . .

> Lust is redefined as love.
>
> Marriage, not as a covenant of lifelong fidelity but a contract for personal fulfillment.
>
> Divorce, as an act of courage and authenticity rather than the breaking of vows.
>
> The objectification of women's sexuality through porn, as female empowerment.
>
> Greed, as responsibility to shareholders.
>
> Gross injustice toward factory workers in the developing world, as globalism.
>
> Environmental degradation, as progress.
>
> The deracination of once-thriving local economies, as free-market capitalism.

Racism, as a past issue.

Marxism, as justice.

Honestly, I can't think of a more gut-wrenching example than abortion, where the greatest infanticide in human history is re-cast as "reproductive justice."[43] The sheer nerve to use the word *justice* to refer to the dehumanization (not a baby, a "fetus") and destruction of millions of children is inexplicable. The moral reasoning here is just staggering in its complete break from logic and wisdom and even science, and yet it has widespread social acceptance.

My favorite movie of 2019 was *The Peanut Butter Falcon* (what fun!). Reminiscent of Huck Finn, it follows the antics of a down-and-out orphan named Tyler (played by Shia LaBeouf) and Zack (played by Zack Gottsagen himself), a teenager with Down syndrome who escapes from a state home facility as they make a run down the river from the authorities. We watched it multiple times as a family, but on our first viewing, it struck me: I haven't seen an adult person with Down syn-drome in *years.*

Since the 1980s, when screening for Down syndrome be-came more common for pregnant women, most babies with Down syndrome have just been quietly aborted outside the public eye. We don't have reliable statistics, but most esti-mates say America aborts 67 percent of babies with a prena-tal diagnosis of Down syndrome, France 77 percent, and Scandinavian countries like Denmark around 98 percent. Due to widespread testing and abortion on demand, Iceland is close to 100 percent. One Icelandic doctor recently said, "We have basically eradicated, almost, Down syndrome from our society."[44] By *eradicated* he meant "We've killed all the babies with Down syndrome." He called it genetic counseling. You now have leading thinkers like Peter Singer—the moral philosopher and professor of bioethics at Princeton—making a case for killing babies with disabilities[45] and others calling for "after-birth abortion," saying parents should wait a few days after birth before they decide to terminate the baby's life or not.[46]

Yet the current iteration of infanticide is not only socially acceptable but also celebrated as a form of liberation and a human right. And here's the kicker: if you dare to insinuate that this thinking is rooted in convoluted logic or that it's scientifically or philosophically (much less scripturally) indefensible, you're instantly labeled regressive or worse—oppressive. If you try to assert that *all* babies, regardless of their intellectual capacity, are worthy of love and celebration, you are instantly labeled as antiprogress. Because in the new moral hierarchy, choice, desire, and sexuality free of responsibility are all more important than the life of the unborn. A baby is seen not as a human soul but as an unwanted responsibility to be terminated.

British journalist Antonia Senior, in her article for *The Times* "Yes, Abortion Is Killing. But It's the Lesser Evil" came to this conclusion after her experience of pregnancy and birth:

> My daughter was formed at conception. . . . Any other conclusion is a convenient lie that we on the pro-choice side of the debate tell ourselves to make us feel better about the action of taking a life. . . . Yes, abortion is killing. But it's the lesser evil.

She ends her case for abortion in the name of women's rights with this chilling line: "You must be prepared to kill."[47]

It's wild to think this is happening in an era renowned for equality and inclusion. I just wish that spirit of justice were extended to these beautiful image-of-God-bearing kids.

And yet "those who refuse to celebrate are condemned."

This is about the best example I can think of—emotionally charged as it is—of the twisted logic of the world. Of the way deceptive ideas appeal to our disordered desires and, tragically, often find a home in society at large.

What must God feel about all this?

I imagine, woe.

Woe not just at the moral dislocation of abortion but at the lost possibility of family. The beauty of *The Peanut Butter Falcon* is the way it prophetically and playfully calls into question the secular assumptions about not only people with Down syndrome but also unwanted children as a whole (personified by Shia LaBeouf's character). As an adoptive father, I'm acutely aware of the pain and complexity of generational poverty, teenage pregnancy, mental health, and substance abuse, yet I've also had a front-row seat to watch my lovely daughter flourish and thrive. And our family is all the richer with Sunday as a Comer.

Google the video of Shia LaBeouf and Zack Gottsagen at the Oscars. Zack was the first person with Down syndrome to ever hold that honor.[48] Tell me if it doesn't make your heart sing.

I know all this conversation can feel very heavy, and we'll get to the hope for the future soon. But for now, the point I'm making is that much of what we call culture (or the arts, entertainment, economics, politics, or the Western way of life),

Jesus and his followers called the world. And they saw the world as an enemy of the soul.

Now, let me be very clear: the *people* of the world are not our enemy; they are the object of Jesus's love. As Paul wrote, "Our struggle is not against flesh and blood,"[49] including people of differing religious, ethical, or political perspectives. "God so loved [the people of] the world that he gave his one and only Son";[50] our fight is not *against* them but *for* them.

Yet—and let's be honest here—the world is something we just don't talk about anymore in the Western church.

Why not?

Here's a theory: we've been colonized.

A remnant

I'm just old enough to remember a few old-school preachers railing against the evils of the world. That's OG, people.

Right out of high school, I spent a few years on staff at a church that was an eclectic mix of Oregon hippy meets Pentecostal revivalist. Think Birkenstocks, folk music, and a bit of hellfire and brimstone. Dating myself yet again, it's the late 1990s, when Abercrombie and Fitch spread preppy style to the masses via a then-less-common sexualized marketing campaign. One of my fellow youth pastors went on vacation and spent $500 on an entire Abercrombie wardrobe; his first Sunday back, the pastor literally gave a sermon railing against the moral depravity of Abercrombie and Fitch.

True story.

As ridiculous as that might sound to us today, we're so far on the other end of the spectrum that I wonder if we would be wise to search for the why behind a sermon on the danger of Abercrombie sweatshirts rather than just mock the idea.

In *The Screwtape Letters,* C. S. Lewis (who was anything but an angry fundamentalist) had the senior demon, Screwtape, write this to his apprentice demon, Wormwood. (If you're not familiar with his book, everything is flipped, so "the Enemy" is Jesus.)

> The Enemy's servants have been preaching about "the World" as one of the great standard temptations for two thousand years. . . . *But fortunately they have said very little about it for the last few decades.* In modern Christian writings, though I see much (indeed more than I like) about Mammon, I see few of the old warnings about Worldly Vanities, the Choice of Friends, and the Value of Time. All that, your patient would probably classify as "Puritanism"—and may I remark in passing that the value we have given to that word is one of the really solid triumphs of the last hundred years? By it we rescue annually thousands of humans from temperance, chastity, and sobriety of life.[1]

To clarify, by *rescue* Screwtape means ruin.

Oh, by the way, Lewis published this book in 1942. For upwards of a century, less and less has been said in the Western church about the danger of the world. As a result, many apprentices of Jesus are blind to the threat posed by the cultural milieu we live in—our networks of relationships, our entertainment choices, our economic operating systems, and our intake of news, information, and the Google-sourced wisdom by which we navigate life.

Yet the gravitational pull of the world is greater now than it's been in centuries.

The towering intellect that was Philip Rieff—sociologist of religion and one of the great minds of the twentieth century—broke down Western history into three phases: (1) first culture, (2) second culture, and (3) third culture. Or, for our purposes . . .

1. Pre-Christian culture
2. Christian(ized) culture
3. Post-Christian culture[2]

Pre-Christian culture was the Roman Empire before the gospel, Celtic Ireland before Saint Patrick, or the Norse tribes of Viking legend. It was a culture charged with spirituality and superstition but tribal and violent and cruel.

But as the gospel took root in each of these cultures, they were forever changed. They moved into a new Christianized mode. I say Christianized, not Christian, because there's no such thing as a Christian culture; what Rieff called the second culture was *always* a mix of Christian and pagan or, later, secular ideas, values, and practices. But there was a time in the West when the basic framework of Christian thought was accepted across the social spectrum.

Recently I was reading a historical novel set in Victorian England; in it was a daily schedule from a bank in central London. The day started at 8:30 with morning prayer. Everyone, from the president to the lobby teller, had to be there thirty minutes before opening to pray to Jesus. Can you imagine that happening at Wells Fargo or Chase today?

That time is past; we've now moved into a post-Christian culture. And Rieff's key insight is that post-Christian culture is not the same thing as pre-Christian culture. Nobody has gone back to worshipping Odin or sacrificing their firstborn child to the forest spirits.

Post-Christian culture is an attempt to move *beyond* the Christian vision while still retaining much of its scaffolding. It's a reaction *against* Christianity—the West's rebellious teenager moment. We're the stereotypical adolescent, kicking against our parents' authority and railing against all their flaws while still living in their house and eating all their food.

My friend Mark Sayers said it so well:

> Post-Christianity is not pre-Christianity; rather post-Christianity attempts to move beyond Christianity, whilst simultaneously feasting upon its fruit.
>
> Post-Christian culture attempts to retain the solace of faith, *whilst gutting it of the costs, commitments, and restraints that the gospel places upon the individual will.* Post-Christianity intuitively yearns for the justice and shalom of the kingdom, whilst defending the reign of the individual will.[3]

In Mark's language, we want the kingdom without the King.[4]

In fact, post-Christian culture is still very moral, painfully so at times. There is an unprecedented advocacy for human rights and equality, which I laud and link arms with. But note how its rise comes with cancel culture and online shaming, with the internet mob as judge, jury, and executioner, and majority opinion as the moral arbitrator. The West inherited from Christianity incredibly high standards for human rights, but without Christ's presence and power, it's increasingly devoid of the necessary resources to achieve its moral goals. The result is a culture that can rarely live up to its own standards. And without any means of atonement, as well as an increasing hostility toward the idea of forgiveness, once you sin (as defined by the new morality), you're a pariah.

As Nathan Finochio, teaching pastor and lead singer of Le Voyageur, put it in an Instagram story, "Everything is ethical. Every millennial is ethical. The next generation will be painfully ethical. The one after that will embrace an ethical totalitarianism. This is what happens when people don't have a purpose and their cultural framework is Christian. The end result isn't the playful return to paganism; it's the militant march to legalism."

Or here's Tim Keller, from an excellent essay on how the various visions of social justice align (or don't align) with biblical theology:

> The postmodern view sees all injustice as happening on a human level and so demonizes human beings rather than recognizing the evil forces—"the world, the flesh, and the devil"—at work through all human life, including your own. Adherents of this view also end up being utopian—they see themselves as saviors rather than recognizing that only a true, divine Savior will be able to finally bring in justice.[5]

But here's the insight I'm getting to: what Rieff and Sayers both pointed out is that if you're coming from a Christianized culture to a pre-Christian culture—say from nineteenth-century England to Africa or Aotearoa as a missionary—then the great danger is that you *colonize* the culture. That you dishonor and damage the indigenous culture rather than honor and serve it. We could fill a library with stories of how Western missionaries got this one horribly wrong. Much has been said about this in recent years, and the reckoning is long overdue.

But—and stay with me now—if you're coming from a Christianized culture to a *post*-Christian culture—say you're an immigrant coming from Nigeria to England, a refugee coming from Syria to America, or a follower of Jesus coming from Bridgetown Church to a city like Portland—the great danger is not that you colonize the culture but that you are *colonized by* the culture. I'm referring of course to Pope Francis's "ideological colonization," not the socioeconomic exploitation of former colonial rule.

You see this in a novel like *White Teeth* by Zadie Smith or a film like *The Big Sick* with Kumail Nanjiani, where immigration into Western cities divides multigenerational families. As the younger family members assimilate into Western life, secularism corrodes the previous culture's moral and religious norms. The parents weep; their apostate kids hook up on Tinder; all feel adrift.

As followers of Jesus, we are the epitome of a cognitive minority, whatever our ethnicity is. And the gravitational pull of the world is hard to resist. In part, because it's often so subtle that we miss it.

The political scientist Joseph Nye of Harvard coined the language of hard power versus soft power to talk about different types of sociopolitical influence. His ideas became the basis of strategies for both the Clinton and Obama White Houses. Basically, hard power is coercion by brute force. For a government, this would mean military violence or economic sanctions. It's North Korea's police state and labor camps or China's tanks in Tiananmen Square and "deradicalization" of the Uyghurs via internment camps.

Hard power eventually sparks a backlash. As Foucault said, "Where there is power, there is resistance."[6] Push people too hard, and they inevitably push back.

But soft power is a different beast. It's "the ability to shape the preferences of others" and "the ability to attract."[7] Hollywood is the epitome of soft power. It's done more to change Western mores around sex, divorce, adultery, vulgar speech, and consumerism than most anything, simply by making movies that are fun to watch. Another example is the advertising industry, which is an attempt to control our behavior, not through coercion, but consumerism, simply by appealing to our desires.

The cultural analyst Rod Dreher called the emerging culture of the West a "soft totalitarianism," and wrote, "This totalitarianism won't look like the USSR's. It's not establishing itself though 'hard' means like armed revolution, or enforcing itself with gulags. Rather, it exercises control, at least initially, in soft forms. This totalitarianism is therapeutic. It masks its hatred of dissenters from its utopian ideology in the guise of helping and healing."[8]

For followers of Jesus in the democratic West, soft power is the far greater threat. It's subtle, yes, but corrosive. It eats away at your heart, appealing to your flesh, until you wake up one day and realize, *Daaang, I've been colonized.*

Every follower of Jesus, in *every* culture, has to constantly ask the question, In what ways have I been assimilated into the host culture? Where have I drifted from my identity and inheritance?

The temptation for us in the West is less to atheism and more to a DIY faith that's a mix of the Way of Jesus, consumerism, secular sex ethics, and radical individualism.

All of which brings us full circle to Jesus as the revealer of reality. We're finally ready to revisit this book's central thesis and put all three pieces together.

Everything starts with *deceptive ideas,* or lies we believe (put our trust in and live by) about reality—mental maps that come from the devil, not Jesus, and lead to death, not life.

But deceptive ideas get as far as they do because they appeal to our *disordered desires,* or our flesh.

And then the world comes in to complete the three enemies' circular loop. Our disordered desires are *normalized in a sinful society,* which functions as a kind of echo chamber for the flesh. A self-validating feedback loop where we're all telling each other what we want (or what our flesh wants) to hear.

It's like when I ask my wife if she'd like me to get her some dessert. As any married couple knows, I'm not actually asking her if she wants dessert. I'm asking her to enable *me* to get dessert guilt free. If I can trick my brain into thinking I'm eating dessert as an act of love for T rather than a craving for sugar, then I can justify my behavior (eating strawberry ice cream on a Monday night). The world is this dynamic at a society-wide level.

So, critique over. On to business: How do we resist the enemy of the world?

Well, our working theory has been that *spiritual disciplines are spiritual warfare.* Or said another way: the practices of Jesus are how we fight the world, the flesh, and the devil.

Now we come to the most basic practice of all. So basic, I often think of it as less a practice and more as the milieu in which we practice the Way of Jesus: the church.

Whether you define church as a Sunday gathering around a stage, a much smaller community around a table, or, as I would recommend, a mixture of both, *we can't follow Jesus alone.* Jesus did not have a disciple (singular); he had disciples (plural). The call to follow Jesus was—and still is—a call to join his community of the Way. And by following Jesus *together,* not alone, we are able to (1) discern Jesus's truth from the devil's lies, (2) help one another override our flesh by the Spirit, and (3) form a robust community of deep relationships that functions as a counterculture to the world. In doing so, we're able to resist the gravitational pull of all three enemies of the soul.

But here's a crucial idea we need to recapture in our generation: *the church is a counterculture.* It is, as my friend Jon Tyson from New York City put it, a "beautiful resistance"[9] to the world and its vision of life of rebellion against God.

Or since the Western, secular world is currently more of an anti-culture than a culture, more about tearing down than building up, more about deconstruction than construction, then maybe it's better to say the church is a counter-anti-culture. In the language of Anabaptist thought, the church is an "alternative society."[10] A group on the margins of the host culture, living in an alternative but compelling and beautiful way. A prophetic signpost to kingdom life in a culture of death.

This is Jesus's vision of the church as a "town built on a hill" and his call to "let your light shine before others, that they may see your good deeds and glorify your Father in heaven."[11] It's Peter's call to be "exiles" in modern-day Babylon and to "live such good lives among the pagans that, though they accuse you of doing wrong, they may see your good deeds and glorify God on the day he visits us."[12] It's the church of Acts 2, Romans 13, and Revelation 3. It's the confessing church under the Third Reich, the house-church movement in Mao's China, the orthodox Christians in Syria today. Increasingly, it's you and me.

There's a tremendous opportunity in our cultural moment for the church to come back to her roots as a counter-anti-culture. And while I hope I don't end up crucified in fifty years in some kind of Huxleyan secular, progressive dystopia, I've already made peace with the obvious reality:

I will never fit in.

I will never be cool.

I will never be liked or well respected or admired by the culture.

And that's okay.

The word *church* itself (ἐκκλησία in Greek) means those who are "called out."[13] It's not a community of comfort but of calling.

But what we mean when we talk about the practice of church is not just regular attendance of Sunday services in a religious building. I'm all for Sundays, now more than ever. After dozens of hours of secular programming coming into our minds all week long, we *need* the anchor of Sunday gatherings to re-center our minds on truth and open our hearts back to God for healing and renewal. Every time I walk in on Sunday and see other followers of Jesus all around me, I remember: I'm not alone. I'm a part of the new humanity—the future rulers of the world, ordinary and flawed as we may be.

But while church is not *less* than Sunday services, it is *far more.* It must be more to survive the Western spiritual apocalypse. Church must become a thick web of interdependent relationships between resilient disciples of Jesus deeply loyal to the Way.

Whether your church is Anabaptist or Anglican; urban, suburban, or rural; a megachurch or a house church; in a theater, cathedral, or living room—we must move beyond Sunday services and a network of loose ties to become a robust counter-anti-culture not just against the world but for the world. Because we're not just against evil; we're *for good.* We're for love, joy, thriving marriages and families, children brought up in loving delight, adults moving off the egocentric operating system to become people of love, *true* freedom, justice for *all,* and unity in diversity.

Let me give you three salient examples that I see as especially key for our cultural moment. To become a church for our time, we must become . . .

1. A community of deep relational ties in a culture of individualism and isolation

In a world of "you do you" and "keep your laws off my body" and "don't tread on me," we must choose—of our own free will—to live under the authority of the New Testament charter, as best exemplified by the Sermon on the Mount, *and* we must do so together. In deep, vulnerable, interdependent relationships that stand in sharp relief to the superficiality and autonomy of our day. Think of the inviolable honesty and intimacy of Alcoholics Anonymous, not the posturing of the golf club; think of the confession of sin, not chitchat; think of the trust within relationships formed over decades, not the fast-burning social connections of like-attracts-like.

This could look like rigorous commitment to a small group, home community, or table fellowship.

It could look like starting a multigenerational kinship group and welcoming people into the experience of family.[14]

It could look like a regular meeting with two or three other followers of Jesus to unburden your heart, confess your failures, and extend one another love, compassion, and wisdom.

It could look like doing your annual budget with the members in your community and setting a threshold on what you spend without the community's approval. (In mine, it's $1,000. For anything over that, we go to the group.)

Or it could just look like a regular meal around a table with people you follow Jesus with and who hold you to that pursuit.

Next . . .

2. A community of holiness in a culture of hedonism

The word *holy* in Hebrew, קָדוֹשׁ (*qadosh*), literally means "set apart" or "unique" or "different." To live holy is to live differently from the world—different in how we spend our money and our time, in how we steward power (hint: we give it away), in how we engage (or refuse to engage) with systems of evil and injustice, in how we talk, in how we engage in social media (think, "quick to listen, slow to speak and slow to become angry"[15]), and of course in how we do marriage and family and sex and romance and dating and singleness and what Christians have long called chastity.

In a world where the body is "just meat," sex is "just play for grown-ups," and gender is "just plumbing," we must choose to "offer [our] bodies as a living sacrifice, holy and pleasing to God," and to "not conform to the pattern of this world, but be transformed."[16]

We must embrace what Pope John Paul II called a "theology of the body,"[17] where we treat our bodies not just as biological vehicles for pleasure, or what Melinda Selmys called a "wet machine, a tool that you can use and exchange for whatever purpose suits your fancy,"[18] but as "temples of the Holy Spirit"[19]—the locus point of our relationship to God himself. We must reject the neo-Gnosticism of our day and honor God with our bodies. "Then you will be able to test and approve what God's will is—his good, pleasing and perfect will."[20]

I know I've hit on sexuality a lot in this book; I've hesitated to do so, knowing how complex and tender it is for all of us and hating when people are used for ideological positions. But I keep coming back to sexuality because (1) I think it's the primary test of our generation's fidelity to the Way of Jesus or to the world's ideas and ideologies, (2) it's one of *the* most common New Testament examples of non-Christian behavior, and (3) sexuality has always been an arena where followers of Jesus stand in sharp contrast to the world. From the acropolis of Athens to the sidewalks of Brooklyn.

The Economist called the writer Nancy Pearcey "America's pre-eminent evangelical Protestant female intellectual."[21] In her stunning book *Love Thy Body,* Pearcey wrote, "What Christians do with their sexuality is one of the most important testimonies they give to the surrounding world."[22]

It's important; it matters deeply.

Remember, what we now think of as traditional values, like marriage between a man and a woman until death do us part, were *radical* when they were introduced by Jesus and the writers of Scripture. To Jews, in a patriarchal culture of easy divorce (for men, that is), Jesus's teachings on the equality of women (which we now take for granted) and the evil of divorce were stunning. To Greco-Romans, for whom pretty much any form of promiscuity you could possibly imagine was A-okay, Jesus's call to limit your sexuality to one partner (of the opposite sex) for life was mystifying. These ideas *became* traditional because so many people realized they led to human flourishing. But in our post-Christian, deconstructionist zeitgeist, they've become radical yet again.

We must discover "the joy of conviction in a culture of compromise."[23] Finally . . .

3. A community of order in a culture of chaos

When you read church history, you notice a trend: in times of chaos, the church moved toward order.

For example, in the fourth century, when the Roman Empire fell into disarray and the Mediterranean world began to come apart, followers of Jesus began to start monasteries. First, they were far from the cities in the deserts of North Africa or Syria; then with Saint Patrick and the Celtic Christians in Ireland, they *became* cities. But the monastery was always a rock of order in a sea of chaos.

Many very intelligent people have drawn parallels between the decline of the Roman Empire in the fourth and fifth centuries and Western culture today. I don't know if we're living through the end of Western civilization or just a few rough years (hopefully the latter); but I do think the impulse of the Spirit right now is toward what the ancients called *stabilitas,* a kind of stability, structure, and peace in our time of anxiety, freedom in excess, and transience.

The way followers of Jesus have long done this is by developing a Rule of Life. If that's unfamiliar language to you, don't think rules (plural), but rule (singular). The Latin word was *regula,* where we get the words *ruler* or *regulation.* It was the word for a straight piece of wood.[24] Many scholars think it was the Greek word used for a trellis in a vineyard.[25]

A Rule of Life is simply a schedule and set of practices and relational rhythms that organize our lives around Jesus's invitation to abide in the vine. It is how we live in alignment with our deepest desires for life with God in his kingdom.

Prior to Saint Benedict, in the sixth century, the moniker *rule of life* was used interchangeably with *way of life.* Your Rule is just the way you live and follow Jesus in community.

We've spent the last few years at our church in Portland developing a Rule of Life, specifically designed to create a "beautiful resistance" in the city we call home and the days we are living through. Next, we're working on starting a neo-monastic church order with other churches across the world.

You can do this too.

Get together with your community, and write your own Rule.[26] Heck, start your own miniorder. Do it with friends; I am. The point isn't to take over the world but to stand in our place in the world and to stay loyal to Jesus no matter what comes.

To end, let me run one last idea by you . . .

A few pages back, I said the church is a minority in the West—not an ethnic minority but a moral and spiritual one. But the kind of minority we're talking about here is what the historian Arnold Toynbee called a creative minority, which he described as a small but influential group of committed citizens who—motivated by love—bless the host culture, not from the center, but from the margins.[27]

Here's Jon Tyson's definition:

> A Christian community in a web of stubbornly loyal relationships, knotted together in a living network of persons, in a complex and challenging cultural setting, who are committed to practicing the way of Jesus together for the renewal of the world.[28]

Of course, the Jews are the example par excellence of a creative minority. Our spiritual ancestors have long thrived on the margins of society, not just as spiritual survivalists, but as some of the most influential writers, poets, scientists, philosophers, politicians, entrepreneurs, and businesspeople to ever live.

But as any Jew will tell you, exile isn't easy.

I was introduced to the idea of the church as a creative minority through Chief Rabbi Jonathan Sacks. In a lecture for *First Things,* Sacks said this:

> To become a creative minority, is not easy, because it involves maintaining strong links with the outside world while staying true to your faith, seeking not merely to keep the sacred flame burning but also to transform the larger society of which you are a part. This is, as Jews can testify, a demanding and risk-laden choice.[29]

What Sacks called a creative minority, the writers of the Bible called the remnant.

The *remnant* is the label used all through the library of Scripture for the small group inside Israel (and later the church) that was loyal to God when the majority of people were not—what Barna called resilient disciples.

It's Paul to the Romans: "At the present time there is a remnant chosen by grace."[30]

It's God's word to Elijah in 1 Kings 19v18: "I reserve seven thousand in Israel—all whose knees have not bowed down to Baal and whose mouths have not kissed him." Seven thousand here is a symbolic number, meaning "There are more than you think." We are not alone even when, like Elijah, we feel alone.

It's those with a courageous fidelity to orthodoxy in a time of widespread syncretism on both the Left and the Right.

Of course, Jesus is the ultimate example of the remnant. His was a minority report to the host culture—both a challenge to the status quo of compromise and complicity and a catalyst for healing and renewal from the margins to the wider society. And through his life and teaching and suffering and persecution and death and resurrection from the dead to stand at the right hand of the Father as Lord and King, he literally changed the course of history—not only for Israel but for the world.

The question before us today is this: *Will we join Jesus in the remnant?*

While many of us are new to the current level of hostility and opposition from secular culture toward followers of Jesus, the church has been in exile before. She thrived there. She didn't lose her identity; she discovered it. She didn't fall asleep; she came awake.

This could look like a thousand different things . . .

In Portland, it looks like Every Child Oregon, a faith-based nonprofit that is bringing together churches and foster children. A lethal combination of Western sexual ethics, the breakdown of the family, generational poverty, the opioid epidemic, and the war on drugs has left thousands of little kids without a home or family. Families across our church are meeting this crisis, not with an angry tweet at a politician, but with quiet, humble love, welcoming children into their homes for as long as it takes the families to heal. Around twelve hundred of the fifteen hundred foster families in my city are Christians recruited from local churches.

On a similar note, a crew of over seventy people in our church put on a monthly Foster Parents' Night Out, where they throw a killer party for the kids and give the foster parents a night to go out on the town or just catch their breath.

My friends Pete and Gav in London have started Ark, a co-working space for creatives and entrepreneurs in the Kings Cross neighborhood; they are creating community in a hyper-transient city and giving a hefty portion of the proceeds to local charities.

My friends at Praxis in New York City have started a business accelerator for "redemptive entrepreneurship,"[31] giving a new generation of Christians a vision for business on the bleeding edge of the kingdom.

I could go on for *pages* with examples of intelligent, humble, ardent followers of Jesus who are living as a creative minority right in the middle of some of the most secular cities in the world.

They awaken my heart to dream again, to pivot from anxiety to possibility.

They show me the way of fidelity to Jesus in digital Babylon.

They give me vision of what's possible in exile.

Honestly, I have more hope now than I have in years. The post-Christian West is failing. The challenges of 2020 just about did us in. The anxiety and anger are still off the charts. The polarization in my country is deep and raw. The gap between the haves and the have-nots is gut wrenching, and it's getting worse, not better. The promised utopia is turning into something more akin to *Brave New World* or *The Hunger Games* than to Jesus's vision of the kingdom of God. It's not delivering on its promise of the kingdom without the King. And with the rising specter of China, the spread of the internet, and the growing diversity of Western nations, we're entering a true globalism, which is now disrupting the disrupter that is post-Christianity. As Western cities continue to diversify through immigration, the label "post-Christian" is increasingly inaccurate.

What if this isn't a threat to fear but a chance for something new to be born?

What if there's a conspiracy of God in all of this?

Anything could happen next.

The idols of ideology are failing. What if in the aftermath people were to turn back to the living God?

People can't live without meaning, purpose, and community. The secular world can't seem to offer that; Jesus can and does. What if the church were to come back to her call as a community radiant with the love of God?

Nobody knows where the West will go in the years to come. The smartest people can only guess.

But this could be our finest hour.

We could be days away from a sweeping renewal across the Western church. It's happened before, at the moment it was least likely.

It could happen again.

So, I'll wake up tomorrow and go about my life in Portland. I'll carry the city's joy and pain in the inner recesses of my heart. I'll raise my children here. I'll pay my taxes, go grocery shopping, and have my neighbors over for dinner. I'll volunteer with my kids to serve the houseless. I'll make my small, nondramatic contribution to the peace and prosperity of the city I call home.

And I'll fight the three enemies that prowl the city's streets.

I'll stand with the beautiful resistance.

I'll live, and if I must, I'll die—in hope.

But I won't do it alone.

Part 3 step sheet

Definitions:

- **The world**—a system of ideas, values, morals, practices, and social norms that are integrated into the mainstream and institutionalized in a culture corrupted by the twin sins of rebellion against God and the redefinition of good and evil
- **Pre-Christian culture**—a culture of gods and goddesses
- **Christianized culture**—a cultural moment where the societal norms push you toward a vision that is a mix of Jesus and pagan or secular ideas
- **Post-Christian culture**—a reaction against Christianized culture that attempts to hold on to some core elements of Jesus's vision, while rejecting others, and attempts to bring about the kingdom of God without the King. Utopian trending dystopian.
- **Hard power**—coercive force, such as legal or military force
- **Soft power**—the attempt to control or influence behavior by appealing to people's sensual desires
- **Creative minority**—a small group operating on the margins of society who live together in a thick web of relationships and, through their lives and work, bless the host culture with healing and renewal

Key texts to meditate on: John 17 and 1 John 2v15–17

Working theory of the devil's strategy: deceitful ideas that play to disordered desires that are normalized in a sinful society

Key practice for fighting the world: gathering with your church

In summary: The devil's deceptive ideas get as far as they do because they appeal to our flesh's animal cravings. But these in turn find a home in our bodies through the echo chamber of the world, which allows us to assuage any guilt or shame and live as we please. As a result, evil is often labeled good, and good, evil; and the soul and society devolve into a reign of anarchy via the loss of a moral and spiritual true north. In such an exilic moment, the church as a counter-anti-culture has the potential to not only survive but also flourish as a creative minority, loving the host culture from the margins.

Epilogue: Self-denial in an age of self-fulfillment

Before Gandhi.

Before Dr. King.

Before Madiba.

There was Jesus of Nazareth.

Who—*two millennia ago*—said things like,

> Love your enemies.[1]

> Pray for those who mistreat you.[2]

> Those who live by the sword die by the sword.[3]

The irony of writing about fighting our enemies in a book based on the life and teachings of a rabbi who taught us to *love* our enemies is not lost on me.

And yet Jesus was a warrior, as the ancient prophecies predicted he would be. He was the Messiah, the long-awaited king. Unlike political leaders today, in the ancient world, a king was synonymous with a warrior at the head of an army—think of King David or Julius Caesar. In the US, we call the president the commander in chief but would never let him within miles of an actual battle. But in Jesus's time, the king was *expected* to be the one to lead the charge, literally.

It comes as no surprise that Jesus's most ardent followers just assumed he would take up the sword, rally an army, and kick off a war with Rome. He was the king, and that's what kings did: they used violence to seize political power and take what they wanted.

Instead, a central theme in Jesus's teaching was nonviolence and enemy love—an idea that's still far too radical for many people in our modern, enlightened world, including many Christians, on both the Left and Right. And instead of shedding blood, he went to the cross to *give* his own blood, for the very people jeering him from the crowd.

In doing so, Jesus radically redefined both the nature of our war and the means by which we fight it.

For Jesus, our fight isn't against Rome, the "barbarians" to the north, or even the corrupt Jewish aristocracy that supported his torture and death in the name of religion, any more than our fight today is against Russia, ISIS, or the "other" political party. Rather, it's against the triumvirate of the world, the flesh, and the devil. And our victory isn't won by swords, spears, or predator drone strikes but with truth embodied in self-sacrificial love.

This is why it is absolutely crucial for us to recapture the idea of spiritual war; because as long as we deny the reality of demonic evil, we will demonize *people*—the very people we are called to love and serve. Instead of fighting Satan, we will turn people or even entire groups of people into Satan. As a result, instead of fighting back the hate and violence and darkness of the three enemies, we will just add even *more* hate and violence and darkness to a culture in desperate need of healing.

So, it comes as no surprise that Jesus calls on his apprentices, not to pick up a sword and kill but to follow his example and die.

Yes, die.

Listen to Jesus's most common invitation:

> Whoever wants to be my disciple must deny themselves and take up their cross and follow me.[4]

Jesus put one evocative symbol at the center of apprenticeship to him—not a sword but a cross. The cross was a symbol of death. Jesus's call to follow him was a call to die—if not literally in body, then at least figuratively in self-denial. As Dietrich Bonhoeffer once said, "When Christ calls a man, he bids him come and die."[5]

Bonhoeffer was later martyred by the Gestapo.

So for him, it was literal.

But this call to self-denial sounds alien to our modern ears, right? The barrage of cultural messaging we receive constantly through the digital IV of our myriad devices says the exact opposite—everything is about *self-fulfillment,* not self-denial. The idea of saying no to your self to say yes to Jesus sounds, well, crazy. Many of us just can't fathom a vision of the good life that doesn't involve our getting what we want.

So what exactly is Jesus calling us to deny?

The best way I can frame it is to say this: we're to deny our *self,* not ourselves.

The self in Jesus's call isn't our inner essence or personality type or Enneagram number. Under our rubric of the world, the flesh, and the devil, the self is akin to our flesh, the axis point of the three enemies' assault on our souls. It's where the devil's deceptive ideas on one side and a sinful society's normalized behaviors on the other meet and direct their attack against the fulcrum point of our disordered desires.

We get a little hint from Paul's famous declaration:

> I have been crucified with Christ and I no longer
> live, but Christ lives in me.[6]

Clearly, Paul was still breathing. So, what part of Paul was crucified? The answer comes in a later paragraph:

> Those who belong to Christ Jesus have crucified
> *the flesh* with its passions and desires.[7]

Paul had died to his flesh and, in doing so, had come alive.

A deep happiness and calm spirit come over those who have died to self. Their desires have been put to death or, at least, put in their proper place below God. As a result, they have been set free from the domination of want.

For Jesus, the cross is the *entry* point into the life "to the full" of the kingdom. It is how we step into life—we die.

But take note, the reciprocal is also true: the refusal to deny self is the entry point of the devil into our own minikingdoms. When we reject the cross, we open our souls to enemy infiltration.

This is why Jesus places the cross squarely in front of his invitation to apprentice under him. It's also why we find this invitation to "come and die" in all four Gospels. It's repeated over and over again. It's not an ancillary idea but *central* to Jesus's Way. John Calvin once used the phrase *self-denial* to summarize the entire spiritual journey.[8]

To say yes to Jesus's invitation is to say no to a thousand other things. As the monks used to say, "Every choice is a renunciation."[9] To say yes to Jesus is to say no to living by my own definition of good and evil, to spending my time and money however I want, to the hyperindividualism, antiauthoritarianism, and full-tilt hedonistic pursuit of our day. It's a thousand tiny deaths that all lead up to one massive life. It's not a futile grasping for control, but the freedom of yielding to Love. It's saying to Jesus, *Whatever, wherever, whenever, I'm yours.*

We look back on the Crusades as a low point in the history of the church (though historians tell a much more complex story than that of popular imagination). Legend has it that before going into battle, the Knights Templar were baptized, but they would hold their swords above their heads as they went under the water. As if to say, "Jesus, you can have all of me except this. Not my violence. Not my quest for glory."

Legend or history, the imagery is piercing. *We all do this.* We might not hold up a sword; for us it could be a debit card, a relationship, a sexual ethic, a wound, an entertainment habit, a political or even a theological position. It could be anything. But how often do we say, if not in word, then by our actions, *Not this, Jesus. Not this.*

Many followers of Jesus don't yet realize that the cross isn't just something Jesus did *for us;* it's also something we do *with him.* Even in church traditions with a high value for the cross, their interpretation of Jesus's death on the cross is often more *transactional* than *transformational.* I'm not remotely questioning the doctrine of substitutionary atonement: that Jesus died for our sins is central to the gospel. But think about it: *we still die.* Jesus didn't die so we don't have to; he died to teach us *how* to die—how to follow him through death and into life.

Now, I'm guessing that for many of you, this sounds like a tough sell (not to mention a really depressing way to end a book). Your inner skeptic might be thinking, *Why would I do that?*

Jesus, ever the master teacher, anticipates your question and goes on to tell you why:

> Whoever wants to save their life will lose it, but
> whoever loses their life for me and for the gospel
> will save it.[10]

The word *life* here can also be translated "soul."[11] Jesus is warning us about the gravity of our decision to practice self-denial or pursue self-fulfillment, and about the trajectory of that decision for our souls.

Notice, this is a statement, not a command. You *will* lose or save it. Not that you *could* lose or save it. Jesus frequently ended his teachings not with a command but simply with a statement about reality. He has access to the moral knowledge we need to thrive. Whether or not we trust Jesus's mental maps over our own or those of our culture is left up to us to decide.

For Jesus, you have two choices:

Option A: *you deny Jesus and follow your self.* Put another way, you put desire on the throne of your life. You make getting what you want the ultimate authority and driving motivation for your life.

Or option B: *you deny your self and follow Jesus.* Meaning, you crucify the desires of your flesh and tap into your deeper desires for God himself.

The results?

Losing your life.

Or saving it.

According to Jesus, those are your options.

Now, either-or thinking is anathema in our postmodern age. We hate black-or-white approaches; we prefer gray. Yet

Jesus, subversive as ever, doesn't let us get away with a lazy opt out. His binary choices are designed to shock listeners out of apathy and prompt us to make a decision.

To follow him or not.

Circling back to Bonhoeffer, his book *The Cost of Discipleship* was one of the great books of the twentieth century. But to push just a little on his language, yes, we need to weigh the cost of discipleship. But we also have to calculate the cost of *nondiscipleship.*

Meaning, it's true it will cost us to follow Jesus, *but it will cost us even more to not follow him.*

Jesus is just trying to get you to run a simple cost-benefit analysis: your soul versus your self.

Are you really willing to trade long-term happiness for short-term pleasure?

To trade mental maps to reality for autonomy from authority?

Love for a fleeting sexual encounter?

The intimacy and trust of a marriage for the matchstick thrill of an affair?

Contentment with what you have for the feeling of buying a shiny new thing?

The cumulative, compound interest of blessing and reward accrued over decades of fidelity to Jesus and his Way for the easy out of quitting when you hit a rough patch?

Do the math.

How much is your soul worth to you?

We've come back full circle to the need for trust.

When Jesus laid out the good news of God's kingdom availability to all, he ended by calling people to "repent and believe the good news!"[12]

Or to paraphrase: "Rethink everything you think you know about what will lead you to the good life, and put your trust in me."

To "believe the good news" is to trust, to commit to, to live in unswerving fidelity to Jesus. To enter his kingdom, we have to trust that Jesus's mental maps are the accurate and true guide to the life we seek.

Why else would the devil target our trust in God above all? From Eve in the garden to you and me today, his fiercest assault is upon our confidence in Jesus. Because without a deep trust in Jesus, we will never take up our cross, which means we will never enter the kingdom.

Why is it we resist crucifying our desires? Why this gut-level, inner resistance to Jesus's call? It's not necessarily because we're evil or even narcissistic; it's because we're scared. We're scared of losing something we value, something we think (or feel) we need to live a happy life. Until we come to the place where we genuinely trust Jesus's mental maps over our own intuition or feelings, and trust that God is a loving and wise Father with good intentions for our joy, death to self will remain an unwinnable war of attrition between the torn factions of our fragmented souls.

To win, we must release our hearts to Jesus in radical surrender.

And to clarify one last time, Jesus is not calling you to live by faith. You're already doing that. We *all* live by faith; we all trust someone or something to lead us to the life we ache for, whether our faith is in a politician or professor or scientist or subculture or ideology or just our own inner compass of desire. The question isn't "Do you live by faith?" but "Who or what do you put your faith *in*?" Jesus is calling you to live by faith *in him*.

Even if it means we must die.

Three weeks before Hitler committed suicide and the Third Reich crumbled, Bonhoeffer was stripped naked and executed in the woods outside his prison camp. We have one record of his death, from his prison guard, who was utterly captivated by Bonhoeffer's sacrifice. Listen to the account of the morning he was sent to transport Bonhoeffer to the firing squad:

> Through the half-open door of a room in one of the huts I saw Pastor Bonhoeffer, still in his prison clothes, kneeling in fervent prayer to the Lord his God. The devotion and evident conviction of being heard that I saw in the prayer of this intensely captivating man, moved me to the depths.[13]

This towering life is *still* moving people not just to live by faith, but to die in faith.

To end, one last deep breath . . .

Pastor/writer Eugene Peterson said, "Honestly written and courageously presented words reveal reality and expose our selfish attempts to violate beauty, manipulate goodness and dominate people, all the while defying God. . . . Honest writing shows us how badly we are living and how good life is."[14]

In this book, I've done my very best to expose "how badly we are living and how good life is." But I'm not a pundit; I'm a pastor, a companion and guide for the spiritual journey, for the soul's return to its home in God. My job is "admonishing and teaching everyone with all wisdom, so that we may present everyone fully mature in Christ."[15]

I've been following Jesus for more than three decades now, and even with the rising cultural hostility of recent years, I can tell you in complete honesty: life is hard, but it's so good. With each passing year, with each tiny death to self, with each small victory over the three enemies, I feel more and more of the increasing joy of the Trinity's inner life. I feel at peace, happy, and more alive than I ever thought possible.

Yet it's not me you need to trust; it's Jesus.

Remember Ignatius's definition of sin? "Unwillingness to trust that what God wants for me is only my deepest happiness."

Until we come to a place of deep trust that what God wants for us is only our deepest happiness and that what we actually want—the desire beneath all the other desires—is God himself, we will fight to control our lives. We will continue to think that we know better than God what will lead to our happiness. And we will chase the wind and reap the whirlwind.

But friends, here's the good news, *and it really is the best of news:* we already have *all* we need to live a happy, free, beautiful life—access to life with the Father, through Jesus, by the Spirit.

That, honestly, is it.

Everything else is bonus.

So, how do we fight the war for our soul in a secular age that claims we don't even have one? How do we defeat the three enemies—the world, the flesh, and the devil?

We die.

And then . . .

We live.

I am coming soon. Hold on to what
you have, so that no one will take your
crown. The one who is victorious I will
make a pillar in the temple of my God.
Never again will they leave it. I will write
on them the name of my God and the name
of the city of my God, the new Jerusalem,
which is coming down out of heaven from
my God; and I will also write on them my
new name. Whoever has ears, let them hear
what the Spirit says to the churches.

—Jesus, in Revelation 3v11–13

Appendix:
A monastic handbook
for combating demons

Here's a short guide to make your own monastic handbook for combating demons. Evagrius did it; you can too. His handbook had five hundred entries; yours can have five. Just start where you are.

The goal is to follow Jesus's example in Matthew 4. These entries will help you retrain your mind to turn from the enemy's obsessive thoughts rooted in lies to the truth of Scripture. When the lies come, don't open a dialogue with them. Just "change the channel" to truth. Resist by redirection. Evagrius and the ancients called this *antirrhesis,* or "countertalking."

In box 1, write out an obsessive thought that keeps coming to mind, a lie that you just can't shake, a toxic feeling (like shame or worry), or a sensation in your body (like tightness of chest, shallow breathing, or a sense of dread). Thoughts, emotions, and sensations are separate only when they are written about as different chapters in a book. In your body, they overlap, collide, and mix together like a chemical reaction.

> **What's the thought, feeling, and/or sensation?**
>
> *I'm worried about losing my job and not being able to make my car payment.*

In box 2, see if you can articulate the lie *behind* the thought, feeling, or sensation. If you're feeling scared and your chest is tight, it could be a lie like *I'm not safe if people criticize me.* If so, what's the attachment under the anxiety? Could it be an attachment to living a suffering-free life where all people speak well of you? Safety isn't bad, but the need to be constantly safe can become a prison that holds us in fear and out of love.

> **What's the lie beneath the thought, feeling, and/or sensation that reveals your attachment?**
>
> *My safety and security are in my job, and owning newer, nicer things will make me happy.*

In box 3, write out a scripture or word from the Spirit that *counters* the lie. Then turn your mind to this truth whenever the lie reappears in your mind stream. It will, many times. Don't be discouraged. It happens to all of us, constantly. Resist.

What's the truth?

*"Keep your lives free from the love of money and
be content with what you have, because God has
said, 'Never will I leave you; never will I forsake you.'"
(Hebrews 13v5)*

Okay, dear reader, it's time to start building your own monastic handbook for combating lies:

What's the thought, feeling, and/or sensation?

What's the lie beneath the thought, feeling, and/or sensation that reveals your attachment?

What's the truth?

Thank yous

Behind every book you've ever read is an army of kind, intelligent souls who make an author like me sound *way* smarter and better than he really is. This was by far the most difficult project I've ever done, and I did not do it alone. So, in the overflow of gratitude from my heart, let me name names.

Thank you to my literary agent, Mike Salisbury, and the entire cast at Yates & Yates; this *never* would have happened without your advocacy. Mike, you are my Yoda. I so appreciate how you've gone far beyond what's expected.

Thank you to the array of beautiful people at WaterBrook and Penguin Random House. To my editor, Andrew Stoddard, can we please start the next project immediately? I *love* working with you—your wisdom, theological acumen, and congeniality are such a joy. Laura Wright and Tracey Moore, you literally saved me weeks of work. Copyeditors are the unsung heroes of all book lovers. I promise one day I will actually know what page number a quote is from. Tina Constable, I finally get to work with a New Yorker! Your belief in this book was the beginning of it all. Laura Barker, thank you for your patience with all the delays. Douglas Mann—so many phone calls, what a patient man you are. Lisa Beech, professional podcast scheduler, well done. And so many more I never even get to meet. Thank you all.

Thank you to Ryan Wesley Peterson for endless revisions on design. Dude, this one took forever, but I love it.

Thank you to my Searock Fraternity brothers; I'm not sure I'd still be doing any of this without your ongoing presence in my life. Your "courageous fidelity to orthodoxy," your inner flame of love for God, your cultural intelligence, your prophetic words over my life, and above all your friendship have made it possible to go the distance.

Here in Portland, thank you to Bridgetown Church. The last eighteen years have been chock-full of pinch-myself moments; yes, we've had our hard moments too, but we're still together. This book was borne out of our experience of practicing the Way of Jesus, together, in this city. I love you so much. Thank you to the elders for the gift of time to write, and especially to Gerald Griffen and Bethany Allan for our many years of partnership. Working with you all has been one of the great joys of my life.

Thank you to all those who have played the role of mentor to me. I am in large part what you have sown into me: Chris and

Meryl Weinand, Dr. Jim Lundy, John Ortberg, Jim McNeish, and so many more.

Thank you to my family and community: all the Comer clan, especially my mom and dad for a lifetime of support, and to you, Beks, for basically working part time as a second editor on all my projects; you're the smartest Comer/Opperman/Kenn by far! And to all those who sit around our table on Sabbath evenings and during the week—Yinka, Christian, Jay, Pam, Hannah, Hooks, Normans—you see us as we actually are and still love us; with you we feel safe and warm.

Thank you to Dave Lomas for being the kind of friend I can bare my soul to one moment and laugh the next as you educate me in all things internet culture. You're a friend for the whole soul.

Last, thank you to my family: T, twenty years; I love you. I don't think I would have had the courage to release this book without your strength as a daily anchor. Jude, Moses, and Sunday, I wrote much of this book for you. You aren't the future of the church; you *are* the church. My greatest dream in all of life is to see you follow Jesus no matter what comes. I'm for you all the way.

Notes

The war on lies

1. "'The War of the Worlds' Radio Script from October 30, 1938," Wellesnet, October 9, 2013, www.wellesnet.com/the-war-of-the-worlds-radio-script. You can listen to a recording on YouTube at www.youtube.com/watch?v=nUsq3fLobxw.

2. "'The War of the Worlds' Radio Script from October 30, 1938."

3. Dawn Mitchell, "Hoosiers Swept Up in Martian Invasion of 1938," *IndyStar,* October 30, 2019, www.indystar.com/story/news/history/retroindy/2015/10/28/hoosiers-swept-up-martian-invasion-1938/74755844.

4. Hey, that last one could still be true.

5. A. Brad Schwartz, "The Infamous 'War of the Worlds' Radio Broadcast Was a Magnificent Fluke," *Smithsonian Magazine,* May 6, 2015, www.smithsonianmag.com/history/

infamous-war-worlds-radio
-broadcast-was-magnificent
-fluke-180955180. In 1877, the
Italian astronomer Giovanni Schiaparelli drew a detailed map of
the Martian surface and marked
a series of dark lines as *canali,*
Italian for "channels." Schiaparelli
was agnostic as to the nature of
the lines, but his work was translated into English as "canals,"
making it sound like they were
built by an intelligence of some
kind. Later astronomers specu-
lated Mars was home to a dying
race whose inhabitants built
massive canals to siphon water
from the polar ice caps to survive. Few scientists took this
theory seriously, but still it spread
in the public imagination. Translation: a lot of people seemed to
think there were aliens on Mars,
and some worried they were
coming for our home.

6. "The Great New England Hurricane of 1938," National
Weather Service, September 21,
2020, www.weather.gov/okx/
1938HurricaneHome.

7. Schwartz, "The Infamous 'War
of the Worlds' Radio Broadcast
Was a Magnificent Fluke." It's re-

ally interesting to see the drift of
sci-fi from its origins—as social
and political commentary written
by critics and intellectuals (such
as H. G. Wells, George Orwell,
Aldous Huxley, Isaac Asimov,
C. S. Lewis, and Ursula Le Guin)
to a genre more known for pop-
corn and nerd jokes than literary
criticism.

8. His announcer began the
broadcast by saying, "The Co-
lumbia Broadcasting System
and its affiliated stations present
Orson Welles and the Mercury
Theatre on the Air in The War of
the Worlds by H. G. Wells."
" 'The War of the Worlds' Radio
Script from October 30, 1938."

9. Christopher Klein, "How 'The
War of the Worlds' Radio Broadcast Created a National Panic,"
History, October 28, 2019, www
.history.com/news/inside-the
-war-of-the-worlds-broadcast.

10. A. Brad Schwartz, *Broad-
cast Hysteria: Orson Welles's
War of the Worlds and the Art of
Fake News* (New York: Hill and
Wang, 2015), 7.

11. "*New York Daily News* Front
Page October 31, 1938 Headline," Getty Images, www

.gettyimages.com/detail/news
-photo/daily-news-front-page
-october-31-1938-headline-fake
-radio-news-photo/97298590.
12. Richard J. Hand, *Terror on
the Air!: Horror Radio in America,
1931–1952* (Jefferson, NC:
McFarland, 2006), 7.

A manifesto for exile

1. We find this language as far
back as Thomas Aquinas's towering work *Summa Theologica*
in 1265, which scholars still
point to as one of the most important theological works of all
time. It shows up again in the
Council of Trent in 1543, a key
moment in the Protestant Reformation. From there, it enters
the English-speaking world
through *The Book of Common
Prayer* in 1549: "From all the
deceytes of the worlde, the
fleshe, and the deuill: God lorde
deliuer us."
2. For example, Ephesians 2v1–3.
3. Ephesians 6v10–20, 2 Timothy 2v4, etc.
4. 1 Timothy 6v12.
5. Ephesians 6v11.
6. 1 Timothy 1v18.

7. Ephesians 6v12.
8. 2 Corinthians 10v4.
9. *Pacifist* isn't really a great
word, as it's emotionally loaded
and has various connotations.
But most followers of Jesus prior
to Constantine and Augustine
understood killing to be incompatible with following Jesus's
teachings. For an excellent case
for nonviolence, read the stimulating book *Fight* by my friend
Preston Sprinkle.
10. John Mark Comer, "Fighting
the World, the Flesh, and the
Devil: The Truth About Lies: Part
2," Bridgetown Church, October
7, 2018, https://bridgetown
.church/teaching/fighting-the
-world-the-flesh-the-devil/the
-truth-about-lies-part-2.
11. Well, that's the common
quotation. What he *actually* said
was "If you know the enemy and
know yourself, you need not fear
the result of a hundred battles. If
you know yourself but not the
enemy, for every victory gained
you will also suffer a defeat." Sun
Tzu, "3. Attack by Stratagem,"
The Art of War, https://
suntzusaid.com/book/3/18.
12. This is my adaptation of Jon

Tyson's teaching from his *Creative Minority* sermon series. It's excellent! Read or watch: Jon Tyson and Heather Grizzle, *A Creative Minority: Influencing Culture through Redemptive Participation* (self-pub., 2016); Jon Tyson, "A Creative Minority Discussion Guides," sermon series, January–February 2021, www.church.nyc/a-creative-minority?rq=a%20creative%20minority.

13. "In U.S., Decline of Christianity Continues at Rapid Pace," Pew Research Center, October 17, 2019, www.pewforum.org/2019/10/17/in-u-s-decline-of-christianity-continues-atrapid-pace.

14. "What Do Young Adults Really Mean When They Say They Are Christians?," Barna Group, December 11, 2019, www.barna.com/research/resilient-discipleship.

15. Hebrews 12v4.

16. Lee Beach, *The Church in Exile: Living in Hope After Christendom* (Downers Grove, IL: InterVarsity, 2015), 21. See also Walter Brueggemann, *Cadences of Home: Preaching Among Exiles* (Louisville: Westminster John Knox, 1997), 115.

17. Wendy Everett and Peter Wagstaff, "Introduction," in *Cultures of Exile: Images of Displacement* (Oxford: Berghahn, 2004), x.

18. Paul Tabori, *The Anatomy of Exile: A Semantic and Historical Study* (London: Harrap, 1972), 32.

19. "Digital Babylon: Our Accelerated, Complex Culture," Barna Group, October 23, 2019, www.barna.com/research/digital-babylon.

20. Judy Siegel-Itzkovich, "Stars of Hollywood's Golden Era Were Paid to Promote Smoking," *Jerusalem Post,* September 24, 2008, www.jpost.com/health-and-sci-tech/health/stars-of-hollywoods-golden-era-were-paid-to-promote-smoking.

21. C. S. Lewis, *Surprised by Joy: The Shape of My Early Life* (New York: Harcourt Brace, 1955), 200–201.

22. Evan Andrews, "8 Reasons It Wasn't Easy Being Spartan," History, September 1, 2018, www.history.com/news/8-reasons-it-wasnt-easy-being-spartan. All other work was done by noncitizens.

23. M. E. Bradford, "Faulkner, James Baldwin, and the South," *The Georgia Review* 20, no. 4 (Winter 1966): 435, www.jstor.org/stable/41396308?seq=1.

He said this to a crowd of students in Nagano, Japan, at a 1955 literary event, commenting on the wave of creative output in Japanese literature and poetry after the disasters of Nagasaki and Hiroshima.

The truth about lies

1. For example, he was able to articulate preverbal thought, how emotions are made, mindsight, and more.

2. For an easy-to-read, excellent summary of the Desert Fathers and Mothers' thought world, I'd recommend *A Beginner's Introduction to the Philokalia* by Anthony M. Coniaris.

3. *Encyclopaedia Britannica Online,* s.v. "seven deadly sins," www.britannica.com/topic/seven-deadly-sins. The theologians conflated pride and vainglory because of their similarity.

4. Evagrius of Pontus, *Talking Back: A Monastic Handbook for Combating Demons,* trans. David Brakke (Collegeville, MN: Liturgical Press, 2009), www.amazon.com/Talking-Back-Monastic-Combating-Cistercian/dp/0879073292.

5. A little nod here to my friend Tim Chaddick's book *The Truth About Lies: The Unlikely Role of Temptation in Who You Will Become* (Colorado Springs: David C Cook, 2015).

6. This line and the story I'm about to summarize are found in John 8v31–47.

7. John 8v44.

8. Blue Letter Bible, s.v. *"diabolos,"* www.blueletterbible.org/lang/lexicon/lexicon.cfm?Strongs=G1228&t=KJV.

9. Many of us think of Satan as a proper name, but in Hebrew, it has the article in front of it, *ha satan,* or "the satan." It carries the same meaning as *diabolos* in Greek—"the accuser." "Job 1," *The Pulpit Commentary,* Bible Hub, 2010, https://biblehub.com/commentaries/pulpit/job/1.htm. "The great dragon . . . who deceives the whole world" is found in the NKJV.

10. John 12v31; 14v30; 16v11.

11. Matthew 4v8–10.

12. Ezekiel 28v15.

13. Job 1v6–12; 2v1–7; Matthew 4v1–11; see also "Job 1," *Cambridge Bible for Schools and Colleges,* Bible Hub, https://

biblehub.com/commentaries/
cambridge/job/1.htm.

14. Genesis 3; Isaiah 14v12–13; Ezekiel 28v12–15. See also "God's Divine Council," Truth or Tradition?, July 2, 2018, www .truthortradition.com/articles/ gods-divine-council.

15. Ezekiel 28v15–17; Revelation 12v1–9; 14v9–12; Luke 10v18; Isaiah 14v12–17.

16. This is a minority position, but it's growing in popularity. My seminary professor Dr. Gerry Breshears introduced me to this idea, but you can read more in *Satan and the Problem of Evil* by Gregory A. Boyd.

17. Isaiah 14v12–15; Ezekiel 28v16–19; Luke 4v5–8; 10v18; Revelation 12v1–9.

18. John 14v30; 2 Corinthians 4v4; 1 John 5v19.

19. Greg Boyd makes the case for this most convincingly in *Satan and the Problem of Evil,* but of course this opens a whole can of worms not only over evolution but also with the free-will-versus-sovereignty debate. As weird as this may sound, we actually have a bit of a category for augmented evolution in dogs in that humans somehow interacted with the natural process to index wolves toward being man's best friend. Who's to say nonhuman intelligences couldn't interject themselves into the process in a similar way but to more nefarious ends? We're well into conjecture now; I'm just saying it's a fascinating concept that could aid our quest for a plausible theodicy (theology of evil). If this all sounds ridiculous, here's a short, accessible teaching my friend Josh Porter gave at our church on the topic, called "God of Evil" (November 4, 2018): https:// bridgetown.church/teaching/ fighting-the-world-the-flesh-the -devil/god-of-evil.

20. 1 John 3v8.

21. Mark 3v27.

22. John 8v32, 36.

23. Colossians 2v15.

24. Matthew 16v18, KJV.

25. 1 Peter 5v8.

26. Lisa H. Trahan et al., "The Flynn Effect: A Meta-analysis," *Psychological Bulletin* 140, no. 5 (2014): 1332–60, www.ncbi.nlm .nih.gov/pmc/articles/ PMC4152423.

27. Bernt Bratsberg and Ole Rogaberg, "Flynn Effect and Its Reversal Are Both Environmentally Caused," *Proceedings of the National Academy of Sciences* 115, no. 26 (June 2018): 6674–78, www.pnas.org/content/115/26/6674.

28. Lea Winerman, "Smarter Than Ever?," *Monitor on Psychology* 44, no. 3 (2014), www.apa.org/monitor/2013/03/smarter; see also Daniel Engber, "The Great Endumbening," *Slate,* September 19, 2018, https://slate.com/technology/2018/09/iq-scores-going-down-research-flynn-effect.html.

29. Bratsberg and Rogaberg, "Flynn Effect and Its Reversal Are Both Environmentally Caused." The *Slate* article referenced above also gives a fun summary.

30. Yuval Noah Harari, *Sapiens: A Brief History of Humankind* (New York: HarperCollins, 2015), 21.

31. "Quotes," *The Usual Suspects,* directed by Bryan Singer, PolyGram Filmed Entertainment, 1995, www.imdb.com/title/tt0114814/quotes/?tab=qt&ref_=tt_trv_qu.

32. John 10v10.

33. A great line from James K. A. Smith, *How (Not) to Be Secular: Reading Charles Taylor* (Grand Rapids, MI: Eerdmans, 2014), 4.

34. C. S. Lewis, *Christian Reflections,* ed. Walter Hooper (Grand Rapids, MI: Eerdmans, 1967), 41.

35. C. S. Lewis, *The Screwtape Letters* (New York: Macmillan, 1982), 3.

36. John 8v44–45.

37. I would recommend you read one of these three: *Supernatural* by Michael S. Heiser (Bellingham, WA: Lexham, 2015), a great, easier-to-read intro; *Deliverance* by Jon Thompson (to be published by Summer 2021) for the best overview of demonization I know of; and *God at War* by Gregory A. Boyd (Downers Grove, IL: InterVarsity Academic, 1997), for the heavyweight theology stuff. By far my favorite book on this is *Deliverance* by Jon Thompson.

Ideas, weaponized

1. One well-known work on this is Jordan B. Peterson, *Maps of Meaning: The Architecture of Belief* (New York: Routledge, 1999).

2. See Lisa Cron, *Wired for Story: The Writer's Guide to Using Brain Science to Hook Readers from the Very First Sentence* (New York: Ten Speed, 2012), chap. 1.

3. Dallas Willard, *Renovation of the Heart: Putting on the Character of Christ* (Colorado Springs: NavPress, 2002), 96–97.

4. Diane Kwon, "Neanderthal Ancestry in Europeans Unchanged for Last 45,000 Years," *The Scientist,* January 23, 2019, www.the-scientist.com/news-opinion/neanderthal-ancestry-in-europeans-unchanged-for-last-45-000-years-65364.

5. Yuval Noah Harari, *Sapiens: A Brief History of Humankind* (New York: HarperCollins, 2015), chap. 2.

6. Dallas Willard, *Hearing God: Developing a Conversational Relationship with God,* updated and expanded ed. (Downers Grove, IL: InterVarsity, 2012), 12.

7. This line was inspired by Dallas Willard's better line: "Reality does not adjust itself to accommodate our false beliefs, errors, or hesitations in action." *Knowing Christ Today: Why We Can Trust Spiritual Knowledge* (New York: HarperCollins, 2009), 39.

8. 1 Corinthians 5v12. I continue to come back to this passage as a template for how we consider sexuality in the church. It opens with a marriage against God's design, then has warnings about how "a little yeast leavens the whole batch of dough" (1 Corinthians 5v6), then clarifies that our posture toward sexual immorality outside the church is totally different than inside.

9. Brittany Almony, "Attachment Theory and Children of Divorce," Bartleby Research, May 10, 2015, www.bartleby.com/essay/Attachment-Theory-And-Children-Of-Divorce-F3UTUVQ3FV8X.

10. Corie Lynn Rosen, "Men v. Women: Who Does Better in a Divorce?," LegalZoom, September 16, 2020, www.legalzoom.com/articles/men-v-women-who-does-better-in-a-divorce.

11. Alicia Vanorman, "Cohabiting

Couples in the United States Are Staying Together Longer but Fewer Are Marrying," Population Reference Bureau, November 5, 2020, www.prb.org/cohabiting -couple-staying-together -longer.

12. Scott Stanley, "Premarital Cohabitation Is Still Associated with Greater Odds of Divorce," Institute for Family Studies, October 17, 2018, https://ifstudies .org/blog/premarital-cohabitation -is-still-associated-with-greater -odds-of-divorce.

13. Juliana Menasce Horowitz, Nikki Graf, and Gretchen Livingston, "Marriage and Cohabitation in the U.S.," Pew Research Center, November 6, 2019, www.pewsocialtrends .org/2019/11/06/marriage-and -cohabitation-in-the-u-s.

14. Abigail Tucker, "What Can Rodents Tell Us About Why Humans Love?," *Smithsonian Magazine,* February 2014, www .smithsonianmag.com/science -nature/what-can-rodents-tell-us -about-why-humans-love -180949441.

15. "The Long-Term Effects of Abortion," Epigee Women's Health, www.epigee.org/the -long-term-effects-of-abortion .html.

16. "The Proof Is In: Father Absence Harms Children," National Fatherhood Initiative, www .fatherhood.org/father-absence -statistic.

17. "The Consequences of Fatherlessness," fathers.com, https:// fathers.com/statistics-and -research/the-consequences-of -fatherlessness/.

18. See this simple but excellent overview of the largest study so far: Ryan T. Anderson, " 'Transitioning' Procedures Don't Help Mental Health, Largest Dataset Shows," The Heritage Foundation, August 3, 2020, www .heritage.org/gender/ commentary/transitioning -procedures-dont-help-mental -health-largest-dataset-shows.

19. Audrey Conklin, "Hawley, Sasse Lead Charge Against Pornhub, Human Trafficking," FoxNews, December 9, 2020, www.foxnews.com/politics/ hawley-sasse-lead-charge -against-pornhub-human -trafficking; see also Exec. Order No. 13903, Fed Reg. Doc. 2020-02438 (January 31, 2020), www.federalregister.gov/

documents/2020/02/05/2020
-02438/combating-human
-trafficking-and-online-child
-exploitation-in-the-united
-states.

20. Matthew McNulty, " 'Fifty
Shades of Grey' Tops Decade's
Best Seller List," Fox Business,
December 19, 2019, www
.foxbusiness.com/markets/
penguin-random-house
-dominates-top-selling-books-of
-the-decade-one-day-after-news
-of-675-bertelsmann-sale; Scott
Mendelson, "Box Office: Hugh
Jackman's 'Greatest Showman'
Is Still Leggier Than 'Titanic,' "
Forbes, February 25, 2018, www
.forbes.com/sites/
scottmendelson/2018/02/25/
box-office-hugh-jackmans
-greatest-showman-is-still
-leggier-than-titanic/?sh=
72c6869b2c13.

21. Mary Eberstadt, introduction
to *Adam and Eve After the Pill:
Paradoxes of the Sexual Revolution* (San Francisco: Ignatius,
2012).

22. Robert D. McFadden, "Philip
Rieff, Sociologist and Author on
Freud, Dies at 83," *New York
Times,* July 4, 2006, www
.nytimes.com/2006/07/04/us/
04rieff.html.

23. Jeffrey Schwartz, *A Return
to Innocence* (New York: Harper,
1998).

24. Willard, *Renovation of the
Heart,* 100.

25. Genesis 3v4.

26. M. Scott Peck, *People of the
Lie: The Hope for Healing
Human Evil,* 2nd ed. (New York:
Touchstone, 1998), 207.

27. David G. Benner, *Soulful
Spirituality: Becoming Fully Alive
and Deeply Human* (Grand Rapids, MI: Brazos, 2011), 135.

28. Willard, *Renovation of the
Heart,* 100–101.

29. Willard, *Renovation of the
Heart,* 99.

30. Hannah Arendt, *The Origins
of Totalitarianism,* new ed.
(Orlando: Harcourt, 1968), 474.

31. Winston S. Churchill, "The
Gift of a Common Tongue"
(speech, Harvard, Cambridge,
MA, September 6, 1943),
https://winstonchurchill.org/
resources/speeches/1941-1945
-war-leader/the-price-of
-greatness-is-responsibility.

32. Inés San Martín, "Pope Francis: Ideological Colonization a

'Blasphemy Against God,'"
Crux, November 21, 2017,
https://cruxnow.com/vatican/
2017/11/pope-francis
-ideological-colonization
-blasphemy-god.

33. See Timothy Keller's *The Reason for God: Belief in an Age of Skepticism* (New York: Dutton, 2008) and *Making Sense of God: An Invitation to the Skeptical* (New York: Viking, 2016), and Zadie Smith's novels, especially *White Teeth* (New York: Vintage International, 2000) and *Swing Time* (New York: Penguin, 2016).

34. David Foster Wallace, *Infinite Jest* (New York: Back Bay Books, 1997), 389.

35. 2 Timothy 2v26.

36. John 18v37.

37. John 18v38.

38. For a popular version of these ideas, read Willard's *Knowing Christ Today,* one of my favorites! Or go for it and read the tome that is his *The Disappearance of Moral Knowledge.*

39. Willard, *Knowing Christ Today,* 30–31.

40. The phrase *separation of church and state* actually isn't in the Constitution, as many assume, but in a letter from Thomas Jefferson to the Danbury Baptists in 1802. It takes only a few minutes to read their correspondence, and you can easily see the thrust was to keep the state out of the church and assure "religious liberty." See "Letters Between Thomas Jefferson and the Danbury Baptists (1802)," Bill of Rights Institute, https://billofrightsinstitute.org/primary-sources/danburybaptists.

41. Willard, *Knowing Christ Today,* 32–33.

42. Acts 20v35.

43. Willard, *Knowing Christ Today,* 19–22.

44. John 17v3.

45. 2 Timothy 1v12.

46. Colossians 2v2–3.

47. Willard, *Knowing Christ Today,* 21.

48. Actually, it's more interesting: in the traditional parable, the king is the one watching the blind men in the court. Used by Westerners, it's saying "we enlightened Westerners see what these people beneath us can't"; that is, more ideological colonization.

49. John 8v12.

50. Luke 4v18.

51. Willard, *Knowing Christ Today,* 20–21.

52. D. Elton Trueblood, "Chapter 3: The Impotence of Ethics," in *The Predicament of Modern Man* (New York: Harper and Row, 1944), www.religion-online.org/book-chapter/chapter-3-the-impotence-of-ethics.

53. Mark 1v15.

Dezinformatsiya

1. Sarah E. Needleman, "As FaceApp Goes Viral, So Do Concerns About Privacy, Russia Ties," *Wall Street Journal,* July 18, 2019, www.wsj.com/articles/as-faceapp-goes-viral-so-do-concerns-about-privacy-russia-ties-11563485572.

2. Colin E. Babb, "Dezinformatsiya and the Cold War," Naval Science and Technology Future Force, March 17, 2020, https://futureforce.navylive.dodlive.mil/2020/03/dezinformatsiya-and-the-cold-war.

3. Garry Kasparov (@Kasparov63), Twitter, December 13, 2016, 11:08 a.m., https://twitter.com/Kasparov63/status/808750564284702720, emphasis added. This quote is just too good.

4. Colossians 2v15.

5. In theology, this is called a theory of atonement. Theologians separate out the fact of the atonement (Jesus died at the hands of Rome and the Jewish leaders; he was buried in a tomb; three days later God raised him from the dead) from theories of the atonement (what it all means). There are six major views from church history; I ascribe to all of them in what Dr. Gerry Breshears, my theological mentor and seminary professor, called "a multifaceted, diamond view of the atonement."

6. A term from the title of Shoshana Zuboff's fine book on this subject: *The Age of Surveillance Capitalism: The Fight for a Human Future at the New Frontier of Power* (New York: Hachette, 2019).

7. Mark Sayers, "The Devil's Disinformation Campaign," Bridgetown Church, October 21, 2018, 28:46, https://bridgetown

.church/teaching/fighting-the
-world-the-flesh-the-devil/the
-devils-disinformation-campaign.

8. "Syria's War Explained from
the Beginning," Al Jazeera,
April 14, 2018, www.aljazeera
.com/news/2018/4/14/syrias-war
-explained-from-the-beginning.

9. This story is fascinating:
Raphael Satter, "Deepfake Used
to Attack Activist Couple Shows
New Disinformation Frontier,"
Reuters, July 15, 2020, www
.reuters.com/article/us-cyber
-deepfake-activist/deepfake
-used-to-attack-activist-couple
-shows-new-disinformation
-frontier-idUSKCN24G15E.

10. True story. Hundreds
showed up to protest and counterprotest, but the whole thing
was organized by Russia. Claire
Allbright, "A Russian Facebook
Page Organized a Protest in
Texas. A Different Russian Page
Launched the Counterprotest,"
Texas Tribune, November 1,
2017, www.texastribune.org/
2017/11/01/russian-facebook
-page-organized-protest-texas
-different-russian-page-l.

11. Alana Abramson, " 'We Don't
Share a Common Baseline of

Facts.' Barack Obama Reflects
on Divisiveness in Politics," *Time,*
January 12, 2018, https://time
.com/5099521/barack-obama
-david-letterman-interview.

12. Glenn Kessler and Meg Kelly,
"President Trump Made 2,140
False or Misleading Claims in His
First Year," *Washington Post,*
January 20, 2018, www
.washingtonpost.com/news/fact
-checker/wp/2018/01/20/
president-trump-made-2140
-false-or-misleading-claims-in
-his-first-year.

13. "Full Text: Jeff Flake on
Trump Speech Transcript," *Polit-
ico,* January 17, 2018, www
.politico.com/story/2018/01/17/
full-text-jeff-flake-on-trump
-speech-transcript-343246.

14. "Countering Truth Decay,"
RAND Corporation, www.rand
.org/research/projects/truth
-decay.html.

15. Michiko Kakutani, *The Death
of Truth: Notes on Falsehood in
the Age of Trump* (New York:
Tim Duggan Books, 2018),
47, 54.

16. Stephen J. Burn, ed., *Conversations with David Foster
Wallace* (Jackson, MS: University

Press of Mississippi, 2012), 49. For someone who was not a follower of Jesus, Wallace had an uncanny read on the tragic flaw of secularism. I find his more-journalistic writings incredibly insightful.

17. Matthew 24v4–12.

18. 1 Corinthians 6v9.

19. Colossians 2v4.

20. 2 Timothy 3v13.

21. Titus 3v3.

22. 2 Corinthians 11v3.

23. 1 John 3v7.

24. Romans 1v25; 1v18.

25. Jude 4.

26. See Revelation 18v23; 19v20; 20v3, 8, 10.

27. Revelation 12v9, NKJV.

28. A significant portion of the New Testament was written to combat false teachers/teachings. That's worth thinking about.

29. God can, but he usually chooses not to, though that is a long-running debate in theology. I'll utilize self-restraint and not take you down that rabbit hole—you're welcome!

30. See his book *Duped: Truth-Default Theory and the Social Science of Lying and Deception* (Tuscaloosa, AL: University of Alabama, 2020).

31. Malcolm Gladwell, *Talking to Strangers: What We Should Know About the People We Don't Know* (New York: Little, Brown, 2019), 74.

32. See, for example, the work of Dr. John Gottman at The Gottman Institute, www.gottman .com/about/research/couples.

33. That said, I'm well aware a lot is at stake with the *Genesis* narrative, and I don't mean to make light of the historical reading at all. There are far-reaching implications: the historicity of Adam and Eve, how that ties into Paul's language in Acts, how original sin passed into humanity, how all this dovetails with evolutionary biology (if current theories of human origins are accurate), and so on. And when I say *mythology,* I don't mean it in the popular slang sense of a lie but in the academic or technical sense of a grand narrative that makes sense of the big questions of human existence. Not that my opinion matters much, as I'm anything but a scholar of Hebrew exegesis or ancient

Near Eastern history, but my *current* hypothesis is that Genesis 1–11 is parabolic in the same way Jesus's parable of the ten minas, about the king who went to a far country and left his servants behind, was (Luke 19v11–26). There's some historical background underneath that story: In 4 BC, Archelaus, son of Herod the Great, traveled to Rome to have Caesar crown him king of Israel in a dispute over who was the rightful heir to Herod's throne. But the way Jesus tells the story, it's not journalism; it's still clearly a parable designed not to teach history so much as to give the listeners a vision of life in the kingdom of God. My guess is something like that is going on in the early chapters of *Genesis.*

34. Genesis 3v1.

35. Bible Hub, s.v. "crafty," https://biblehub.com/topical/c/crafty.htm.

36. Genesis 3v1.

37. Genesis 3v4–5.

38. How about a quote from the sixteenth-century Scottish Calvinist John Knox? "By what means satan first drew mankind from the obedience of God the Scripture doth witness. Namely, by pouring into their hearts that poison—*that God did not love them;* and by affirming that by transgression of God's commandments they might attain to felicity and joy; so that he caused them to seek life where God had pronounced death to be." John Knox, *Writings of the Rev. John Knox* (London: The Religious Tract Society, 1830), 308, emphasis added.

39. Genesis 3v6.

40. *Strong's Hebrew Lexicon* (NIV), s.v. "H120, *'adam,*" Blue Letter Bible, www.blueletterbible.org/lang/lexicon/lexicon.cfm?Strongs=H120&t=NIV.

41. *Strong's Hebrew Lexicon* (NIV), s.v. "H2332, *Chavvah,*" Blue Letter Bible, www.blueletterbible.org/lang/lexicon/lexicon.cfm?Strongs=H2332&t=NIV.

42. "Jeff Goldblum: Malcolm," *Jurassic Park,* directed by Steven Spielberg, Universal Pictures, 1993, www.imdb.com/title/tt0107290/characters/nm0000156.

43. Of course, we absolutely

cannot place all the blame on "evil secularists." Many secularists I know are deeply good people. The church itself bears a hefty degree of responsibility for the West's secularism. Christian hypocrisy, the abuse of power by church leaders in a pre-separation-of-church-and-state world, and the slow acceptance of scientific findings around evolution, not to mention the reluctance of (some) Christians to advocate for human rights, all fall at our feet and make it very hard for many of our secular friends to trust in Jesus.

44. Scotty Hendricks, " 'God Is Dead': What Nietzsche Really Meant," Big Think, August 12, 2016, https://bigthink.com/scotty-hendricks/what-nietzsche-really-meant-by-god-is-dead.

And having done all, to stand

1. "G.I. Joe—'Don't Jump Your Bike Over Downed Power Lines' PSA," YouTube, May 8, 2014, www.youtube.com/watch?v=1NwvJlbnD5E.

2. Laurie R. Santos and Tamar Gendler, "Knowing Is Half the Battle," 2014: What Scientific Idea Is Ready for Retirement? series, Edge, 2014, www.edge.org/response-detail/25436. I took Laurie Santos's Coursera course "What Is the G.I. Joe Fallacy?" and loved it.

3. John 4v23–24.

4. See his book by the same name: Gordon D. Fee, *God's Empowering Presence: The Holy Spirit in the Letters of Paul* (Peabody, MA: Hendrickson, 1994; Grand Rapids, MI: Baker, 2009).

5. Hebrews 4v15.

6. M. Scott Peck, *The Road Less Traveled: A New Psychology of Love, Traditional Values, and Spiritual Growth,* 25th anniversary ed. (New York: Simon & Schuster, 2002), 50. This is one of my top ten favorite books of all time.

7. Corrie ten Boom, *Not Good If Detached* (Fort Washington, PA: CLC Publications, 1957), chap. 21 epigraph.

8. I was first exposed to this idea by Patrick Deneen in *Why Liberalism Failed* (New Haven, CT: Yale University Press, 2018), a book I'll nod to toward the end of this book. He wrote about how the Left and Right are far more similar than most people care to admit and focused on the 80 percent they have in common—namely, hyperindividualism and the shift from creation to "nature" that shows up in everything from transgenderism to environmental degradation. Stay tuned for more.

9. Louis Brandeis, *Other People's Money: And How the Bankers Use It* (New York: Frederick A. Stokes, 1914), 92.

10. 2 Corinthians 2v11.

11. Luke 4v1–2.

12. Luke 4v3.

13. Luke 3v22.

14. Luke 4v13.

15. Edwin H. Friedman, *A Failure of Nerve: Leadership in the Age of the Quick Fix* (New York: Seabury Books, 2007), 230.

16. For example, see Steven Porter, "Living in a Material World with an Immaterial God," Dallas Willard Center, June 28, 2018, https://vimeo.com/277532616.

17. This definition is from a lecture he gave at Westmont College in 2018 for the fortieth anniversary of Richard J. Foster's book *Celebration of Discipline.* It's taken from my notes of his talk.

18. From my all-time favorite Henri J. M. Nouwen book, *The Way of the Heart* (New York: Ballantine Books, 1981), 13–14.

19. Romans 8v6.

20. Evagrius of Pontus, *Talking Back: A Monastic Handbook for Combating Demons,* trans. David Brakke (Collegeville, MN: Liturgical Press, 2009), 49–50.

21. Jeffrey M. Schwartz and Rebecca Gladding, *You Are Not Your Brain: The 4-Step Solution for Changing Bad Habits, Ending Unhealthy Thinking, and Taking Control of Your Life* (New York: Avery, 2011), 21.

22. See 1 Corinthians 2v16.

23. Psalm 23v1.

24. Matthew 19v6; Ephesians 5v25; 1 Peter 3v7.

25. Hebrews 13v5.

26. Dallas Willard, *Renovation of the Heart: Putting on the Character of Christ* (Colorado Springs: NavPress, 2002), 95.

27. New hashtag? #curate yourinputs.

28. Habakkuk 1v13.

29. Hwee Hwee Tan, "In Search

of the Lotus Land," *Quarterly Literary Review Singapore* 1, no. 1 (October 2001), www.qlrs.com/essay.asp?id=140.

30. "The State of Traditional TV: Updated with Q1 2020 Data," Marketing Charts, September 14, 2020, www.marketingcharts.com/featured-105414.

31. Chris Holmes, "5 Ways to Limit Screentime at Bedtime," WhistleOut USA, November 5, 2020, www.whistleout.com/CellPhones/Guides/5-ways-to-limit-screentime-at-bedtime#screentime.

32. David Kinnaman and Mark Matlock, *Faith for Exiles: 5 Ways for a New Generation to Follow Jesus in Digital Babylon* (Grand Rapids, MI: Baker, 2019), 26.

33. Mary Oliver, *Upstream: Selected Essays* (New York: Penguin, 2016), 8.

34. Romans 12v1–2.

35. Ephesians 6v10–14.

36. 1 Peter 5v8–9.

The slavery of freedom

1. Her exact birthday is unknown, so approximately seven.

2. See the interview here: Walter Isaacson, "The Heart Wants What It Wants," *Time,* June 24, 2001 (first published August 31, 1992), http://content.time.com/time/magazine/article/0,9171,160439,00.html.

3. Actually, the line originated in an Emily Dickinson letter. But Allen was the one to inject it into the mainstream.

4. Ephesians 2v1–3.

5. Ephesians 6v12.

6. *Thayer's Greek Lexicon,* s.v. "Strong's NT 4561: σάρξ," Bible Hub, https://biblehub.com/greek/4561.htm.

7. Philippians 3v3.

8. 2 Peter 2v10.

9. 2 Peter 1v4.

10. Eugene H. Peterson, *A Long Obedience in the Same Direction: Discipleship in an Instant Society,* commemorative ed. (Downers Grove, IL: InterVarsity, 2000), 113.

11. Guatama Buddha, verse 326 in *Dhammapada,* quoted in Jonathan Haidt, *The Happiness Hypothesis: Finding Modern Truth in Ancient Wisdom* (New York: Basic Books, 2006), 2.

12. Plato, *Phaedrus,* quoted in Haidt, *The Happiness Hypothesis,* 2–3.

13. Rabbi Schneur Zalman, *Tanya*, pt. 1, chap. 28, Chabad .org, www.chabad.org/library/ tanya/tanya_cdo/aid/1028992/ jewish/Chapter-28.htm.

14. Henry David Thoreau, *Walden* (New York: Thomas Y. Crowell, 1910), 290.

15. Haidt, *The Happiness Hypothesis,* 22.

16. Jeffrey M. Schwartz, "Neuroplasticity and Spiritual Formation," *The Table,* Biola University Center for Christian Thought, April 18, 2019, https://cct.biola .edu/neuroplasticity-and-spiritual -formation.

17. "Full Transcript: #1169—Elon Musk," *Joe Rogan Experience,* September 26, 2018, 11:03, 34:27, https://sonix.ai/ resources/full-transcript-joe -rogan-experience-elon-musk.

18. Jordan Peterson, *12 Rules for Life: An Antidote to Chaos* (Toronto: Random House Canada, 2018), 9–10.

19. Charles Taylor, *A Secular Age* (Cambridge, MA: Harvard University Press, 2007).

20. Genesis 1v28.

21. William Shakespeare, *Hamlet: Prince of Denmark,* The Picture Shakespeare series (London: Blackie and Son, 1902), 32.

22. This, of course, is an ethical minefield. What is morality if not a place to stand *against* our desires? Any effective morality must draw lines that desire cannot cross.

23. Jonathan Grant, *Divine Sex: A Compelling Vision for Christian Relationships in a Hypersexualized Age* (Grand Rapids, MI: Brazos, 2015), 30.

24. Robert C. Roberts, "Psychobabble," *Christianity Today,* May 16, 1994, www.christianitytoday .com/ct/1994/may-16/ psychobabble.html.

25. David Wells, *No Place for Truth: Or, Whatever Happened to Evangelical Theology?* (Grand Rapids, MI: Eerdmans, 1993), 183.

26. Cornelius Plantinga Jr., *Not the Way It's Supposed to Be: A Breviary of Sin* (Grand Rapids, MI: Eerdmans, 1995), 83.

27. David G. Benner, *The Gift of Being Yourself: The Sacred Call to Self-Discovery,* expanded ed. (Downers Grove, IL: InterVarsity, 2015), 50.

28. I'm referring here to David Bennett's excellent book by the same name—*A War of Loves*—which, to be clear, isn't about food; it's about sexuality. I've given a much less serious example.

"Their passions forge their fetters"

1. Seymour Drescher, "The Atlantic Slave Trade and the Holocaust: A Comparative Analysis," in *Is the Holocaust Unique?: Perspectives on Comparative Genocide,* ed. Alan S. Rosenbaum (New York: Routledge, 2018), 105.

2. Robert Bellah et al., *Habits of the Heart: Individualism and Commitment in American Life* (Berkeley, CA: University of California, 1985), vii–viii.

3. Obama said, "In a time of growing inequality, accelerating change, and increasing disillusionment with the liberal democratic order we've known for the past few centuries, I found this book thought-provoking. I don't agree with most of the author's conclusions, but the book offers cogent insights into the loss of meaning and community that many in the West feel, issues that liberal democracies ignore at their own peril." "These Are the Six Books Barack Obama Thinks You Need to Read," *Harper's Bazaar,* June 20, 2018, www .harpersbazaar.com/uk/culture/ culture-news/a21696261/barack -obama-book-recommendations.

4. Galatians 5v13–15.

5. Jeffrey Schwartz and Patrick Buckley, *Dear Patrick: Life Is Tough—Here's Some Good Advice* (New York: HarperCollins, 1998), 245.

6. For an in-depth analysis, see Matt Jenson, *The Gravity of Sin: Augustine, Luther, and Barthe on homo incurvatus in se* (New York: T&T Clark, 2006).

7. Galatians 5v16–17.

8. Laura Snapes, " 'It's All About What Makes You Feel Good': Billie Eilish on New Music, Power Dynamics, and Her Internet-Breaking Transformation," *Vogue,* May 2, 2021, www.vogue.co.uk/news/ article/billie-eilish-vogue-interview.

9. Kaitlyn Engen, "Former EWU Professor Rachel Dolezal Charged with Welfare Fraud," *The Easterner,* May 31, 2018, https://theeasterner.org/42882/

news/former-ewu-professor-rachel-dolezal-charged-with-welfare-fraud.

10. Galatians 5v19–21.

11. Galatians 5v22–23.

12. Galatians 5v24–25.

13. Planned Parenthood of Southeastern Pa. v. Casey, 505 U.S. 833 (1992), 851, https://tile.loc.gov/storage-services/service/ll/usrep/usrep505/usrep505833/usrep505833.pdf.

14. In the absence of transcendence, some kind of ultimate meaning to life, most people devolve to the base instincts for survival and feeling good. So everything becomes about power and pleasure, and since power is best defined as the ability to shape your life as you see fit, for most people, personal happiness becomes the telos of life. This is not true of all secular people, but it is for most of the West, including many Christians in the West.

15. 2 Peter 2v19.

16. Proverbs 11v6.

17. Titus 3v3.

18. Andrew Sullivan, "The World Is Better Than Ever. Why Are We Miserable?," *New York,* March 9, 2018, https://nymag.com/intelligencer/2018/03/sullivan-things-are-better-than-ever-why-are-we-miserable.html.

19. *Cambridge Dictionary,* s.v. "compulsion," https://dictionary.cambridge.org/us/dictionary/english/compulsion.

20. From Gerald G. May's wonderful book, *The Dark Night of the Soul: A Psychiatrist Explores the Connection Between Darkness and Spiritual Growth* (San Francisco: HarperSanFrancisco, 2004), 60–61.

21. Edmund Burke, *A Letter from Mr. Burke, to a Member of the National Assembly, in Answer to Some Objections to His Book on French Affairs,* 2nd ed. (London: J. Dodsley, 1791), 68–69, emphasis added.

22. Augustine, *On Reprimand and Grace,* quoted in James K. A. Smith, "Freedom: How to Escape," in *On the Road with Saint Augustine: A Real-World Spirituality for Restless Hearts* (Grand Rapids, MI: Brazos, 2019).

23. Timothy Keller, *Making Sense of God: An Invitation to the Skeptical* (New York: Viking, 2016), 102.

24. Jim McNeish, thank you for everything.

25. Gustave Thibon, quoted in Gabriel Marcel, *Homo Viator: Introduction to a Metaphysic of Hope,* trans. Emma Craufurd (New York: Harper Torchbooks, 1962), 28.

26. John 8v34; 8v32.

27. Michael Green, *Who Is This Jesus?* (Vancouver, BC: Regent College, 1992), 26.

28. In context, he was actually writing about masturbation. Here's a great essay on it: Wesley Hill, "Escaping the Prison of the Self: C. S. Lewis on Masturbation," February 10, 2014, www.firstthings.com/blogs/firstthoughts/2014/02/escaping-the-prison-of-the-self.

The law of returns

1. Leslie Jamison, *The Recovering: Intoxication and Its Aftermath* (New York: Back Bay Books, 2018), 9.

2. Galatians 6v7–9.

3. Galatians 6v8.

4. Luke 6v38.

5. Matthew 7v2.

6. Here's a graph with more details: "Reflections," Windgate Wealth Management, https://windgatewealth.com/the-power-of-compound-interest-and-why-it-pays-to-start-saving-now.

7. Cornelius Plantinga Jr., *Not the Way It's Supposed to Be: A Breviary of Sin* (Grand Rapids, MI: Eerdmans, 1995), 68.

8. Sara Chodosh, "Muscle Memory Is Real, but It's Probably Not What You Think," *Popular Science,* January 25, 2019, www.popsci.com/what-is-muscle-memory.

9. Augustine, *Confessions,* trans. Sarah Ruden (New York: The Modern Library, 2018), 52.

10. Augustine, *Confessions,* trans. Henry Chadwick (Oxford: Oxford University, 1992), 140.

11. Plantinga, *Not the Way It's Supposed to Be,* 70.

12. Note, this doesn't clash with the Christian doctrine of original sin at all. By "evil" he meant pervaded by evil to a point where evil isn't something people do; it's someone people are.

13. M. Scott Peck, *People of the Lie: The Hope for Healing Human Evil,* 2nd ed. (New York: Touchstone, 1998), 82.

14. Erich Fromm, *The Heart of Man: Its Genius for Good or Evil*

(New York: Perennial Library, 1964), 173–75, 178, emphasis added.

15. C. S. Lewis, *The Great Divorce* (New York: Macmillan, 1946), 72.

16. Gregory A. Boyd, *Satan and the Problem of Evil: Constructing a Trinitarian Warfare Theodicy* (Downers Grove, IL: IVP Academic, 2001), 190.

17. C. S. Lewis, *Mere Christianity* (New York: Macmillan, 1952), 86–87. It's easily one of the best Christian books in the last century.

18. C. S. Lewis, *The Weight of Glory; And Other Addresses* (New York: Macmillan, 1949), 15.

19. Lewis, *The Great Divorce,* 127.

20. Dallas Willard, quoted in John Ortberg, *Soul Keeping: Caring for the Most Important Part of You* (Grand Rapids, MI: Zondervan, 2014), 22.

21. I don't personally think God sends anyone to hell; I think he respects and honors our human dignity and freedom of choice. And I don't buy the idea of hell as an eternal torture chamber. I understand many people believe that, and I respect that, but I don't. I don't think it comes from Jesus's teachings or the New Testament but from medieval fantasy and fundamentalist anger. The opposite of life isn't torture; it's death. Most of my secular friends assume that when they die, they will cease to exist. While I don't claim to know the specifics, I imagine they aren't that far off the mark. Of course, Jesus was very clear that there is a postmortem judgment coming, so there's mystery here I can't entirely explain. But my favorite read on this is Edward William Fudge, *The Fire That Consumes,* 3rd ed. (Eugene, OR: Cascade, 2011). Consider it.

22. Timothy Keller, *The Reason for God: Belief in an Age of Skepticism* (New York: Dutton, 2008), 78.

23. C. S. Lewis, *God in the Dock,* in *The Collected Works of C. S. Lewis* (New York: Inspirational Press, 1996), 404.

24. Ronald Rolheiser, "Purgatory as Seeing Fully for the First Time," ronrolheiser.com, November 4, 2012, https://ronrolheiser .com/purgatory-as-seeing-fully -for-the-first-time/#.X_i_lNhKjIU.

25. Revelation 22v5.

So I say, live by the Spirit

1. Ruth Burrows, *Before the Living God* (Mahwah, NJ: HiddenSpring, 2008), 5.

2. *New Catholic Encyclopedia,* s.v. "guilt (in the Bible)," Encyclopedia.com, December 21, 2020, www.encyclopedia.com/religion/encyclopedias-almanacs-transcripts-and-maps/guilt-bible.

3. 1 Timothy 4v2.

4. Colossians 2v19.

5. Dr. Jim Wilder distinguishes between healthy shame and toxic shame. Different language but same idea. See Jim Wilder and Michel Hendricks, *The Other Half of Church: Christian Community, Brain Science, and Overcoming Spiritual Stagnation* (Chicago: Moody, 2020), chap. 6.

6. Saint Thérèse of Lisieux, *Collected Letters of St. Thérèse of Lisieux,* trans. F. J. Sheed (New York: Sheed and Ward, 1949), 3030, quoted in M. Scott Peck, *People of the Lie: The Hope for Healing Human Evil,* 2nd ed. (New York: Touchstone, 1998), 11.

7. Galatians 5v24–25.

8. "Where Does *Mortification* Come From?," Dictionary.com, www.dictionary.com/browse/mortification.

9. "Commentaries: Genesis 4:7," Bible Hub, https://biblehub.com/commentaries/genesis/4-7.htm.

10. Jeffrey Schwartz and Patrick Buckley, *Dear Patrick: Life Is Tough—Here's Some Good Advice* (New York: HarperCollins, 1998), 185.

11. 2 Peter 2v10, 12.

12. Leslie Jamison, *The Recovering: Intoxication and Its Aftermath* (New York: Back Bay Books, 2018), 304.

13. Again, see his book by the same name, *God's Empowering Presence,* or his magisterial commentary on 1 Corinthians.

14. Romans 8v3.

15. Romans 8v3–4.

16. Romans 8v5–6.

17. This was language used by René Descartes and others, such as Thomas Edison, who is credited with saying, "The chief function of the body is to carry the brain around." While biblical theology gives us a very high view of the mind, *res cogitans* is not a biblical view of the human person.

18. Richard Foster, *Celebration of Discipline: The Path to Spiritual Growth,* 20th anniversary ed. (San Francisco: HarperSanFrancisco, 1998), 55.

19. Dietrich Bonhoeffer, *Life Together* (New York: Harper & Row, 1954), 112.

20. James 5v16.

21. Jamison, *The Recovering,* 328.

22. James 1v13–15.

23. Henri J. M. Nouwen, *The Way of the Heart* (New York: Ballantine Books, 1981), 60.

24. 1 Peter 2v11. The New International Version says "sinful desires," but the Berean Study Bible and other versions say "desires of the flesh" or "fleshly lusts," which is more accurate.

25. 1 Timothy 6v9.

26. Galatians 6v9.

The brutal honesty about normal

1. Watch it here: Carson Daly and Shawn Fanning, "Lars Ulrich," 2000 MTV Video Music Awards, YouTube, September 7, 2000, www.youtube.com/watch?v=_q0Z3gBActg.

2. You can read about the case here: Jonathan Bailey, "20 Years Later: Metallica v. Napster, Inc.," *Plagiarism Today,* April 13, 2020, www.plagiarismtoday.com/2020/04/13/20-years-later-metallica-v-napster-inc.

3. "Piracy. It's a Crime," YouTube, December 4, 2007, www.youtube.com/watch?v=HmZm8vNHBSU.

4. Luke 9v25.

5. John 15v18–20.

6. John 12v31.

7. John 17v14–18.

8. 1 John 2v15–17.

9. Bible Hub, s.v. "2889. *kosmos,*" https://biblehub.com/greek/2889.htm.

10. Johannes P. Louwe and Eugene Nida, *Greek-English Lexicon of the New Testament Based on Semantic Domains,* 2nd ed., Logos research ed. (n.p.: United Bible Societies, 1996), 41.38, Logos.

11. Abraham J. Heschel, *The Prophets*, vol. 1 (New York: Harper & Row, 1969), 190.

12. Dallas Willard, *Life Without Lack: Living in the Fullness of Psalm 23* (Nashville: Nelson Books, 2018), 75.

13. This is from an email when he was prereading my book to correct all my bad theology. ☺

14. Patrick Deneen, *Why Liberalism Failed* (New Haven, CT: Yale University Press, 2018), 39. This is an easy book to disagree with and a very hard book to dismiss.

15. For more on racism in the Constitution and Declaration of Independence, see the work of Navajo activist Mark Charles, or listen to an excellent lecture he gave at our church on the subject: "Saving Justice," Bridgetown Church, January 23, 2017, https://bridgetown .church/teaching/race-justice/ racial-justice-lecture.

16. Eugene H. Peterson, *A Long Obedience in the Same Direction: Discipleship in an Instant Society,* commemorative ed. (Downers Grove, IL: InterVarsity, 2000), 9.

17. Peterson, *A Long Obedience in the Same Direction*, 113.

18. Patrick Devitt, "*13 Reasons Why* and Suicide Contagion," *Scientific American,* May 8, 2017, www.scientificamerican .com/article/13-reasons-why -and-suicide-contagion1.

19. Paul Marsden, "Memetics and Social Contagion: Two Sides of the Same Coin?," *Journal of Memetics—Evolutionary Models of Information Transmission* 2, no. 2 (December 1998): 171–85, http://cfpm.org/jom-emit/1998/ vol2/marsden_p.html.

20. Marsden, "Memetics and Social Contagion."

21. Renée DiResta, "Computational Propaganda," *Yale Review,* https://yalereview.yale.edu/ computational-propaganda.

22. Eugene H. Peterson, *Run with the Horses: The Quest for Life at Its Best* (Downers Grove, IL: InterVarsity, 1983), 135.

23. Jeffrey Schwartz and Patrick Buckley, *Dear Patrick: Life Is Tough—Here's Some Good Advice* (New York: HarperCollins, 1998), 33.

24. Clive Thompson, "Are Your Friends Making You Fat?," *New York Times Magazine,* September 10, 2009, www.nytimes .com/2009/09/13/magazine/ 13contagion-t.html.

25. 1 Corinthians 15v33.

26. Minerva Lee, "Mangala Sutta: 38 Blessings," Lotus Happiness, www.lotus-happiness

.com/mangala-sutta-essential
-blessings-part-1-2.

27. A. W. Tozer, *The Pursuit of God,* Tozer Legacy ed. (Camp Hill, PA: Christian Publications, 1982), 99.

28. Early on in the Enlightenment, secular elites attempted to keep a version of the Judeo-Christian ethical vision alive, but they simply failed at developing any kind of intellectually coherent, alternative source of authority to the Bible.

29. This is Gideon Rosenblatt's summary of Harari's ideas. Gideon Rosenblatt, *"Homo Deus: A Brief History of Tomorrow* (My Notes),*" Vital Edge* (blog), June 15, 2017, www.the -vital-edge.com/homo-deus; see also Yuval Noah Harari, *Homo Deus: A Brief History of Tomorrow* (New York: HarperCollins, 2017).

30. Stephen J. Burn, ed., *Conversations with David Foster Wallace* (Jackson, MS: University Press of Mississippi, 2012), 18.

31. 1 John 2v16.

32. That's a phrase from Ronald Rolheiser in *Forgotten Among the Lilies: Learning to Love Be-*
yond *Our Fears* (New York: Doubleday, 2004), 16.

33. Matthew 4v8.

34. Genesis 3v6.

35. Theo Hobson, *Reinventing Liberal Christianity,* quoted in Tim Challies, *Final Call* (blog), January 17, 2017, www.challies .com/final-call/final-call-january -17.

36. 1 Corinthians 3v19.

37. Luke 16v15.

38. David Brooks, "America Is Facing 5 Epic Crises All at Once," *New York Times,* June 25, 2020, www.nytimes.com/ 2020/06/25/opinion/us -coronavirus-protests.html.

39. "America's New Religious War: Religious Fervour Is Migrating into Politics," *The Economist,* March 27, 2021, www.economist .com/united-states/2021/03/27/ religious-fervour-is-migrating-into -politics.

40. A nod to Lee C. Camp, *Scandalous Witness: A Little Political Manifesto for Christians* (Grand Rapids, MI: Eerdmans, 2020), proposition 11.

41. John Milton, *Paradise Lost* (Chicago: Thompson and Thomas, 1901), 86.

42. Isaiah 5v20.

43. "Reproductive Justice," Sister Song, www.sistersong.net/reproductive-justice.

44. Julian Quinones and Arijeta Lajka, " 'What Kind of Society Do You Want to Live in?': Inside the Country Where Down Syndrome Is Disappearing," CBS News, August 14, 2017, www.cbsnews.com/news/down-syndrome-iceland.

45. Scott Klusendorf, "Peter Singer's Bold Defense of Infanticide," Christian Research Institute, April 16, 2009, www.equip.org/article/peter-singers-bold-defense-of-infanticide.

46. Alberto Guibilini and Francesca Minerva, "After-Birth Abortion: Why Should the Baby Live?," *Journal of Medical Ethics* 39, no. 5 (February 2012), https://jme.bmj.com/content/39/5/261.full; see also Eugene C. Tarne, "The Dark Ladder of Logic: After-Birth Abortion," Charlotte Lozier Institute, April 27, 2012, https://lozierinstitute.org/899.

47. Antonia Senior, "Yes, Abortion Is Killing. But It's the Lesser Evil," *The Times,* July 1, 2010, www.thetimes.co.uk/article/yes-abortion-is-killing-but-its-the-lesser-evil-f7v2k2ngvf8.

48. Alexandra Del Rosario, " 'The Peanut Butter Falcon' Star Zack Gottsagen Takes Stage as First Oscar Presenter with Down Syndrome," *Hollywood Reporter,* February 9, 2020, www.hollywoodreporter.com/news/peanut-butter-falcon-star-zack-gottsagen-makes-history-at-oscars-1277720.

49. Ephesians 6v12.

50. John 3v16.

A remnant

1. C. S. Lewis, *The Screwtape Letters* (New York: Macmillan, 1982), 46–47, emphasis added.

2. John Sutherland, "The Ideas Interview: Philip Rieff," *The Guardian,* December 4, 2005, www.theguardian.com/education/2005/dec/05/highereducation.uk1.

3. Mark Sayers, *Disappearing Church: From Cultural Relevance to Gospel Resilience* (Chicago: Moody, 2016), 15–16. This is my favorite book of Mark's. Every single one is worth a read, but this one is special.

4. The quote is from Sayers, *Disappearing Church,* 80. We want "the kingdom, but do not want to acknowledge the authority of the King."

5. Timothy Keller, "A Biblical Critique of Secular Justice and Critical Theory," *Life in the Gospel,* Gospel in Life quarterly newsletter, https://quarterly.gospelinlife.com/a-biblical-critique-of-secular-justice-and-critical-theory.

6. Michel Foucault, *The History of Sexuality,* vol. 1, trans. Robert Hurley (New York: Vintage, 1990), 95.

7. Joseph S. Nye Jr., *Soft Power: The Means to Success in World Politics* (New York: PublicAffairs, 2004), 5–7.

8. Rod Dreher, *Live Not by Lies: A Manual for Christian Dissidents* (New York: Sentinel, 2020), 7. Rod, I'm so sorry about how similar our titles are! Thanks for being so kind about it.

9. See his book by the same name: *Beautiful Resistance: The Joy of Conviction in a Culture of Compromise* (Colorado Springs: Multnomah, 2020).

10. John D. Roth, "Be Not Conformed," *Christian History,* no. 84 (2004), www.christianitytoday.com/history/issues/issue-84/be-not-conformed.html.

11. Matthew 5v14, 16.

12. 1 Peter 2v11–12.

13. Blue Letter Bible, s.v. "G1577—*ekklēsia,*" www.blueletterbible.org/lang/lexicon/lexicon.cfm?Strongs=G1577&t=KJV.

14. Something like the "forged families" described here: David Brooks, "The Nuclear Family Was a Mistake," *Atlantic,* March 2020, www.theatlantic.com/magazine/archive/2020/03/the-nuclear-family-was-a-mistake/605536.

15. James 1v19.

16. Romans 12v1–2.

17. Pope John Paul II, *The Theology of the Body: Human Love in the Divine Plan* (Boston: Pauline Books and Media, 1997).

18. Melinda Selmys, *Sexual Authenticity: An Intimate Reflection on Homosexuality and Catholicism* (Huntington, IN: Our Sunday Visitor, 2009), 85.

19. 1 Corinthians 6v19.

20. Romans 12v2.

21. J.D., "Rallying to Restore God," *The Economist,* Decem-

ber 10, 2010, www.economist
.com/prospero/2010/12/10/
rallying-to-restore-god.

22. Nancy Pearcey, *Love Thy Body: Answering Hard Questions about Life and Sexuality* (Grand Rapids, MI: Baker, 2018), 74.

23. The subtitle to my friend Jon Tyson's book on the church, *Beautiful Resistance.* Read it!

24. *Online Etymology Dictionary,* s.v. "regular," www.etymonline .com/word/regular.

25. Jane Tomaine, *St. Benedict's Toolbox: The Nuts and Bolts of Everyday Benedictine Living* (New York: Morehouse, 2005), 5.

26. We have an entire teaching series, practice, and workbook all available for free at http:// practicingtheway.org/practices/ unhurry.

27. Arnold J. Toynbee, *A Study of History: Abridgement of Volumes I–VI,* ed. D. C. Somervell (Oxford: Oxford University, 1946); see also Michael Metzger, "The Church as a Creative Minority," Religion Unplugged, January 28, 2020, https:// religionunplugged.com/news/

2020/1/28/the-church-as-a -creative-minority.

28. Jon Tyson and Heather Grizzle, *A Creative Minority: Influencing Culture Through Redemptive Participation* (self-pub., 2016), 12.

29. Take ten well-spent minutes and read it here: Jonathan Sacks, "On Creative Minorities," 2013 Erasmus Lecture, *First Things,* January 2014, www .firstthings.com/article/2014/01/ on-creative-minorities.

30. Romans 11v5.

31. "Our Mission and Model," Praxis, https://praxislabs.org/ mission-and-model.

Epilogue: Self-denial in an age of self-fulfillment

1. Matthew 5v44.

2. Luke6v28.

3. See Matthew 26v52. That's the popular phrase; the actual quote is "All who draw the sword will die by the sword."

4. Mark 8v34.

5. Dietrich Bonhoeffer, *The Cost of Discipleship* (New York: Touchstone, 1995), 89.

6. Galatians 2v20.

7. Galatians 5v24.

8. John Calvin, "A Summary of the Christian Life. Of Self-Denial," in *On the Christian Life,* trans. Henry Beveridge (n.p.: Calvin Translation Society, 1845), Christian Classics Ethereal Library, https://ccel.org/ccel/calvin/chr_life/chr_life.iv.html.

9. Ronald Rolheiser, *The Holy Longing: The Search for Christian Spirituality* (New York: Doubleday, 1999), 9.

10. Mark 8v35.

11. Blue Letter Bible, s.v. *"psychē,"* www.blueletterbible .org/lang/lexicon/lexicon.cfm ?Strongs=G5590&t=ESV.

12. Mark 1v15.

13. Eugene H. Peterson, *A Long Obedience in the Same Direction: Discipleship in an Instant Society,* commemorative ed. (Downers Grove, IL: InterVarsity, 2000), 178.

14. Eugene H. Peterson, *Run with the Horses: The Quest for Life at Its Best* (Downers Grove, IL: InterVarsity, 1983), 128.

15. Colossians 1v28, a text every pastor should live in and live out.

John Mark Comer is the founding pastor of Bridgetown Church in Portland, Oregon, the director and teacher of Practicing the Way, and the bestselling author of *The Ruthless Elimination of Hurry* and four previous books. Much of his writing is focused on the work of spiritual formation in post-Christian culture. The gnawing questions that get him out of bed in the morning are, *How do we experience life with God in the digital age? And how do we change to become more like Jesus in a culture where emotional health and spiritual maturity are rare?* To that end, he is regularly found reading the desert fathers and mothers, ancient saints and obscure contemplatives, modern psychologists and social scientists, philosophers like Dallas Willard, and the weekly op-ed page. When he's not reading, he can be found attempting to learn how to cook for his wife and children, drinking Heart coffee, and walking the family dog in the forest.

John Mark graduated from Western Seminary and has a master's degree in biblical and theological studies.

johnmarkcomer.com
Facebook, Instagram, and Twitter:
@johnmarkcomer

We follow the way of Jesus at the speed of love. But hurry and love are incompatible.

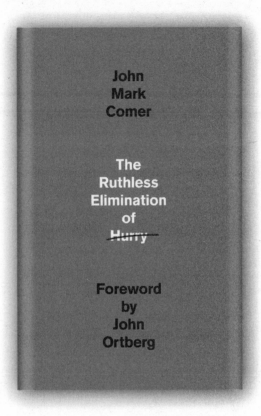

"Desperately needed."

—SCOTT HARRISON